Why People Choose The Wrong Mate

Avoiding The *9* Deadly Booby Traps

by **Gillis Triplett**

Most Valuable
PUBLICATIONS

MVP

Unless otherwise indicated, all Scripture quotations are taken from the King James Version of the Bible.

Scripture quotations noted NIV are taken from the HOLY BIBLE, NEW INTERNATIONAL VERSION. Copyright 1973, 1978, 1984 International Bible Society. Used by permission of Zondervan Publishers.

Scripture quotations noted AMP are taken from THE AMPLIFIED BIBLE. Old Testament copyright 1965, 1987 by the Zondervan Corporation. The Amplified New Testament copyright 1958, 1987 by the Lockman Foundation. Used by permission.

Verses marked (TLB) are taken from *The Living Bible* © copyright 1971. Used by permission of Tyndale House Publishers, Inc. Wheaton, Il 60189. All rights reserved.

Please be advised that the name satan and related names are not capitalized. We will not concede to him any respect, even if doing so causes us to violate established traditional grammatical rules.

Copyright © 2004 by Gillis Triplett

**Why People Choose The Wrong Mate
Avoiding The *9* Deadly Booby Traps**
Library of Congress Control Number: 2002117668
ISBN 1-890292-09-5

For Worldwide Distribution
Printed in the United States of America

Published by
Most Valuable Publications
PO Box 310900
Atlanta, Georgia 31131
Local 404-745-0547
Out of state 888-651-0547

Direct all inquiries to our website at **www.Gillistriplett.com** where you will find complete information on ordering, latest releases, seminars and training opportunities.

All titles by Gillis Triplett are available at special quantity discounts for bulk purchases for bookstores, distributors, bookclubs, ministries, and for educational or institutional purposes worldwide.

Cover design by George Foster: www.fostercovers.com

Dedication

This book was born out of the pain and tears of the multitudes of men and women who chose the wrong mate and found themselves hurt by the very person who claimed to love them and care about them. I pray for the complete mending of your heart.

There is life after a bad relationship and there is healing after a horrific marriage. May you learn from your mistakes and never repeat them.

To those dating, searching for romance, hoping for companionship, engaged to be married or wondering if you found *The One,* in your quest to find *True Love*, may you understand the snares and the booby traps along the way and avoid the people who lay them. My prayer is that you find the love of your life, the two of you become *One Flesh* and live a rich, fulfilling and rewarding life together.

To the voices who have been permanently silenced: the men and women who paid the ultimate price for choosing the wrong mate... the ones who were killed by a disgruntled boyfriend or girlfriend... the ones whose demise came at the hands of a controlling or malicious ex... the ones whose precious lives were snuffed out by a vengeful fiancé or fiancée... and to the ones brutally murdered by a selfish or hateful spouse.

Their voices are truly missed...

Although we can never bring them back, their smiles, their laughter, their memories and the times we shared can never be taken away. With much love in our hearts, we will never forget them...

May the family and true friends they left behind find some degree of solace in knowing that final justice will be served in the Supreme Court of God.

Table of Contents

Preface

Undoubtedly, you know someone who has been affected by a bad relationship, a horrendous marriage or a bitter divorce. Like most men and women, you are reading this book primarily for two reasons.

(1). You want to know the answer to the question, "Why do people choose the wrong mate?" This perplexing question has left many boyfriends, girlfriends, lovers, fiancés, fiancées, spouses and their families cupping their face in between their hands, some in tears, wondering what went wrong and why.

(2). You want to avoid choosing the wrong mate. You want to avoid adding your name to the numerous relationship and marriage casualties lists. To what lists am I referring?

(a) The state court's "list" of people who were forced to file a restraining order(s) against their boyfriend, girlfriend, fiancé, fiancée, spouse or ex.

(b) The "list" of men and women who found themselves being stalked by an "ex" who recorded their phone conversations, tampered with their mail, pestered them with a relentless barrage of unwanted phone calls and e-mails, peeped in their windows, tracked their e-mails with remote Internet surveillance software, hid GPS tracking systems equipment on their vehicle, spied on them while they were on dates and otherwise harassed them.

(c) The sexually transmitted disease clinic's "list" of men and women who have contracted HIV/AIDS, Genital Warts, Chlamydia, Hepatitis B, Herpes, Trichomoniasis, Syphilis or other sexually transmitted diseases from their boyfriend, girlfriend, fiancé, fiancée, casual sex partner or spouse.

(d) The "list" of anguished men and women who now hate God because of their failed relationships or marital fiascos. They met who they thought was the love of their life at church or in a religious setting, the person convinced them it was God who brought them together. After the divorce or betrayal, they vowed never to have anything to do with God or the church again.

(e) The "list" of befuddled spouses who are crying in the dark because they find themselves trapped in a torturous, unbearable marriage.

(f) The "list" of tormented men who found themselves falsely accused of rape by a bitter ex-girlfriend, wife or fiancée who was determined to get revenge because he broke up with or divorced her.

(g) The "list" of heartbroken husbands and wives who have experienced the excruciating torture of having their spouse stab them in the back with the double-edged dagger of adultery.

(h) The District Attorney's Domestic Violence Victims "list" of men and women who were abused, attacked, assaulted or murdered by their boyfriend, girlfriend, fiancé, fiancée, spouse or by their ex.

(i) The silent but ever growing "list" of women who suddenly find themselves pregnant and alone. They were swept off their feet by men they believed to be knights in shining armor. Convinced their relationships would last forever, they each gave their man everything, including their bodies. And why not? They all had men who declared their undying love but when they got pregnant, their boyfriend, live-in lover or fiancé changed from Mr. Nice into Mr. No More. As in no more phone calls. No more candle light dinners or any other dates. No more e-mails. No more, "I can't wait to see you." No more flowers. No more gifts and no more, "I love you." Because their babies' daddy abandoned them, many of these women became lifetime members of the infamous (BSMC) Bitter Single Mothers' Club.

(j) The divorce court microfilm records "list" that stores the names and case numbers of the husbands and wives who were forced by their spouse to go through the combative and traumatizing, blood sucking divorce court mill.

(k) The increasingly angry "list" of men (including ex-husbands) who have been held hostage by a child support system that uses Mafia type tactics to force them to pay child support to women who claimed these men were their babies' daddies. When these men finally took DNA tests, they were shocked to find out that they were not the biological fathers of these children. Although these females committed paternity fraud, the current laws in most states still force the men to continue paying them anyway, or face losing their professional licenses, driver's licenses, or going to jail and losing everything.

(l) The "list" of women who are afflicted with (DWS) Divorced Women's Syndrome and the "list" of men who are suffering from (DMS) Divorced Men's Syndrome. The side effects of DWS and DMS are too many to mention. A few of the symptoms are suicidal thoughts, depression, hostility, resentment, festering bitterness, social withdrawal, shame and unforgiveness. These men and women chose the wrong mate, got married anyway, went through a combative injurious divorce and their life has never been the same.

These lists are real. Sadly, new names are added to each list daily. Behind the names on these lists are real people. They are not just statistics. Like you, they have a life. They have dreams, hopes, a vision and a plan for the future. They all have something else in common. They chose the wrong mate and saw their hopes, visions and dreams dashed before their very eyes. There are no words to express their pain and hurt. But the dark, cold, rough road they were forced to travel down could have been avoided.

Their names did not have to end up on any of the lists you just read, or on any of the other lists compiled for the men and women who chose the wrong mate. Neither does yours. You can avoid all of the drama, stigma and shame that comes with choosing the wrong mate. I need to pause and give a special heartfelt thanks to so many men and women. Through the detailed accounts of painful incidents in their lives, they have relived the trauma and suffering they experienced while dating, courting, living together, being engaged and while married. They didn't have to, but they told their story, some of them in tears, to help you avoid the booby traps in which they found themselves.

In some cases, their statements revealed their own mistakes and ignorance. In other cases, their factual statements revealed their outright rejection of irrefutable life-giving rules, laws and principles. Rules, laws and principles that surely would have protected them from the heart piercing agony they experienced. One thing is certain, there is a clear and present danger when a person chooses the wrong mate.

Not only for them but also for their family and friends. Because of that danger, the individuals within these pages, their families and their friends who love and support them, were forced to suffer. They suffered through heart ripping betrayal, dead-end go nowhere relationships, extra marital affairs, paternity fraud, sexually transmitted diseases, nightmarish marriages, bitter divorces, abandoned children, the aftermath of abortions, physical abuse, financial ruin, date rape and even murder. These are their stories.

As I give you a detailed case-by-case analysis of each relationship, you'll learn why people choose the wrong mate and end up regretting the day they ever laid eyes on the person they had claimed to love. Please be advised, this book contains graphic descriptions of incidents which depict real events and includes material which is intended for mature individuals. Therefore, reader discretion is advised.

In some instances I had to take the necessary precaution of not divulging the identities of some of the parties. Unless indicated by this notation, (*real name*) all names were changed to guard the privacy of and to protect the identity of the individuals involved.

Some of the incidents and accounts have been provided by or recorded from external sources, (*i.e., divorce court proceedings, civil trials, criminal court trials, investigative reporters, families of victims, homicide investigators and other law enforcement agencies*).

By reading this publication you agree to be bound by the Georgia Shield Law and by the First Amendment and under no circumstances attempt to violate the privacy of, nor attempt to divulge or reveal the identity of any of the parties who are not disclosed herein.

Some individuals have cases which may still be pending in a court of law. Others are highly concerned that their "ex," may attempt to defame their name, harass, stalk, slander or try to bring physical harm against them or against their family. To these individuals, the dangers of choosing the wrong mate is all too real.

Introduction

What do most men and women want in a mate?

When a man or a woman thinks about being with that special someone, they usually envision being with a person with whom they are compatible and for whom they have strong romantic feelings.

They seek someone who shares the same beliefs and has similar values as they do. They desire a person they can trust to the utmost, someone they can confide in concerning any issue of life without feeling ridiculed or mocked. They look for a person who is concerned about their well-being, someone responsible, kind, affectionate, loving and lovable. No sane person searching for the love of their life intentionally falls in love with a pathological liar, home wrecker or psychopath.

No woman in her right mind willingly marries a wife beater, a female leach, a whacked out control freak, a momma's boy or a hardened criminal. No man in his right mind seeks to be joined together with a manipulative gold-digger, a domineering diva, an emotionally immature spoiled brat, a quick tempered tongue lasher or a woman suffering from an acute case of girl gone wild.

Yet it always starts out the same way. People believe the best about their chances of finding the love of their life. They usually keep a positive outlook and maintain big dreams about meeting *Mr. Right* or *Mrs. Right*. Then one day, out of nowhere, it just happens.

Their eyes meet. Their hearts start to beat rapidly. Their palms get sweaty and the sparks fly. Romance has been awakened from its sleep. The next thing they know, the two of them are holding hands, dreamily gazing into each other's eyes and expressing their deep feelings and immense love toward each other. That can be one of the most tender moments of a lifetime. Once it happens, there are numerous paths the new couple can take. Some start the dating or courting process to see if the person who caused those sparks to fly is not just another *false positive*. What is a false positive? That's when you experience the, "I'm in love feeling," and believe that he or she is *The One*, yet when you take a second and closer look, you quickly discover that the first look, although seemingly positive, was definitely false. Other men and women meet and take the path of engaging in commitment free casual sex. They use their sexual urges as a barometer to determine who their next mate will be. Then there are those who meet and move in together. First comes love, then cohabiting, then maybe marriage. They become sexually active roommates with the slim possibility of marriage somewhere in the unknown future.

Some take the path of identifying themselves as boyfriend and girlfriend. They intermingle their finances, have children together, take trips together, but that's as far as they go. They never get married.

They don't live together. They just continue to live separate lives while dating each other. Finally, there are those who decide to take the stroll down the aisle and become *One Flesh*. No matter what path they take, it seems like another fairytale love story has unfolded.

At least up until the point where issues begin to surface...

Severe issues... critically severe issues. Take the case of Terence Kirkendall, (*real name*). On May 17, 1998 in a little known town called Findlay, Ohio, Terence's *ex*-girlfriend, Christina Barkman (*real name*), reported to the police that Terence grabbed her outside her apartment, pushed her inside and forced her to have sex. When police arrived, they found what they classified as evidence of an attack.

The room was ransacked and there was a used condom on the floor. Without questioning Terence, a grand jury took his *ex*-girlfriend's word and returned a four count indictment against him. These first degree felonies could have sent him to prison for 40 years. Terence turned himself in, made bail and prepared for the fight of his life.

While he was awaiting trial, his *ex* went back to the police on June 11th and told them that Terence had tied her arms and legs together and forced her to call the prosecutor's office to request dismissal of his rape indictment.

Based on her statement, police filed additional charges of witness intimidation and kidnapping and rearrested Terence; but detectives quickly determined there was no way he could have attacked her at the time she claimed. As a result of the second incident, authorities asked Terence and Christina to take lie detector tests. They wanted to see who was telling the truth.

Prior to taking her test, his *ex*-girlfriend confessed to the police that her accusations were false. She said she made them up because she was angry with Terence for ending their six-month relationship.

When you examine the lengths to which his obviously embittered *ex*-girlfriend was willing to go because he broke up with her, it's unnerving: the ransacked room, the used condom, lying to the police, and deceiving a grand jury. Because of her callous acts, Terence was arrested, not once but twice! The rape accusations along with his name were plastered in the local newspaper. He was suspended from his job and lost more than $15,000 in bail bonds money and attorney's fees.

Had the detectives not asked Terence and his *ex*-girlfriend to take lie detector tests, he would be sitting in prison right now because almost everyone falsely assumed that he was guilty as charged! His life was almost destroyed, all because he chose the wrong mate to date.

Why is it that in the beginning of a relationship a person can seem "so perfect," only to end up betraying, abusing or misusing the person they claimed to love? Why do they intentionally break their partner's heart? Why do they deliberately administer emotional, physical, sexual or financial pain and anguish to their spouse, loved one or to their ex? Make no mistake about it, the statistics and facts don't lie... they paint a crystal clear picture to those looking for love.

In today's world, finding someone special is like traveling through a wild jungle. You have to deal with snakes, dead-ends, dangerous cliffs, poisonous spiders, parasites, booby traps and contagious diseases. Lurking in this lover's jungle is a multitude of liars, cheaters, fakes, users and abusers.

If you get in a relationship with one of these individuals, they will leave you with pounding headaches, sleepless nights, crying in the dark and regretting the day you ever laid your eyes on them.

When Victor Perdessi, (*real name*) met his girlfriend in Minneapolis, Minnesota, they chose the path of casual sex then cohabitation. Perdessi seemed like a dream come true to this single mother. He introduced her 18-month-old daughter to his family and treated her child as if she was his own. He changed her diapers and even rocked her child to sleep. When his girlfriend announced that she was pregnant with his child, Perdessi was bubbling over with joy. But when problems sprouted in their relationship, his girlfriend decided to call it quits. She cut off all contact with Perdessi. After giving her dilemma some thought, the already single mother of one child decided to have an abortion.

When she told Perdessi that she terminated her pregnancy, family members said he cried for days. Then with malice and much forethought, he went to his *ex*-girlfriend's house and told her that he was going to kill her daughter in retaliation for killing his child. For three tense hours she held Perdessi at bay, pleading with him to let her child live.

She was able to break away to try and get help but she did not make it far... he caught up with her, snatched her daughter and returned to the house. When police arrived, they found her baby on a bed wearing a T-shirt and a diaper. Perdessi had shot the child in the face, then committed suicide. His *ex*-girlfriend can testify from firsthand experience, the dangers of choosing the wrong mate. I urge you not to make the mistake many men and women are making by believing in casual dating or casual sex.

There's nothing casual about having to sift through the massive number of normal looking men and women who will electrocute your emotions and high-jack your peace of mind before you have a chance to say, "I thought you loved me?" All of the women who dated Andrew Luster (*real name*), probably believed they were having a casual relationship with a pretty cool dude.

Andrew is the wealthy great-grandson of Max Factor and heir to the Max Factor cosmetics fortune. Andrew had it all. He lived in a beachfront home, supported himself with a trust fund and real estate investments and spent most of his time surfing. Although he lived the glamorous lifestyle of the rich and famous, Andrew Luster was the wrong man for any woman to date. In 1996, 1997 and 2000, Andrew took three different women to his beachfront home and raped them after secretly drugging them with a date rape drug.

A search of his home turned up videotapes of his sexual escapades with women who appeared to be either asleep or unconscious. In one tape played in court, Luster is seen on camera having sex with a woman and declaring: *"That's exactly what I like in my room, a passed-out beautiful girl."* One of his victims, only identified as Tonja Doe, dated Andrew for several months and was unaware of the rape tape, which included vile torturous acts, until authorities showed it to her.

Imagine having a detective warning you to brace yourself, and then showing you a homemade video of a man you once dated, violating your body in unspeakable ways. Was his barbaric acts an aberration? A one in a million crime performed by some psycho? I wish I could answer by saying, "yes!" The fact is that many women are finding themselves booby trapped into similar torturous nightmares.

In March of 2003, in Bryan, Texas, Brennan Brice (*real name*), was sentenced to five years of probation, a month in jail, and was ordered to take out a half-page ad in the Texas A&M student newspaper to apologize to his *ex*-girlfriend.

Prosecutors say Brennan, a former Texas A&M student, videotaped a sexual encounter with his girlfriend without her knowledge and showed the footage to about fifteen of his fraternity brothers.

His *ex*-girlfriend addressed him during an emotional sentencing hearing at the Brazos County Courthouse. Here is what she had to say, *"You violated me in ways I don't think you'll ever understand..."* She went on to say, *"My freshman year of college has been a relentless nightmare."*

Rebekah Revels (*real name*) also had a similar experience. In July of 2002, Rebekah held the coveted crown of Miss North Carolina and was on her way to represent her state in the Miss America Pageant. That was until her dreams were dashed by her *ex*-fiancé Tosh Welch, (*real name*). Rebekah described their relationship as emotionally and physically abusive. When she broke off their engagement, her friends said Tosh did not take the news too well. Three years later, according to court testimony, Tosh did the unthinkable.

He contacted the Miss America Pageant officials via e-mail and alerted them to some topless photos he claimed to have of Miss Revels. The chain of events that followed: Rebekah was forced to give up her Miss North Carolina crown. She was not allowed to participate in the Miss America Pageant. She had to sue her *ex*-fiancé to retrieve the alleged topless photos, and she had to swallow the bitter pill that comes with choosing the wrong mate. Those who date must also deal with the fact that violence occurs in 1 in 4 dating relationships.

The exact statistics are hard to determine because some surveys and studies include verbal aggression, threats and emotional abuse whereas others do not. Either way, it is an indisputable fact that dating violence is widespread. Intermingled with sweet words, gentle caresses, soft glances, tingly blushes, moonlight walks, tender hand-holding and spontaneous laughter, is cursing, slapping, fighting, screaming, kicking, punching, choking, grabbing and murder.

In July of 2003, in San Juan Capistrano, California, accountant Tamara Bohler (*real name*), the former girlfriend of Jean Marc Weber (*real name*) was charged with murder, attempted murder, using a weapon and inflicting great bodily injury. Based on an investigation, the two had an on-again, off-again relationship. When Tamara showed up at Weber's house attempting to reconcile, an argument erupted. Tamara wielded a knife and attacked Weber. As he desperately struggled to get to a neighbor's house to seek medical attention, she attacked and fatally stabbed Weber's 13-year-old son. Always remember, choosing the wrong mate not only affects you; it affects your entire family.

These incidents are not abnormalities. Like clockwork, they take place everyday, running the spectrum from the upper echelons of society all the way down to the ghetto. Whether you are dating, engaged to be married, cohabiting or just having casual sex, it would be unwise to cast caution to the wind and ignore these irrefutable facts.

It is bad enough that certain men and women don't know how to conduct themselves in a relationship. To compound the matter, many individuals have written their own malicious scripts on how to break up. In 1996 in Houston, Texas, when Nathan Dale Campbell (*real name*) proposed marriage to his girlfriend, she had no idea he would not take "no," for an answer. When she said, "no," police say, Nathan nearly choked her to death, then cut her eyes out with a steak knife.

When she faced her *ex*-boyfriend in court, she was dealt another deafening blow. Using the insanity plea, Nathan avoided prison and was instead sent to a mental institution with the potential of being released back into society.

In August of 2003, when Heather Radley (*real name*) saw her *ex*-boyfriend in a Tameside Magistrates Court in the United Kingdom, they probably did not exchange any pleasantries. When he ended their six month romance, Heather admitted that she flew into a *"fit of rage."* After the breakup, her *ex* was away on a business trip and Heather conned one of his friends to let her into his apartment, (*she claimed she had to retrieve some of her clothes*). Once inside, she cut his face out of one his photographs, shredded his wardrobe and killed his Persian cat.

I could cite countless examples of tragic cases like that of Cherica Adams, (*real name*). Cherica represented many of today's 21st century women who express their sexual freedom through casual sex (*commonly known as hooking-up*). When she started having sexual relations with Rae Carruth (*real name*), a professional football player for the Carolina Panthers, she probably thought she had the perfect hook-up.

But things escalated from casual to tense when Cherica informed Carruth that she was pregnant with his child. Court testimony revealed two key points: **1). Carruth insisted that Cherica get an abortion,** and **2). This wasn't Carruth's first confrontation with a female he had gotten pregnant.** One of his *ex*-girlfriends testified how he threatened to kill her if she didn't get an abortion. She must have believed him because she terminated their child. But when Cherica refused, prosecutors say Carruth took matters into his own hands by hiring hit men. They said he was not willing to pay Cherica any child support.

That is how a lot of men feel when they find they have impregnated a casual sex partner. After watching a movie together, Cherica was following Carruth to her house when he (*for no reason*) stopped his SUV in front of her car on the highway, forcing her to stop as well. Moments later, the hit men pulled up alongside Cherica and fired a hailstorm of bullets into her car. Although she was hit four times Cherica managed to dial 911 from her cell phone. Here is part of that chilling 911 transcript and some of Cherica's final words:

Medic: *Okay. How did this happen?*
Cherica: *I was following my baby's daddy. Rae Carruth the football player.*
Medic: *So you think he did it?*
Cherica: *He slowed down. And, a car pulled up beside me.*
Medic: *And, then shot at you?*
Cherica: *Yes..."*
Medic: *"...your boyfriend? The one that you said was with you. Where's he at?*
Cherica: *He was in the car in front of me and slowed down and somebody pulled up besides me and did this.*
Medic: *And then, where'd he go?*
Cherica: *He just left.*

"He just left." Those are the words of a woman who just realized that she had chosen the wrong mate. Sadly, she came to that gut-wrenching revelation too late. Casual dating has produced another lethal threat, a mass number of men and women who have tested positively for the deadly HIV/AIDS virus. However, they purposefully refuse to inform their potential mate or sex partner(s). They know they are infected and they know they are going to infect others, but they do not care.

Of those who marry, the statistics say that about half of them will eventually file for divorce. Many in this group will terminate their marriage before they experience their second wedding anniversary. Two questions must be answered: what is going wrong and, why is it happening to so many people? Those involved in the wedding ceremony process offer absolutely no solutions to stem this tide of heartbreak, pain and emotional distress. The wedding industry has turned into a whopping $21 billion dollar a year automated assembly line. Fees of $15,000 to $30,000 per wedding have become commonplace.

After all of the painstaking planning and tremendous expense, many newlyweds report having serious marital problems. A portion of them exhibit these dire tensions right after exchanging vows. Do you recall the fairytale union between Prince Charles & Princess Diana?

It is estimated that 750 million people worldwide collectively held their breath as they observed that gala event. The world waited for that special moment when the groom saluted his bride. It was a magical moment indeed, but it was short lived. Their love has been described as a lavish wedding, a terrible marriage and then a bitter divorce.

They experienced one hundred and eighty one months of turmoil, betrayal and then broken vows. The questions remain, "What went wrong and why is it happening to so many people?" In the summer of 1990, I started assisting ministers who officiated wedding ceremonies. It was from that vantage point that I began to see a disturbing pattern. The majority of the people who were marrying didn't realize that they had just rolled the dice when it came to choosing their mate.

Many of them met, and usually French-kissed their way through a whirl wind love affair. Others became sexually involved, got married, then braced themselves as they waited to see if they were lucky enough to become lifetime members of the Happily Married Club.

They literally hoped or prayed, in vain, after the fact, that they chose the right mate. The divorce courts, marriage therapists, domestic violence courts, family courts, police blotters and the morgues all sadly testify to the fact that their desperate hopes and futile prayers were too late. No sane person will argue the fact that there is a large segment of men and women in our society who are not fit to be dating, courting and God forbid, exchanging marriage vows.

Yet time and time again, these individuals succeed at booby trapping others into nightmarish relationships. Become clear on this point, choosing the wrong mate will put you at risk. My mission in life is to ensure that whether you are dating, courting, engaged to be married, or divorced with a desire to remarry, that you clearly understand how to avoid choosing the wrong mate.

Why do good hearted people end up choosing the worst possible mate?

Why do nice people end up in dreadful dead-end relationships?

Why do tenderhearted, caring and loving people end up dating or marrying losers, abusers and misusers?

I asked those questions after counseling and praying with multitudes of brokenhearted men and women. The misery and agony they experienced at the hands of the person who claimed to love them was beyond appalling. It was their pain and anguish, coupled with my own dating and courting experiences, that caused me to seek the answers to those three critical questions.

Without a doubt, choosing a mate is *one of* the most important decisions you will ever make in your entire life. Additionally, you must accept the fact that there are certain unscrupulous men and women who are determined to see your dream of having a happy home transformed into a ghoulish nightmare.

You can bend over backwards for them but no matter how hard you try to make things work, they will find a way to dash your dreams and rip your heart out. Their actions will leave you and your family speechless, stunned beyond belief and literally gasping for air. This goes way beyond using the worn-out excuse, *"They made a mistake, everybody makes them..."* The truth is, in some or in all foundational facets of love, sex, relationships or marriage, whether spiritually, morally, mentally, emotionally or financially, these men and women are completely off course. Many of them refuse to change. Yet they consistently find ways to dupe good hearted people into falling in love with them. In **Why People Choose The Wrong Mate - Avoiding The *9* Deadly Booby Traps** I'll answer three primary questions:

(1) Why do these men and women intend on getting you to fall in love with them and then proceed to ruin your life?

(2) What kind of tactics do they use? And,

(3) How do you determine the difference between true love and their false intentions?

I must forewarn you, if you fall for any of these *mis*guided males or females, here are the type of relationships they will lure you into:

- A painful relationship
- An on again, off again relationship
- An abusive relationship
- A deadly relationship
- A combative relationship
- A stormy relationship
- A dead-end relationship
- A volatile relationship
- A tumultuous relationship
- A betrayal based relationship

Their success or failure at misleading you into dating, courting, living together, sexual relations or marriage is based solely on you not knowing or totally ignoring any or all of the *9* deadly booby traps.

Please hear and understand my heart on this issue. I have been sent to protect you and your loved ones from the shock, the trauma and the ensuing horror that comes when a person chooses the wrong mate. As intelligent as you are, if you ignore or don't know the *9* deadly booby traps, you are putting yourself at risk and these smooth operators will take advantage of your lack of knowledge or rebellion.

I classify them as smooth operators because that's exactly what they are. With the seductive skills of Giacomo Casanova, the sexual magnetism of Mati Hari and the cunning sophistication of a black widow spider, these individuals spin their webs, catch their romantic interests off guard, then administer their sting.

They coldheartedly inject their venomous poison into promises they make, into their commitments and into their own wedding vows. The totality of the people they have misled, deceived and damaged has had an absolutely devastating impact on our society.

They are the primary cause of our penal system bursting at the seams. They are the ones who have single-handedly spearheaded the staggering high rate of divorce and the horrendous number of sexually transmitted disease cases. They are the major contributors to the countless number of forlorn children, foster kids and juvenile delinquents. Who are these smooth but cruel operators? What do they look like and how do they sound? They range from the average citizen in middle America, to senators, pro-athletes, movie stars, university deans, music moguls and even those sworn to uphold the law.

You will also find janitors, CEOs, school teachers, postal workers, truck drivers, golfers, race car drivers, architects and many prominent people. Obtaining a high stature in the public's eye does not prevent a person from seeking the false sense of power that comes from wielding pain and anguish into the lives of the people they say they love.

Therefore, I would be remiss if I didn't inform you that within this dastardly collection of deliberate home wreckers, you will also find doctors, pastors, priests, rabbis, well known tele-evangelists and other men and women claiming to be on a divine mission from G-O-D!

In either case, you cannot allow yourself to be swayed by a person's status, power, their influence over others, public opinion or by superficial appearances. As you are immersed in this pivotal life changing book, you will notice that, at times, I use the Scriptures. Make no mistake about it, the Word of God is my foundation. Period!

If you don't believe in God, don't read the Bible or don't go to church, for your sake, don't put this book down. You will be empowered! One of the first steps to finding the love of your life is knowing how to detect and avoid the multitudes of liars, date rapists, unfit mothers, wife beaters, players, psychopaths, slobs, men who leech off females, lazy wives and criminal minds who are seeking to win your heart.

People who don't go to church, don't read the Bible or who don't believe in God have dreams of meeting the love of their life, falling in love, getting married and having a family. You need what I am sharing. So keep reading...

If your position is that you don't desire to get married, that's fine! You may just intend on living with someone, engaging in sexual relations outside of marriage or maybe you're just dating to have some fun and meet new people. Whatever your decision, you will have to choose a mate. In doing so there is a strong possibility that you could choose the wrong mate. Or, even worse, you may become the wrong mate yourself! So keep reading...

This book was written to speak directly to the hearts of the men and women I just mentioned. The ones who are dating, engaged to be married, living together, looking for love or otherwise having sexual intercourse but are not married. If you are already married, you may be reading **Why People Choose The Wrong Mate - Avoiding The *9* Deadly Booby**

Traps because you are facing a severe marital crisis and you are searching for answers. I realize this is a critical time for you, especially if your spouse has forced you to deal with the horrors of domestic violence, filing restraining orders, abuse, infidelity, pornography, drug or alcohol addiction or other marital traumas that lead to divorce, depression, perpetual despair and even spousal murder.

While reading **Why People Choose The Wrong Mate - Avoiding The *9* Deadly Booby Traps** you may come face-to-face with the heart breaking realization that you fell in love with someone whose intentions concerning you were never pure. In some cases they may even be malicious. The decisions your spouse will force you to make may be difficult ones, but you must make them. I'll show you how to obtain proper advice, so keep reading...

Within these pages, I am addressing issues related to the dynamics of love, sex, relationships and marriage. Some of these issues are touchy and have been known to polarize people, provoke divisive debates, stir anger and cause individuals to harbor lingering resentment. It is not my intention to incite or inflame any of the above. Nor is it my intention to offend you or anyone else.

However, if I remain silent, it is highly possible that you may become another victim or casualty of love. If you find yourself fuming over something you've read, that simply means it is time for you to take a detailed inventory of your heart and carefully examine your beliefs. You must ask yourself critical questions such as, "Have I been misinformed, misled or ill-informed about love, sex, relationships or marriage prior to reading **Why People Choose The Wrong Mate - Avoiding The *9* Deadly Booby Traps?** Has this book brought to the surface any festering wounds that I must deal with before I can become a suitable mate? Am I holding firm to any beliefs or philosophies concerning love, sex, relationships or marriage that may be setting me up for continuous relationship failures or successive marital meltdowns?"

Remember, I'm on your side. I want the best for you! It is my earnest prayer that your love life be a joyful blessing to your heart, soul and body and a ray of sunshine to others. Because of that, I must challenge you, probably like you have never been challenged before.

If after reading these potent life-changing words, you realize that you must make some changes in your life, then make them! I assure you, you will be a better person afterward. Finally, I've got some great news for you at the end, so keep reading...

For starters we are going to learn why these men and women intend on getting you to fall in love with them and then proceed to shatter your dreams and ruin your life.

- 1 -

The Glorious Plan Versus The Secret Plot

Michael was a conservative young man who wanted to do things the right way. His dream was to find a prudent woman, get married, settle down and build a family. Michael wasn't the type of man who chased women, or who handled his finances unwisely. He worked hard at his job, faithfully saved his money and stuck to his plan of preparing for his *Mrs. Right*. With no credit card debt, his car paid off, money in the bank and a good job, Michael figured he was ready to find that special woman. Karyn attended church faithfully but not for the purpose of serving or worshipping God. She was on the hunt! Karyn had made up her mind that she was going to catch a nice church going man.

Meanwhile, she had no qualms about sharing her voluptuous body with a string of part time lovers. Those in her inner circle knew she had no intentions of being a good wife or mother. She had already expressed to her close friends that she had no plans to stop seeing or sleeping around with other men just because she got married.

For Karyn, a husband meant nothing more than a steady supply of cash infusions. She was a real life, money hungry, gold-digging home wrecker. Michael met Karyn and began courting her. Against the advice of his family and close friends, the two exchanged wedding vows.

Once they were married, it seemed like Karyn had Michael in a trance. Whatever she said, he did, and that was that. Within months, his wife had depleted all the money he had saved prior to their wedding. By the time they had been married about two and a half years, Karyn had them drowning in an inescapable ocean of debt. Michael's life had spiraled downward like an out of control aircraft.

While his wife ran up the credit card bills, Michael was straining to provide for their kids and take care of their house. He worked multiple jobs just to keep them afloat financially. Karyn was contentious. She didn't like to work at home or on a job. She didn't know how to make or keep a budget, take care of their children, shop for groceries, prepare meals or in any manner be a helpmeet. So how in the world did she snag a nice respectable man like Michael? Keep reading...

Jonathan had a charismatic and electrifying personality. As far as women were concerned, he had the Midas touch. Everyone who met Jonathan said the same thing about him, "He's going to succeed in life!" He had dreams of being a big time movie and record producer, but he was undisciplined in every area of his life: spiritually, mentally, physically, financially and socially. Instead of paying the bills he created, Jonathan would intentionally let them pile up, then open new accounts using assumed names and counterfeit social security numbers. He handled his love life just like he handled his bills.

It didn't take his first wife long before she realized that she had unwittingly married an unrepentant con man and a leech. Bill collectors and irate clients he had outwitted, hounded Jonathan and his new bride day and night. To make matters worse, his erratic behaviors intensified. He would lock himself in the bathroom for hours at a time. He couldn't keep a job. He would sneak out of their apartment in the wee hours of the night and he confiscated all of their incoming mail. His wife looked upon him with a heavy cloud of suspicion.

It turns out that Jonathan was addicted to crack cocaine. Although the signs were there, he masterfully got his wife to ignore the obvious while he pursued her hand in marriage. When she found out, it tore her now fragile heart apart. When he couldn't take the heat anymore, Jonathan simply packed his bags and fled. He left his bewildered wife with a staggering mountain of debt. He also left a long list of very angry clients to whom he had made gigantic promises, promises he never intended to keep. When Jonathan settled into his new city and state, he breathed a sigh of relief. He was starting over.

There were no more bill collectors, no more angry clients and no pestering wife insisting that he get help. In his mind, he didn't have a problem, and now he was a totally free man. Jonathan was back on the prowl. He was searching for another suitable mate and he quickly found one in Barbara. Barbara was the type of woman who was a perpetual optimist. She saw good in everyone she met.

She dreamed of one day being swept off her feet by a knight in shining armor. When she set her eyes on Jonathan, her heart fluttered. She got light headed, thinking, *"This is what true love feels like."* Her search was over. Here was a man who seemed to have it all together. To her, he was the total package: intelligent, confident and successful.

He was what she was looking for in a man. To add validity to his plot to defraud Barbara, Jonathan claimed he had a college degree and somehow landed a great job at a major corporation. He wasn't concerned about the company detecting his false bravado because he only intended to keep the job long enough to pop the big question to Barbara.

When he did, Barbara readily said, "Yes!" There was no hesitation or reservation on her part. As far as she was concerned, Jonathan was her soul mate. He had convinced her that he was a man who truly loved God, one who would be a great husband and father. Barbara had no earthly idea that her newly found romance was an out of control missile, still married, who had just abandoned his first wife.

There would be no words to describe the pain and anguish he would inflict upon her through their fraudulent union. How did Barbara make the mistake of falling head over hills for a time-bomb like Jonathan? How did Michael miss all of the telltale signs that Karyn, although she attended church, was an absolutely terrible choice for a wife? Like many other men and women, both Michael and Jonathan's two wives didn't understand the glorious plan versus the secret plot.

> Jeremiah 29:11 NIV [Emphasis added]
> For I know the plans I have for you," declares the Lord, "PLANS to prosper you and not to harm you, PLANS to GIVE YOU A HOPE AND A FUTURE.

There are three critical points on which we should focus our attention. First, it was the Lord who laid out these plans for you. These are not the iffy, unreliable, always changing plans of a mere mortal man or woman. That's what makes them so glorious. Second, the reason *plans* is in plural form instead of singular, is because His plans cover every aspect of your life: spiritual, mental, social, physical and financial. Third, His plans are designed to give you a hope and a future. Examine His plans for your life concerning love, sex, relationships and marriage.

> Jeremiah 29:5-7 NIV [Emphasis added]
> 5 BUILD HOUSES AND SETTLE DOWN; plant gardens and eat what they produce.
> 6 MARRY AND HAVE SONS AND DAUGHTERS; find wives for your sons and give your daughters in marriage, so that they too may have sons and daughters. INCREASE IN NUMBER THERE; DO NOT DECREASE.
> 7 Also, seek the peace and prosperity of the city...

Did you notice what was missing from the Lord's plan for your life concerning love, sex, relationships and marriage? In His plan there is no daytime soap opera drama. There is no depression, no mental anguish, no heart break, no sleepless nights, no infidelity, no marital discord, no restraining orders and no temporary separations. His plan comes complete with peace of mind, absolute stability and prosperity. Read verse 6 again. Did you notice what else was missing from His plan? His plan has no decrease, no divorce and no child custody battles.

In His plan, children are not forced to watch mommy versus daddy in a bitter knock down, drag out tug-of-war over who gets to keep the kids, who keeps the house, who keeps the cars, who gets to keep the cash and who pays the attorney fees. In His plan, when a man and a woman meet and fall in love, they become husband and wife and their relationship reads like a heart warming poetic love story.

> Proverbs 5:18-19 [Emphasis added]
> [18] Let thy fountain be blessed: and REJOICE WITH THE WIFE OF THY YOUTH.
> [19] *Let her be* as the loving hind and pleasant roe; let her breasts satisfy thee AT ALL TIMES; and be thou ravished ALWAYS with her love.

The word "ravished" means to be intoxicated with her love, not for two years or twenty years and then split-up, but always and forever! With such a glorious plan, why does one in every two marriages end in divorce? Why is the world and the Church filled with so many jilted women like Barbara and with so many defrauded men like Michael? The answer is because of the secret plot.

> Psalm 64:1-6 NIV [Emphasis added]
> [1] Hear me, O God, as I voice my complaint; protect my life from the threat of the enemy.
> [2] HIDE ME FROM THE CONSPIRACY of the wicked, from that noisy crowd of evildoers.
> [3] They sharpen their tongues like swords AND AIM THEIR WORDS LIKE DEADLY ARROWS. (*words such as, "I love you!"*)
> [4] They shoot from ambush at the innocent man; they shoot at him suddenly, without fear.
> [5] THEY ENCOURAGE EACH OTHER IN EVIL PLANS, they talk about HIDING THEIR SNARES; they say, "Who will see them?"
> [6] THEY PLOT INJUSTICE and say, "WE HAVE DEVISED A PERFECT PLAN!" Surely the mind and heart of man are cunning.

For some, the issue of the secret plot to destroy God's glorious plan for their life brings back horrific memories. Take the case of Nicholas & Samantha. Samantha was raised up to believe that one day she would meet a beautiful man, fall in love, get married, have children and build a lasting legacy. When Samantha met Nicholas he convinced her that she had met her *Mr. Right*. Nicholas was raised in a family that had a strong southern heritage. His family firmly believed in passing the family values and business from one generation to the next. Nicholas was running the family empire and was in line to inherit a sizeable estate. Financially, he was set for life.

In the eyes of the women in his community, he was the most eligible bachelor. After the wedding ceremony, the newlyweds headed off to the beautiful Coral Sea for their honeymoon. It was to be a romantic time of physical love to consummate their glorious union. A virgin on her wedding night, Samantha was expecting to experience sexual love for the first time, but Nicholas never touched his gorgeous bride dressed in her sexy lingerie. He wasn't even tempted to try, sending her into a state of shock! She realized their marriage was over before it got started.

She sat in that luxurious newlywed's suite crying and wondering how in the world had she not seen this coming. When they returned home from their passionless honeymoon, Samantha was shrewdly informed by her husband that he would only be spending a few nights a week at their home. The rest of the time he would be staying in town, at his other house, without her.

He gave absolutely no explanation or reasoning. Soon after, Samantha started hearing whispers about her husband's secret life. It turned out Nicholas was an avowed homosexual. He had cleverly hidden his lifestyle from his parents because he didn't want to jeopardize losing his inheritance. He knew that if his father found out about his secret lifestyle, he would be eliminated from the family's will. His dad despised homosexuals with a passion, so Nicholas devised a scheme to get married to convince his dad he was a chip off the old block. He entered into a marriage covenant with Samantha by defraud.

Using love as his bait, his plot was to find and marry a church girl. When he told Samantha that he would love and cherish her forever, those empty words were just part of his [*sic*] plot. Like deadly arrows, his words pierced and wounded Samantha's heart. When she filed for divorce and attempted to get on with her life, Nicholas became furious! He told his wife that he was a homosexual, but he cleverly waited until after she married him to make that disclosure.

He was currently living with and having sex with another male, yet he had the audacity to insist that she stay married because of her religious beliefs against divorce. He was so enraged that he threatened to ruin her if she exposed his secret sin in their divorce proceedings. This was no soap opera. This was real life. Samantha endured that nightmarish marital union for seven long tumultuous years.

If you don't already know it, just as God has men and women who obey His Word and follow His voice, so does the devil. Jesus was having a heated dialogue with a bunch of self-righteous heathens. They were trying to persuade the Lord that they knew and followed God. At the climax of their heated discussion, Jesus revealed their true nature and the sinister intent of their hearts.

John 8:41-44 [Emphasis added]
[41] YE DO THE DEEDS OF YOUR FATHER. Then said they to
him, We be not born of fornication; we have one Father, *even*
God.
[42] Jesus said unto them, IF GOD WERE YOUR FATHER, ye would
love me: for I proceeded forth and came from God; neither came
I of myself, but he sent me.
[43] Why do ye not understand my speech? *even* because ye cannot
hear my word.
[44] YE ARE OF *YOUR* FATHER THE DEVIL, and THE LUST OF
YOUR FATHER YE WILL DO..."

Although these men faithfully attended religious ceremonies and
although they adamantly claimed to know God, it was only for show.
They did not know or follow God. They left their church services and
proceeded to carry out the deeds of their true father, the *devil*. Get this
next critical point engraved into your mind and heart as quickly as
possible. The devil has men and women who obey his voice and like
remote controlled robots, he compels them to carry out his plot to ruin
your love life. He strategically plants these men and women in your
path in an attempt to lure you into falling in love with one of them.

Later on, I'll show you how he influences them to follow his
commands. Right now, read a quick overview of his secret plot. Ladies,
his plot is to constantly mock you with the men he sends into your life.
These men will keep your heart and emotions pinned up against a
jagged brick wall. He intends for you to spin your wheels in dead-end
relationships, one after another. He plans to stain your conscience with
a long list of past sex partners who misuse your body and then quietly
vanish into the night. This will leave you with the bitter feeling of
being exploited by men and taking on the, *"All men are dogs,"* mentality.

His plot is to get you to have sex with a handsome and charming
derelict. Afterward, that irresponsible male brags to his running buddies
about what a player he is. He describes to them the lingerie you wore
for him and gives them intimate details of your sexual encounters. In
the meantime, you discover that you are pregnant by him. With the
news of your expectancy, he stops calling you and he stops coming by.

Even with the accessibility of all of the modern technology: e-mail,
cellular phones, pagers, beepers, regular telephones and postal services,
you still cannot reach him. He has made it crystal clear. He does not
want to see you and he does not want to talk to you anymore! Now
you're sitting at home alone, brokenhearted in a bed of tears. What
happened? It's pretty obvious. You fell for a man who was hired and
inspired by the devil. He toyed with your emotions, played with your
physical body, jerked your heart around and then fled!

The devil's secret plot is to lure you into a relationship or marriage, with a man who thrives on abusing and beating women. For the men, his secret plot is to send into your life one of the many females who has gone buck wild sexually. Her objective is to get pregnant and use the baby to force you to marry her. After you crack under pressure and say, "I do," you will need to brace yourself because these females will adamantly refuse to give up their promiscuous lifestyles.

The devil's plot is to seduce you to fall for a woman who is emotionally unstable. There are a number of paths your life can take if you make that critical mistake. All of them are pretty scary. Aside from filing false rape charges, they will also file false domestic violence charges. These females will physically assault you and dare you to call the police. If you make the call, they will claim that you attacked them. In most cases, you will be the one who is arrested and convicted.

If you decide to break up with her instead of dialing 911, you need to beware. In the past, these females used to stalk you, scratch your car, flatten your tires or crack your windshield. To this new breed of women, that kind of stuff is child's play. Today, they find another man, have sex with him, get pregnant and then swear under oath that you are the baby's daddy. Be advised, most states stand behind this type of fraud and will force you to pay her. When you show up in court, she will growl at you as the judge orders you to pay her or go to jail!

She may attempt the suicide plot. That's when she threatens to commit suicide if you try to break up with her. Or she may try the miscarriage trick. She'll claim she's pregnant, mysteriously have a miscarriage and blame you for the loss of her fictitious child. The trap is to make you feel guilty enough to take her back. If none of those tactics work, she may resort to violence!

Overall, the devil's plot is to fill your memory with broken promises of fidelity, betrayal and love disappointments. His secret plot is to seduce a man to fall for a wanton female or a woman to fall for a rolling stone male, have sex, and get infected with HIV/AIDS, Syphilis, Genital Warts, Herpes, Chlamydia or with (HPV) Human Papilloma Virus.

His plot is to get you to take on a live-in lover who eventually abandons you, leaving you with an enormous stack of bills you could never pay by yourself. With their disappearance, your credit will be ruined and you may be forced to file bankruptcy.

Finally, the devil wanted you to experience living through the nightmare of a stormy marriage and then a bitter divorce, one that pitted you against your spouse in a fierce, expensive and drawn out courtroom battle. Afterwards, you wake up and realize that there has got to be a better way to finding *True Love*. There is a better way!

It all starts with discerning if a potential mate is determined to fulfill the Lord's glorious plan for your love life or if they are dead set on carrying out a secret plot to ruin your life. One issue should be crystal clear, there are certain men and women who are *mis*-guided. Secretly, they live to scheme, connive, abuse, misuse, and get over on others. When it comes to finding *True Love*, they don't suddenly clean up their act and turn from their wayward ways. Notice what the Scriptures say about these malignant males and vixen females.

> Proverbs 6:26 AMP [Emphasis added]
> "...and the adulteress STALKS *and* SNARES [as with a hook] the precious life [of a man.]

> Jeremiah 5:26 [Emphasis added]
> For among my people ARE FOUND wicked men: THEY LAY WAIT, as he that setteth snares; THEY SET A TRAP, THEY CATCH MEN.

Do you understand what your eyes just read? The Scriptures don't lie. These men and women are skilled predators and they are on the hunt. They are desperately seeking to be in a relationship with you, not to shower you with love or to expand your horizons, but for the sole purpose of ruining your life. Multitudes of good hearted people have asked themselves questions like, "How did I end up in such a terrible relationship with such a hurtful person?" Up to this point they never knew the answer to those questions.

Some men and women wallow in self-pity for years wondering, "What did I do wrong?" "What did I do to deserve this?" They didn't have a clue that they had been systematically set up to have their hearts broken by one of the devil's henchmen or hatchet women.

The person they met and fell in love with had a secret agenda that was meted out to them from the synagogue of satan. I'm not trying to discourage anyone, God forbid, but you need to know the truth. If you fall for the bait and allow one of these males or females to lure you into a relationship, you are in major trouble. Be advised that no amount of advice you or anyone else gives them, no long talks the two of you have, or counseling or therapy is going change their callous hearts.

They will passionately swear they are going to change. They will unashamedly plead with you to stay and give them another chance. Some will claim they have found God, but their actions will prove their words to be baseless empty confessions. Smooth operators commonly use church attendance and vain religious talk as a last ditch effort to make you believe they have a heart to follow God.

Praying for and pleading with these type of people hoping to modify their behavior is like pleading with and interceding for the likes of Pharaoh, Hitler and Jezebel. You can pray and intercede for them for the next five decades, but in the end, their tombstone is still going to shamefully read.

> Revelation 2:21 [Emphasis added]
> And I gave her space to repent of her fornication; AND SHE REPENTED NOT.

The only option you have when dealing with these individuals is to be straightforward and get them out of your life immediately! For the love of God, don't marry one of them! You say, "But Brother Triplett, that doesn't sound Christian, does it?"

If believing in God means allowing people to run over your heart with a Mack Truck or torch your emotions with a British Army two ton flame thrower, then we are all in big trouble. Be forewarned and advised - these men and women are not rookies.

They are bona fide masters at using the art of persuasion and seduction. They have hands of silk, eyes of diamonds, voices of angels but HEARTS OF STONE! The tactics they employ to win your heart and convince you they are *The One* can only be compared to the cunning "bait and switch" tactics used by cold blooded, roguish con men. In their plot to snare you and get you to enter into a relationship with them, they put on their best game faces.

Most people will testify under oath that they would have never believed their loved one was capable of intentionally hurting them. However, they now have the emotional, mental, financial or physical scars to prove that what they first believed about this person was completely erroneous. At this point, I must become brutally honest with you. When it comes to choosing a mate, the average person has been taught to use methods that border on utter insanity.

When a person asks the question, "How will I know when I found *The One?*", they need solid information that will help guide them through the maze of liars, fakes, cheaters and abusers.

They need knowledge to assist them in detecting and rejecting the mass number of men and women who are hunting for their next human guinea pig so that they can conduct another destructive love, sex or marriage experiment. But instead of receiving any valuable or useful knowledge, they are given cryptic, worn-out cliches such as, "You'll know when it's right," "Listen to your heart," "Go with your feelings," and "Wait on God." What happens next? They follow that advice and still end up with a jilted heart and torched emotions.

If finding *True Love* was that simple, phrases like "broken vows," "extra marital affairs," "domestic violence" and the words "divorced" and "betrayed" would be some of the least used words and phrases in the English language. That's why I'll continue repeating this next statement until it becomes etched in your mind. "**The secret plot is to lure you into a relationship or marriage from hell.**"

Some men and women are oblivious to that fact and others simply don't get it. Therefore, they go through life constantly being lured into lover's booby traps. Samson is a prime example. He got snared, not once, but three times. We can learn a great deal from his tragic love stories and terrible choices in women.

> Judges 14:1-3,7 [Emphasis added]
> ¹ And Samson went down to Timnath, and SAW A WOMAN in Timnath of the daughters of the Philistines.
> ² And he came up, and told his father and his mother, and said, I HAVE SEEN A WOMAN in Timnath of the daughters of the Philistines: now therefore GET HER FOR ME TO WIFE.
> ³ Then his father and his mother said unto him, Is there never a woman among the daughters of thy brethren, or among all my people, that thou goest to take a wife of the uncircumcised Philistines? And Samson said unto his father, GET HER FOR ME; FOR SHE PLEASETH ME WELL.
> ⁷ And he went down, and TALKED WITH THE WOMAN; and she pleased Samson well.

Samson set his eyes on this woman and one look was all it took! He knew absolutely nothing about her; but that didn't stop him from instantly falling madly in love with her. From that moment on, his heart was dead set on making her his wife. Their marriage hit the jagged rocks as soon as they said, "I do!" Within seven days, the secret plot to ruin Samson's life through his wife was revealed.

> Judges 14:15 [Emphasis added]
> And it came to pass on the seventh day, that they said unto Samson's wife, ENTICE THY HUSBAND...

Samson had put forth a riddle to his wife's fellow countrymen, it was a common practice in those days to give riddles during festivities. If they answered the riddle properly, he promised to give them thirty linen undergarments and thirty changes of raiment.

Those garments were a sign of wealth, sort of like wearing Rolex, Armani, Gucci or Jean Bourget. Those men wanted that clothing so badly that they coerced Samson's wife to use her womanly charm to entice Samson into giving her the answer.

Judges 14:16-17 [Emphasis added]
¹⁶ AND SAMSON'S WIFE WEPT BEFORE HIM, and said, Thou dost but hate me, and lovest me not: thou hast put forth a riddle unto the children of my people, AND HAST NOT TOLD IT ME... ¹⁷ AND SHE WEPT BEFORE HIM THE SEVEN DAYS, while their feast lasted: and it came to pass on the seventh day, that HE TOLD HER, because she lay sore upon him: AND SHE TOLD THE RIDDLE TO THE CHILDREN OF HER PEOPLE.

Instead of forsaking these men and watching her husband's back, this woman betrayed her husband just so her countrymen could flex their new designer wardrobes. After committing marital treason she added insult to injury. She abandoned Samson and moved in with one of his friends. It's safe to say that Samson chose the wrong mate.

Judges 14:20 NIV [Emphasis added]
And Samson's wife WAS GIVEN TO THE FRIEND who had attended him at his wedding.

Here is a quick recap of Samson's first love. It was love at first sight. They made the "**One Hundred Yard Dash To The Wedding Altar.**" His bride immediately turned traitor, deceived him and then ran off with one of his new found friends. His second attempt at love fared no better. Samson's midnight fling with this female put him just a few hours away from becoming another robbery and homicide victim.

Judges 16:1-2 NIV [Emphasis added]
¹ One day Samson went to Gaza, where HE SAW A PROSTITUTE. He went to spend the night with her.
² The people of Gaza were told, "Samson is here!" So they surrounded the place and LAY IN WAIT FOR HIM all night at the city gate. They made no move during the night, saying, "At dawn WE WILL KILL HIM."

After escaping that ill-advised one night stand, Samson met the third girl of his dreams, the infamous Delilah. Contrary to popular belief, the Scriptures will prove these two never married. They remained lovers until Delilah completed her assignment to rip Samson's heart out. Just like his previous two relationships, Samson fell head over heels in love in three seconds flat. He had no idea that his new female heart throb helped write the book on how to set a lover's booby trap.

Delilah wasted no time digging her razor sharp claws into Samson's backside. The 16th chapter of Judges reveals five critical issues concerning Delilah's secret plot against her boyfriend: **1). The ease in which she betrayed Samson 2). The dogged persistence she used to ruin his life 3). How she convinced him to think that she loved him 4). How she gained his** complete trust 5). **The obvious callousness of her heart.**

<u>**The Timeline of Delilah's Booby Trap**</u>

Judges 16:4 [Emphasis added]
And it came to pass afterward, that HE LOVED A WOMAN in the valley of Sorek, WHOSE NAME WAS DELILAH.

Judges 16:16 [Emphasis added]
"...she pressed him daily WITH HER WORDS, and urged him..."

Judges 16:17 [Emphasis added]
"...he told her ALL HIS HEART..."

Judges 16:18 [Emphasis added]
And when Delilah saw THAT HE HAD TOLD HER ALL HIS HEART, she sent and called for the lords of the Philistines, saying, Come up this once, for HE HATH SHEWED ME ALL HIS HEART. Then the lords of the Philistines came up unto her, and brought money in their hand.

Judges 16:19 [Emphasis added]
AND SHE MADE HIM SLEEP UPON HER KNEES; [a sign of complete trust] and she called for a man, and she caused him to shave off the seven locks of his head; AND SHE BEGAN TO AFFLICT HIM, AND HIS STRENGTH WENT FROM HIM.

The final act of Delilah's secret plot against Samson was to gently lull him to sleep. Samson was thoroughly convinced that he had found *True Love*, but that was before Delilah woke him up to a brutal nightmare. Read the final script again, "**She began to afflict him.**" The woman he loved did this to him! They are out there, cunning souls whose hearts are inspired by evil. They lurk in the shadows hunting for prey, desperately searching for someone to fall into their snare.

They are itching to seduce, aching to connive and burning to manipulate someone into becoming their girlfriend or boyfriend, casual sex partner, live-in-lover or their lawfully wedded husband or wife.

You need to know how to spot them! Sincere, good-hearted people primarily choose the wrong mate because of the secret plots females like Delilah and brutish men like Nabal have engraved in their hearts.

I Samuel 25:2-3 [Emphasis added]
[2] And there was a man in Maon, whose possessions were in Carmel; and THE MAN WAS VERY GREAT, and HE HAD THREE THOUSAND SHEEP, and A THOUSAND GOATS: and he was shearing his sheep in Carmel.

I Samuel 25:2-3 [Emphasis added] Continued...
³ NOW TIID NAME OF THE MAN WAS NABAL; and the name of
his wife Abigail: and SHE WAS A WOMAN OF GOOD
UNDERSTANDING, AND OF A BEAUTIFUL COUNTENANCE:
but the man was CHURLISH AND EVIL in his doings; and he
was of the house of Caleb.

Did you read Abigail's biography? She was a woman of good
understanding and she was beautiful. She was the type of woman a
man dreams of. So how in the world did she connect with a man
described as churlish and evil in his doings? The word "churlish" means
to be cruel, severely disrespectful, stiff necked and always in trouble.
It means to be grievous and hard-hearted. Here's how one of Nabal's
hired hands described his employer, I Samuel 25:17 AMP [Emphasis added].
"...For he is such a wicked man that one cannot speak to him." Now read
how Abigail described the man she exchanged marriage vows with:

I Samuel 25:25 AMP [Emphasis added]
Let not my lord, I pray you, regard THIS FOOLISH *and* WICKED
FELLOW NABAL, for as his name is, so is he- Nabal [foolish,
wicked] is his name, and FOLLY IS WITH HIM..."

She wasn't describing a serial rapist. She was talking about her
spouse! How low could Nabal go? While Abigail was pleading with
David to spare his life, her husband was at home throwing an all night
party, complete with strippers and free flowing liquor.

I Samuel 25:36 [Emphasis added]
AND ABIGAIL CAME TO NABAL; and, behold, he held a feast in
his house, like the feast of a king; and Nabal's heart *was* merry
within him, FOR HE *was* VERY DRUNKEN: wherefore she told
him nothing, less or more, until the morning light.

Nabal was in such a drunken stupor, Abigail had to wait until he
sobered up before she could tell him that he had been given a death
sentence. She had to plead with David to give him a stay of execution.

Her entire marriage to Nabal was spent despairing at his
drunkenness, cleaning up after his disgraceful acts and putting up
with his cruelty to her and his harshness to others.

Some people try to appear super spiritual by claiming this was
merely an unfortunate union. They claim it teaches those who have
fallen into similar pitfalls how to never let the despicable acts of their
unruly spouses hinder their devotion to God. That is one possible lesson
you could learn from such a dismal marriage; but the most crucial
thing you will ever learn from Abigail's marital plight is this:

Never become someone's boyfriend or girlfriend, fiancé, fiancée or spouse until you have discerned one of two things. Is your potential mate dead set on dragging your heart and emotions through the abrasive lover's gauntlet? Or, are they determined to fulfill the Lord's glorious plan for your love life? If you are unable to make that determination, you are headed into big trouble.

Nabal and Abigail had an arranged marriage. Nabal convinced Abigail's parents that he was an honorable man who would love, protect and cherish their daughter. They believed him, (*they had no discernment*) and they agreed to allow him to take their daughter's hand in marriage. But you just read the play-by-play analysis; Nabal was everything but honorable. He pulled off the scam of a lifetime.

He won Abigails's heart and then held her hostage in a disgraceful marriage. It is imperative that I get this point ingrained in your mind. What Nabal did to Abigail was intentional and deliberate. He never intended on being a kind, loving or faithful husband. Never!

Not in a million years. His secret plot from the beginning, was to find a good woman. Make a note of this crucial point - he was not looking for a female who bodaciously flashed her nakedness on 'Girls Gone Wild' videos. He avoided gold-diggers and females with bad nasty attitudes. He set out to find the cream of the crop, a diamond in the rough, a Proverbs 31 woman, marry her and then show her first hand what it felt like to be a worn out dirty floor mat.

All the promises he made to her and to her parents during the time he courted her were LIES! When he recited his wedding vows... ADDITIONAL LIES! When he told her that he loved her... MORE BOLD-FACED LIES! Nabal had *pre*-planned on having all-night parties while his loving wife lay awake wondering if he was committing adultery with some wanton female homewrecker.

The earth is filled with Nabals and Delilahs! The true intent of these men and women is to smooth talk their way into your life. Once they snare you, they will proceed to torch your emotions, physically abuse you, sexually misuse you, destroy you financially and basically ruin your life. To avoid these cunning relationship assassins, you need to become thoroughly familiar with three critical phrases.

- 2 -

Smooth Operators, The Baits and The Booby Traps

When it comes to finding *True Love*, there are three critical phrases you must engrave into the recesses of your mind. Get to know them intimately because without this knowledge you are playing Russian roulette with your love life. If you lose, (*as most people do*) the penalty is that you will probably find yourself wondering how you got booby trapped into a relationship from hell. Here are those phrases:

- *Smooth Operators*
- *The Baits*
- *The Booby Traps*

• *Smooth Operators* - On May 26th, 2002, America was forced to brace itself, once again, and deal with another grim tragedy. A towboat pushing two barges along the Arkansas River rammed into the Interstate 40 bridge and caused it to collapse. It was a horrible scene as trucks and vehicles plunged from the bridge into the cold murky waters. Fourteen people died.

Two hours into the tragedy a man arrived on the scene wearing a green beret and camouflaged fatigues. He called himself Captain William Clark and claimed he was from the Army's Special Forces Unit. He kept telling the Mayor of Webbers Falls that he was in charge. With persuasive words, he took command of the launch site that sent rescue boats to where the section of the bridge had collapsed and started giving orders. Away from the site, Clark wasted no time.

He went to a car dealership and told them he needed a truck to transport supplies to the accident site. Without giving them a penny, he left with a truck valued at ten grand. Employee Mike Milligan, (*real name*) said, "The man's manner was very convincing; he knew what he was doing." Next, Clark went to the Super 8 Motel in Van Buren and told them he needed eight rooms for additional military personnel who were coming to assist with the disaster. He stayed in one of the rooms and placed "Do Not Disturb" signs on the other seven, which were never occupied.

A few days later, the motel staff discovered that Clark had left without paying his bill. To add insult to injury, military officials said they had no record of a Captain William Clark. So who was this man? Authorities quickly identified him as Billy Clark of Tallapoosa, Missouri.

According to Van Buren police, Lt. Brent Grill, Billy has an extensive criminal record and was known for posing as police, fire and military officials. Bertha Weaver, former police chief in Tallapoosa, said Billy Clark spent time in her town staying at his grandmother's residence. "He's a con and he's good at it," Weaver told one reporter. "He can get money ...any place." How was he and other people like him, able to deceive so many people and get away with so much?" The answer is revealed in the Written Word of God.

> Proverbs 26:24-26 NIV [Emphasis added]
> ²⁴ A malicious man DISGUISES HIMSELF WITH HIS LIPS, but in his heart he harbors deceit.
> ²⁵ THOUGH HIS SPEECH IS CHARMING, DO NOT BELIEVE HIM, for seven abominations fill his heart.
> ²⁶ HIS MALICE MAY BE CONCEALED BY HIS DECEPTION, but his wickedness will be exposed in the assembly.

Verse 24 says, a malicious man disguises himself with his lips. In other words he conceals his true character and hides his true intentions. The next verse says his speech is charming. These men and women are masters at convincing others to believe their lies and exaggerations, that is why I have classified them as smooth operators. Do you realize how smooth a person has to be, to walk into a Super 8 Motel and convince them to give him eight rooms without giving them any money or using a credit card?

Come on now? This was no Mom & Pop operation. That motel is part of a major corporation. They have strict rules and regulations that employees must follow and this impostor still jerked their chain. Then, he was brazen enough to look the mayor straight in her eyes and claim he was running things! Did he care that he could have hampered the true rescue efforts and possibly caused someone to die unnecessarily while he masqueraded around as some big shot super-trooper? No! Smooth operators care little about the lives of the people they injure or destroy. When it comes to relationships, they will talk their way into becoming your boyfriend, girlfriend, lover or spouse.

Once they have captured your heart, brace yourself, because the next thing you will feel can only be compared to a near-sighted dentist trying to drill out your wisdom teeth with a Black & Decker 1/4 inch Cordless Drill. We hear and read about their horror stories everyday.

Disgruntled ex-boyfriend says "no way," to breakup, kills *ex*-girlfriend, then commits suicide. Wife files for divorce, adamantly demands the house, cars, jewelry, 401k, alimony, child support plus everything else they own. Meanwhile, the husband takes paternity tests and finds out that he is not the biological father of their three children. These smooth operators are able to ease their way into a person's life and cause such great pain because of their two secret weapons: their bait, it is irresistible and their well laid booby traps.

• **The Baits** - If you asked the men and women who have had their emotions engulfed in flames and their hearts dragged through the mud by a smooth operator, to describe how they viewed their former love or *ex*-spouse when they first met, here is how they would describe them:

• My soul mate	• A godsend	• My princess
• My knight in shining armor	• Attractive	• Charismatic
• Charming	• Irresistible	• Captivating
• The love of my life	• Hypnotizing	• My one and only love
• Magnetic personality	• Enchanting	• A great catch
• Sexually appealing	• A breath of fresh air	• A voice of authority
• A really good friend	• Fun loving	• Alluring
• Just what I was looking for	• Swept me off my feet	• Indescribable
• Love at first sight	• Easy going	• Impressive
• Made me laugh	• A dream come true	• Took my breath away

What you just read is a comprehensive list of the most popular baits used by smooth operators. The real life case of Jill Coit shows us just how these well-trained henchmen and hatchet women use this bait to hook their prey. Jill was an intelligent vivacious dark-haired fox from Louisiana. With her wits and beauty, she could have done just about anything. Instead, the one-time fashion model used her good looks, magnetic smile and charm to prey on unsuspecting men.

Using more than a dozen aliases to spin a tangled web of marriages, Jill said, "I do," nine times. Her life was a series of betrayals involving adultery and bigamy that ended when she killed her ninth husband. After being sentenced to prison with no possibility of parole, Jill got access to the Internet and began advertising for a husband, falsely claiming she was being released soon.

She destroyed every man she decided to date or marry. Why did she intentionally spin a web of deceit to ruin these men's lives? Investigators, psychologists and other specialists have tried to probe her mind to find out why. Is she crazy? No! Does she have a borderline personality? A thousand times no! You should know the answers by now. Read (John 8:44) again, this time in the Amplified Bible Version.

YOU ARE OF YOUR FATHER, THE DEVIL, and it is your will to practice the lusts *and* gratify the desires [WHICH ARE CHARACTERISTIC] OF YOUR FATHER. He was a murderer from the beginning and does not stand in the truth, because there is no truth in him. WHEN HE SPEAKS A FALSEHOOD, HE SPEAKS WHAT IS NATURAL TO HIM, FOR HE IS A LIAR [himself] and THE FATHER OF LIES *and* ALL THAT IS FALSE.

The Scripture reveals that these men and women follow and practice the characteristics of their father, the devil. Deceiving their way into relationships while hiding their cruel intentions is instinctive for them. Jill was just doing what came naturally for a woman who lived her life hired and inspired by the devil. She used her good looks, charming personality and quick wits as bait.

Let me make this point crystal clear. These relationship assassins look and sound like normal people. That's part of their lure and that's why they get away with ruining so many people's lives.

They are masters at touching a person's heart and then manipulating their emotions. They are ruthlessly proficient at detecting a person's vulnerabilities and then exploiting them. They can pick up on a person's natural desires and play them like a violin. That's why they have the ability to snare even those who are considered intelligent, sophisticated and highly educated.

• *The Booby Traps* - A booby trap is a concealed or camouflaged device designed to seize, injure, maim, or destroy. They are most commonly used to snare bears, mice, bugs and other animals but the deadliest of all booby traps are the ones used to capture or hurt human beings.

During the Viet Nam War, what the Viet Cong and the People's Army of Vietnam lacked in high-tech weaponry, they made up for by using cleverly concealed booby traps. Their devices of destruction were so hazardous that at one point, Charlie Company of the First Battalion, 20th Infantry, sustained over 40% casualties in a thirty-two day period. Almost half of their Company was wiped out by booby traps.

They had to face perilous devices such as the virtually invisible Bouncing Betty. This booby trap was a tomato can sized bomb hidden in the ground and covered in dirt. When an unsuspecting soldier stepped on the arming mechanism, the Bouncing Betty would shoot up in the air and explode at chest height with a devastating effect.

The Viet Cong hid Punji stakes along well-traveled paths and in rice paddies. Punji stakes were sharpened lengths of bamboo or metal with fire-hardened needle-like tips at the end. When a soldier stepped on, or laid on a Punji stake, it would pierce through his flesh and leave him in excruciating pain.

The needles were often smeared with human feces or with some other substance to induce blood poisoning. The soldiers had to avoid other deadly booby traps such as, *Spiked Mud Balls, Toe Poppers, Crossbow Traps, Bamboo Whips, Swinging Man Traps and Scorpion Filled Boxes.* Imagine being under enemy fire, and jumping into a fox hole for cover, only to find out that what you assumed to be a safe haven, turned out to be a deadly booby trap filled with venomous scorpions.

Anyone engaging in a conflict, who believes their enemy is going to fight fairly is foolish! Get this point etched in your mind. Your enemy, the *devil*, is not going to fight fairly. In his secret plot to destroy God's glorious plan for your love life, he is pulling out all stops. Here's what the Word of God says about the booby traps he places in our paths.

> II Timothy 2:26 NIV [Emphasis added]
> and that they will come to their senses and escape from the TRAP OF THE DEVIL, who has taken them captive to do his will.

There are other Scriptures that shed light on satan's diabolical scheme to booby trap us, (See I Timothy 3:7 and Revelation 2:14). Here is a critical statement concerning his secret plot that you must never forget.

To Avoid a Booby Trap You Must First Be Aware Of Its Existence

In dealing with booby traps, the key words are *conceal* and *camouflage*. Booby traps must be concealed or camouflaged in order to snag their prey. Once a sane, coherent person recognizes they are being snared into a lover's booby trap, the next logical action should be to exit the relationship. Smooth operators realize this fact, that's why they work so hard to camouflage their true character and conceal their secret plot at least until they feel they have captured your heart.

Take the case of Dylan & Jasmine. Dylan was a smooth operator with a history of exhibiting controlling and violent behaviors toward women. As fast as Clark Kent could change from a mild mannered reporter into Superman, that's how quickly Dylan could change from being a gentle and affectionate man into being a heartless abuser.

He felt absolutely no guilt about slapping, hitting, choking or kicking a female. When he lured Jasmine into falling in love, she had no idea that he was a violent time-bomb. Dylan made one mistake. He thought he had Jasmine's emotions under his complete control. He figured she was madly in love with him and wouldn't leave him no matter how he treated her.

She was in love with him but when he verbally threatened her, Jasmine smartly poured a bucket of ice water over her feelings and made a fast exit from her tormenting Casanova. When Jasmine informed the smooth operating Dylan their relationship was over, that should have been the end. But as you learned in the introduction, most smooth operators won't let go easily.

Inflamed with the breakup, Dylan waited until dark and went to the home of his *ex*-girlfriend with revenge on his mind. He slashed the tires of her car and cut the telephone lines so no one could dial 911. Thankfully, a family member in the house used a cellular phone to call the police. Deputies arrived on the scene and found Dylan hiding in the shrubbery with two large knives. When they questioned him, he was fuming. He had bitterness in his voice and hatred in his eyes.

He admitted that he came to kill his *ex*-girlfriend because she had broken up with him. After examining the knives, the cut telephone lines and the slashed tires, the only word to describe the crime scene was, "eerie." Dylan was charged with criminal attempt to commit murder, criminal trespass and other charges. You don't have to be a rocket scientist or an FBI profiler to know that had Jasmine stayed with Dylan, she would have become another battered woman statistic.

Like Nabal, Dylan was a relationship assassin. His actions are one of the many reasons why you must be made aware of the existence of these 9 deadly booby traps. The tests that Jasmine should have performed to let her know that she was being snared by a smooth operator are called, "*Booby Trap Acid Tests.*" With each booby trap, I'll give you a battery of these tests to perform. The "*Booby Trap Acid Tests*" are critical. They will help you to determine if your potential mate has used or is attempting to use a booby trap to snare you into a union from hell. You need to know right up front, if your mate fails this battery of *Booby Trap Acid Tests*, you must put the emergency brakes on that relationship! You need to stop the procession immediately! Not tomorrow! Not next week or next month!

It must happen today! You say, "But Gillis, we have the wedding date set already! We have already arranged for family and friends to come in from out of town! She already said, Yes! I'm already wearing his engagement ring! If I stop this now, I'll be embarrassed! I don't want to hurt his or her feelings."

"What will my family, friends and co-workers think? I'm pregnant! We've known each other for a long time. We're so soooo in-love! We've sent out invitations already! We live together for God's sake! This is my high school sweetheart! We already have children together!" I have had men and women give me those and various other seemingly compelling reasons why they went through the motions and stayed in a relationship doomed for failure. The things some of them did next, was completely mind boggling. Numerous men have married women just because they had a pretty face and a fine body. Before their pompous strut down the aisle, they knew these females had snotty ice maiden attitudes, but these men had their eyes focused on the bait!

Many women have tried their best to change heartless womanizers into sincere, caring, loving and moral men. In each case, their efforts proved similar to the task of trying to photograph aliens from another planet. They knew in their heart of hearts they should have pulled the emergency brakes and walked away from the relationship.

However, their decision to stay transformed their lives into a miserable pain based lover's nightmare. Tragically, some of them died in these relationships. Don't ever forget this next law. Make it the screensaver on your computer. Paste it any and everywhere you can, and keep reading it and repeating it until it's drilled into your brain.

Being in love with the wrong person will ruin your life!

It's a simple statement; but its value to you is priceless. More men and women need to know and truly understand this unforgiving law before they allow themselves to fall in love or before allowing themselves to become emotionally attached to someone. They would altogether avoid the trap of spinning their wheels trying to change their wayward or abusive mate into a dependable, trustworthy one. In the search to find the love of your life, you need to look in the mirror and ask yourself this vital question, "Am I fully prepared and absolutely willing to be my mate's: **Surrogate Parent, False Alibi, Anger Management Warden, Floor Mat, Punching Bag, Pornographic Material Monitor, Victim of Love, Emotional Haywire Security Guard, Infidelity Investigator or Drug and Alcohol Interdiction Agent?"**

If your answer is, "no," then you had better take the rule you just read extremely seriously. People who took that rule lightly have been forced by their mates to stand in one or more of those shoes, shoes that were never designed for their feet. Before we analyze the 9 deadly booby traps, you need to know the answers to two other very critical questions. **1). How do smooth operators get trained? And, 2). Who trains them?**

Buckle up, brace yourself and then take your time to digest this next chapter with utmost concern because you don't want to end up like Gavin. After ten years of marriage, Olympia, Gavin's wife, seemingly out of the blue sky filed for divorce. Gavin was a faithful, loving husband and a doting father. These were things his wife could not and would not deny. On the surface, there was no rhyme or reason for her actions. I'll show you her reasoning in a later chapter.

In a mean-spirited manner, she slapped Gavin with a $100,000 dollar lump sum alimony suit, plus a $1500 per month alimony & child support bill. As part of the divorce process, Gavin was advised by his attorney to take DNA paternity tests. He was stunned to find out that he was not the biological father of either of their two children.

Wait a second, there must be a terrible mistake! There was a mistake and Gavin was the one who made it. He chose the wrong mate! An investigation revealed that his wife, who claimed to be a Christian, never broke off the relationship with her life-long boyfriend. She had been committing adultery throughout her entire marriage.

The smooth operating Olympia finalized her secret plot to rip out her husband's heart when she and the broken hearted Gavin stood in front of the judge, recited the divorce decree and signed the paperwork, officially dissolving their marriage.

Olympia walked away from the proceedings grinning like a jovial fat cat! She had just won the relationship lottery. The way the paternity laws were written, Gavin was forced to pay his *ex*-wife child support even though the DNA confirmed the children were not his.

The judge also ordered Gavin to pay Olympia alimony and pay her attorney's fees despite the fact that his wife was a confirmed adulteress. In spite of all the shameful evidence against her, Olympia didn't blink or stutter in court. She adamantly stated her demands and sent Gavin to the poorhouse with her blood sucking greed.

By the time the dust had settled, Gavin was living in a cramped apartment, eating Nissin's Instant Cup Noodles, barely making ends meet, while his *ex*-wife was out "*...livin la vida loca.*" That's Spanish for the *crazy life*. Ten years of marriage, two children who adored and needed him, and the great memories meant nothing to Olympia.

She traded in a great husband and loving father for a boyfriend who didn't give two cents about her or her children. Poor Gavin should have seen it coming.

All the signs that his *ex*-wife was a relationship assassin was evident when they first met. You are about to go behind closed doors and find out how Olympia and other smooth operators get trained.

How "Smooth Operators" Get Trained!

If I asked you to describe the type of training necessary to become an elite Navy Seal, could you tell me? The correct answer: you must first be enlisted in the U.S.Navy, then you must be accepted into the BUD/S Training. This training includes 5 weeks of Indoctrination, 8 weeks of Basic Conditioning, 7 weeks of Diving, 10 weeks of Land Warfare, 3 weeks of Parachute Training, followed by two other intense courses. If you survive, you are assigned to a Navy Seal Team for another round of six to twelve months of rigorous on-the-job training.

If I asked you to tell me how a man learns how to lure a woman into thinking he is her knight in shining armor, marries her and then resorts to beating, slapping and punching her silly, what would you tell me? Or can you explain how a woman gets trained to convince a man that she is a sweet little princess when she is, *in fact*, a manipulative male-bashing female shopping for a disposable dad?

You must be crystal clear on two extremely vital points. First, men like Nabal and women like Delilah are smooth operators! They are smooth operators because they must successfully seduce, trick, lure, lie, manipulate or coerce someone into a relationship before they can commit an act of paternity fraud, infidelity, betrayal or abuse.

That is why it is imperative that you know how to detect these cunning relationship predators. Secondly, men like Nabal are *pre*-trained to be emotionally detached husbands, abusive boyfriends and to impregnate females then abandon them.

Women like Delilah are *pre*-programmed to be gold-diggers, she-devils and combative wives with ornery attitudes. What you don't want to do is spend two years of your life dating a man, get married and waste seven more years before it becomes apparent that your husband will never qualify to be anything more than a BOY in a man's body. You don't want to blow a year of your life courting then marrying a woman, only to be rudely awakened to the fact that your bride, who appeared to be the sweet, adorable girl next door, actually has the temperament of a black widow spider. She came from a family of females who have a successful track record of emasculating men and crushing the male ego. After the honeymoon, the nature of your marriage becomes crystal clear. Anytime your wife doesn't get her way, she sets out to ruin your day. By understanding how smooth operators get trained, who trains them and the type of training they receive, you won't waste valuable time pursuing or being pursued by one of these *pre*-programmed relationship assassins. Did you notice that in order to become a Navy Seal, a person must go through an indoctrination, conditioning and then specialty training? I've got some startling news for you; smooth operators go through similar indoctrination and conditioning.

After the indoctrination process they also receive specialized training. Their training covers areas such as: how to abuse a female and avoid prosecution, how to commit fornication and not get caught and how to get a girl pregnant and disappear from sight. They have other areas of schooling such as how to marry for money and then bleed their husband dry and how to use their child as an extortion tool. You read it right. That is not a misprint. What I am about to share with you in this chapter is not designed to frighten or discourage.

It is designed to help you to understand... **before you agree to become someone's girlfriend, boyfriend, fiancé, fiancée or husband or wife, you must confirm that they are not a trained relationship assassin.** These people are versed on how to waltz into a relationship with the ease of a cat burglar.

They are *pre*-conditioned to be pathological liars, users, abusers and homewreckers and it is the training they receive that we are going to focus on in this chapter. As I have stated, these men and women are *pre*-programmed to shred your heart into pieces. Please read that again!

If you enter into a relationship with one of them, you will know first hand how the 1,523 passengers felt right before they perished on the maiden voyage of the Titanic. It will be just a matter of time before your relationship resembles an aircraft crash and burn investigation site. Knowing how they get trained will give you a better understanding of how to properly screen potential mates and distinguish them from these Kamikaze relationship assassins.

We are going to examine a number of relationship and family hate groups. I classify them as such because they are the ones who recruit, train and deploy smooth operators to ruin God's glorious plan for your love life. Only a person who hates family values, despises marriage and has a menacing attitude towards mankind would teach people the things these groups teach.

It all starts with their indoctrination, which they perform through a little understood but powerful process called **influence by association.** I need to define the words "influence" and "association."

- To **influence** means to cause a change in a person's character or to change the way a person thinks or acts
- An **association** is a mental bonding of ideas, beliefs, thoughts, feelings or interests

Go back and *re*-read both of those definitions again because they set the tone for clearly understanding the ugly process of indoctrinating relationship assassins. A person's character, whether good or bad, is shaped by the associations that influence their life. For instance, when a man joins the U.S. Navy, he mentally bonds with their core values, which are honor, courage and commitment. Their values become his values. From their indoctrination process he builds character and confidence. He learns to accept responsibility and he learns that he must be accountable for his own actions.

Because of his association with the Navy, he is influenced to become disciplined, obedient and brave, and to uphold the highest degree of moral character. On the flip side, there are organizations, groups, clubs, secret societies and individuals who use their associations with others to *influence*, but not to do good or to be good. They influence people to do wrong, to become wicked and to commit evil acts. Associations can happen over a period of time or they can happen very quickly.

They can take place at school, at work and at church. They can develop at entertainment venues, at bars or at nightclubs, at religious gatherings or practically anywhere. Take the case of 16-year-old Luke Woodham (*real name*). On October 1st, 1997, Luke killed his 16-year-old *ex*-girlfriend. They had only dated two months, but booby traps don't take long to unfold. At his trial, he testified that Grant Boyette, (*real name*) whom he had met during his freshman year in high school, influenced him to read the works of Adolf Hitler.

Luke was influenced by his classmate to admire and follow after a man whose legacy and footprint on society was pure hatred, mayhem and brutal murder. According to sources, Luke idolized Hitler. Once you read excerpts from Luke's personal journal, you'll see that Hitler's influence on Luke's life was unmistakable. Luke recorded these eerie words about five months before taking out revenge on his *ex*-girlfriend for breaking up with him. Read and listen to Luke's heart...

From Luke's private journal, April 1997
"...Hate what humanity has made you! Hate what you have become! Most of all, hate the accursed (sic) god of Christianity. Hate him for making humanity. Hate him for making you! Hate him for flinging you into a monsterous (sic) life you did not ask for nor deserve! Fill your heart, mind, and soul with hatred; until it's all you know. Until your conscience becomes a firey (sic) tomb of hatred for the goodness in your soul. Hate everyone and everything. Hate where you were and

are. Hate until you can't anymore. Then learn, read poetry books, philosophy books, history books, science books, autobiographies and biographies. Become a sponge for knowledge. Study the philosophies of others and condense the parts you like as your own. Make your own rules. Live by your own laws. For now, truly, you should be at peace and your own true self. Live your life in a bold, new way. For you, dear friend, are a superman."

From Luke's private journal, April 14, 1997
"...On Saturday of last week, I made my first kill. The date was April 12, 1997 about 4:30 p.m. The victim was a loved one. My dear dog Sparkle. Me and an accomplice had been beating the (*curse words*)... Then we put her in the burned bag and chunked her in a nearby pond. We watched the bag sink. It was true beauty..."

There are three critical points that need to be examined.

1). Notice how Luke described his dog, "**...a loved one. My dear dog...**" Carefully analyze his words. He expressed those warm sentiments right before viciously attacking this helpless animal and then berating her with obscenities. That's just one of the ways men learn how to abuse the women they claim to love. They start by torturing animals.

2). Why was he able to depict this barbaric act as, "true beauty?" The answer is found in a sinister declaration he made in his first excerpt. Read it again, this time very slowly "**...Fill your heart, mind, and soul with hatred; until it's all you know. Until your conscience becomes a firey (sic) tomb...**"

As he filled his mind and heart with hatred through the writings of Hitler and others, his conscience became a lifeless tomb. Luke conditioned himself to be a relationship assassin.

3). The third and most critical point is found in the bottom portion of the first excerpt. In it, Luke reveals three rules adopted by all smooth operators: a. **Create your own philosophies** b. **Make your own rules** c. **Live by your own laws**. Every smooth operator lives by those rules.

Womanizer, New Age philosopher and charismatic counterculture figure, Ira Einhorn, (*real name*) created his own philosophy concerning love, sex and relationships. He was compelled to recite his beliefs to jurors in a courtroom of law. He stated, "**to kill what you love when you can't have it seems so natural" and "violence always marks the end of a relationship.**" You can tell by his warped view of love that he graduated from the smooth operators training course.

Sadly, others have adopted this fatalistic relationship belief and like Ira, have murdered the person they claimed to love. Once a person's mind has been contaminated, the next step is the intense training. This is where recruits are taught to treat the people they claim to love with deception, malice, indifference abuse and domestic violence.

The Three Primary Methods Used to Train "Smooth Operators"
- Conscience Corrupted by Immoral Men/Women
- Conscience Corrupted by the Media, Music and Hollywood
- Victims of Circumstances

- *Conscience Corrupted by Immoral Men/Women* - There are certain men and women who are responsible for influencing the minds of millions. They are not at all bashful about their mission in life, which is to persuade others to become relationship razor blades and marriage missiles. I must forewarn you, the teachings these people publish are quite offensive but you need to understand- these training camps really do exist. The first is **www.Philanderers.com**. They provide instructions for those seeking help on how to commit adultery. Another website **www.bdsm-online.com** claims to educate over 8 million visitors a month, (*at publishing their site appeared to be down*). In one of their articles, **Adultery For Adults A Guide for Self Development**, they provide over twenty-eight do's and don'ts for having an illicit affair. Tips such as:

- Do shower using the same soap you use at home because women can smell new fragrances
- Don't take your adultery partner to your favorite restaurant
- Don't become a friend of your adultery partner's family

The web page **www.ishipress.com/how2rape.htm** may seem like a parody to some, but others take it as training on how to rape a woman without leaving any evidence. Still another website **www.Askmen.com** boasts of serving 198 million readers and having 7,420 articles available online as of April 2003. Are you adding up the numbers? 8 million? 198 million? These people are being indoctrinated to get in a relationship and then hurt you. Some of the past articles on **www.Askmen.com** include

- **How To Lie To Women**
- **Top 10 Ways To Date Two Women At Once**
- **Waging Revenge On Your Ex**
- **Cheating Can Be Healthy For a Relationship**
- **Power Will Get You Sex**
- **Player's Secret Sex Guide**
- **Patience With Seduction**
- **The Shelf Life Of Sex Partners**

In the article **How To Lie To Women**, they show men how to respond to such questions as, "Do you love me?" "How do you feel about me?" They instruct men to appear caring and committed and look a woman straight in her eyes and say, "I have never been in love before, but I am falling in love with you." They tell the men to practice saying, "I love you," in the mirror so they don't choke or vomit at the thought of saying those words. They claim that the rewards of lying and claiming you love her even though you don't, is that you will get some sex.

In an article on **8 Ways To Break-Up With a Female**, they teach such tactics as "Find some way to show her total disrespect; sleep with her friends or have sex with her sister." People who claim they don't believe men and women are buying into these fiendish doctrines obviously have their brains parked on the lower basement level!

In another article on **www.Askmen.com** they claim that women want men who are sexually experienced, so they advise men to, "Sleep with as many women as you can..." They even have a membership only "Player's Club." Once a man joins, they assert that they are able to teach him how to be an expert at approaching and seducing women.

As part of his membership, he'll receive the *players'* secret sex guide, video tutorials, high resolution pictorial guides and access to all of the *players'* articles such as **How To Date Two Women At Once** and **Mastering One Night Stands**. Is this sinking in yet? These individuals spend millions of dollars every year learning how to lie, defraud and deceive their way into your heart. Here are some of the other apprenticeship programs they pay for and learn from:

www.seductionscience.com	**www.getgirls.com**
www.makeeverygirlwantyou.com	**www.pickupmagic.com**

Their training books cover everything from seduction and dating tricks, to destructive marital ploys and cunning mind games:

The 50-Mile Rule: Your Guide to Infidelity and Extramarital Etiquette
by Judith Brandt

How to Have an Affair and Never Get Caught!
by Jay D. Louise, Alan Foreman (Illustrator), Charlotte Hartford (Designer)

Make Every Girl Want You: How to Have Sex with Hot Girls (Without Even Dating Them!)
by John Fate, Steve Reil

How to Make a Man Fall in Love with You: The Fail-Proof, Fool-Proof Method
by Tracy Cabot

Many of the instructors responsible for putting together these teachings, claim they have no ill intentions. Read how they advertise their websites, seminars and books and then you decide for yourself.

- Secrets of seducing any woman even if she has a **husband, fiancé, or boyfriend**
- This book intelligently reveals and uses **all the natural needs and desires of women** to help you get into their panties!

- You will learn how to **destroy her emotional defenses**
- Learn how to **use her key emotional vulnerabilities** to your advantage
- Get females to want to have **casual sex** with you and afterwards introduce you to their girlfriends. This book is your complete guide to meeting girls, getting **great sex** from them, **and remaining their booty call for life!**
- **Simple tricks** to get your partner back - even if you hurt them!!!
- Learn to Cheat at the Dating Game - Twenty-Two Tricks To Help You **Get The Booty Every Time!!!**

Did you notice the blatantly manipulative language they use and how they reduce females to being an inanimate piece of booty? They brazenly teach other heinous tactics such as:

- **Get Pregnant** and **Get Paid** - How to Land an NBA, NFL or MLB Player!
- Have The Best of Both Worlds... **Seduce a Church Girl or a Church Man.** They'll Always Forgive You of Your Sins!
- How To **Control a Woman's Mind**, She'll Believe Your Every Word...
- How to **Deflower a Virgin** - Learn The Secrets from True Players. Bust Those Cherries (*hymens*)! You Could Become The All-Time **Virgin Slayer** Record Holder!
- **How to Seduce a Married Man** and The Benefits of Being a Mistress
- Use These Amazing Tricks To Prevent Your Mate From Finding Out About **Your Checkered Past**.

I keep telling you these men and women are trained relationship assassins. They are not novices! They are dead serious about their mission, which is to charm, disarm, then harm! When corporate executives meet to determine what information they want in their company training manuals, they always have a clear agenda of how they want to shape and mold the minds of their employees.

Before we proceed any further, let's sit in on one of the many secret meetings held by the architect of evil, concerning the indoctrination of smooth operators. You need to know satan's true agenda and clearly understand the net effect this type of training has on the recruits. It is imperative that you get this next point, so pay close attention.

Titus 1:15-16 NIV [Emphasis added]
[15] To the pure, all things are pure, BUT TO THOSE WHO ARE CORRUPTED and do not believe, nothing is pure. In fact, both THEIR MINDS and CONSCIENCES are CORRUPTED.
[16] THEY CLAIM TO KNOW GOD, but by their actions they deny him...

The devil's game plan is to use every available means, weapon and tool at his disposal to corrupt a person's mind and conscience. Once their conscience is deep fried, then get them into a relationship. To corrupt means: **1)**. To ruin morally and to make perverted.

2). To undermine a person's good character. **3).** To taint the integrity of, and to cause to err. **4).** To cause an honest person to become dishonest. Jeffrey Lionel Dahmer, (*real name*) is a prime example of someone whose mind and conscience was totally corrupted.

He converted his now infamous apartment, apartment 213 of the Oxford Apartments, into a torture chamber and human slaughterhouse of unspeakable horrors. When police entered his abode, they were shocked to find the putrid odor of rotting flesh, photographs of mutilated men and various body parts strewn around his apartment.

Dahmer confessed to some of the goriest crimes imaginable. He was sentenced to 1070 years for murder, necrophilia and cannibalism. Read his own chilling words as he describes how he was able to inflict such mayhem without a semblance of having a conscience. -- **"I trained myself to view people as objects of potential pleasure instead of people."** He trained himself. Did you get that?

Smooth operators spend many hours in training, corrupting their minds and torching their consciences. They convince themselves that females are nothing but a piece of booty. That's why some men can take a female to dinner and a movie and feel as if she's obligated to have sex with them. They view females only as inanimate objects of potential pleasure. Read how Dahmer describes the net effect of his training. **"For years now my mind has been filled with gruesome, horrible thoughts and ideas..."** Now read what Dahmer said about his own corrupted conscience. **"I don't even know if I have the capacity for normal emotions..."**

That is the *pre*-planned path for all smooth operators to travel. Once the devil succeeds at corrupting a person's mind and scorching their conscience, they automatically come to the place where they have no capacity for normal emotions.

Invariably, these questions always arise, "Gillis, what type of person is subject to becoming a smooth operator? How can I tell if it's possible that I could become a relationship assassin? And how can I protect my mind and my conscience from being corrupted?" There are four types of people who are subject to becoming relationship assassins:

1. The **God-haters** - these people have either brazenly rejected God or they believe the Bible is an outdated cryptic code book written for people who don't have a life. Instead of serving God, they cleverly replace Him with entertainment, education, sports, politics, corporate gigs and various forms of religion, relativism and new age spiritualism. Mention Christ to these people and they will get offended.
2. The **spiritually immature** - these people go to church faithfully, but the truth is, they are part of the multitude of church going, pew warming, Bible toting, verse quoting, scripturally illiterate worshippers who don't understand God, Jesus, the Holy Spirit or the kingdom of God. Aside from the fact that they attend church, their lifestyle gives little or no indication at all that they know Christ.

3. The **rebellious** - to be rebellious means to oppose, ignore, resist or defy authority. The law states, don't drink and drive. These people say, "it's my car, my body and I'll drink and drive if I very well please!" They rebel against the laws of the land and against the laws of God, it doesn't matter to them. Some rebellious people are so bodacious, they thumb their nose up to heaven, commit sin and literally dare God to do or say something about it.

4. The **feeble-minded** - to be feeble-minded means to be weak willed. To be easily convinced, swayed or persuaded. With the right bait or prodding, these individuals will break their promises, violate their marital vows, foolishly jeopardize their own life, freedom and physical health, and abandon their own flesh and blood. Once they are enticed to sin, break the law or desecrate their conscience, the issue is not if they are going to do it or not. They are going to cross the line. You can count on it. It is just a matter of time!

If any of these four profiles describes you, make no mistake about it, you are subject to becoming a relationship assassin. In all likelihood you will do just like Darma did. You will get someone to fall in love with you and then ruin God's glorious plan for their life. Darma completely fit the profile of a feeble-minded person. It didn't take much to persuade her to have sex or to move-in with a man. She learned at an early age how to, "hook up, get some booty, make out and get jiggy with it," rather than how to demand patient courtship and *True Love*.

It was like she poured high octane racing fuel on her conscience and then lit a match to it. She'd catch a man, become lovers, breakup with him and find someone new. Her body had become a revolving door for indiscriminate men. By the time she married, Darma had gotten pregnant by three different men and had had four abortions. Her attitude was, "It's my body and I have a right to enjoy my sexuality!"

To make matters worse, the abortionists thoroughly convinced her, "That's not a human being in your womb, it's just an inanimate clump of tissue and bones. It has no life or value." They swore to her there would be absolutely no side effects from having an abortion.

She was just a teenager when she terminated her first pregnancy. When she raised concerns about telling her parents, the people at the clinic told her not to worry. They told her the law says she didn't have to inform her parents. With each abortion, the clinics collected their fee, gave her a tranquilizer, performed the procedure, discarded her baby, gave her oreo cookies and a cup of orange juice and dismissed her saying, "Have a nice day!" Before and during her first abortion, Darma wept profusely. Her conscience was screaming at her saying, "No! No! Please don't do it!" But it was too late.

Darma had already conditioned herself to ignore the internal compass engraved in her heart. She had already trained herself on how to numb any emotional attachment towards men and babies.

She could turn on a man and walk away from him at the drop of a dime. Darma had become hard-hearted, manipulative, cold and calculating. Having an abortion had become as easy as changing a flat tire and each time, it seemed like there were no downsides.

But one day, the effect and consequences of her corrupted conscience hit her like a ton of bricks. Shortly after she got married, she became racked with bouts of depression, anger and overwhelming guilt. The numbness she so cleverly crafted in her mind through her pro-choice beliefs, were now replaced with flashbacks and recurring nightmares. None of the abortionists prepared her for this. Darma was in such emotional turmoil that she couldn't bring herself to have sexual relations with her husband. There was just no way!

Her inability to be intimate with her spouse compounded the tension and anger in their already highly stressed marriage. The stress was brought about due to the startling revelations of her abortions and her loose *pre*-marital sex life. Darma and her husband were receiving counseling. They even joined a church. But Darma could not erase the imprints etched on her mind. She kept visualizing those tiny feet and those precious little hands that came out of *her* womb, and then were tossed into a garbage disposal like leftover food.

Those were no longer inanimate, lifeless clumps of tissue. They were her babies that she had willfully given consent to be killed! She could no longer rationalize away her transgressions. She knew on her own that she needed to seek forgiveness. No one preached to her. No one pointed their finger in her face. No one beat her upside the head with the Bible. There were no pro-lifers camped out at her front door.

So why the change of heart? Darma became pregnant for the fifth time in her life, this time by her husband. She carried the baby in her womb to term and gave birth to a beautiful child. That's when the reality of what she had done and how she used to live, turned her life and their marriage into an inescapable house of anguish. When she cuddled the fruit of her womb, listened to their baby cry and looked into the sparkling glimmer from their baby's eyes, her hardened heart began to soften and her corrupt conscience did a 180 degree turn.

It was then that the voice of the Lord, whom she had ignored all those years, was finally able to get her to listen. It was then that she came to the realization that she had lost her capacity to have normal emotions, something she desperately wanted to regain. It was then that she cried out to the Father of heaven and earth. She repented of the sins of her past, and God, through the Blood of His Son, Jesus the Christ, graciously forgave her. But would she ever be able to forgive herself? Not even she could make that guarantee.

Would the nightmares, flashbacks or crying spells ever go away? Who could say with absolute surety? Would she ever stop hating herself or be able to be intimate with her spouse? Darma does not know. Her husband had some heated issues on his heart also. He was coming to grips with the revelation of his wife's past and his increasing resentment toward her. He simply could not or would not let go of her past. He had a menacing way of reminding her of how immoral she used to be. Please hear me! That is not God's glorious plan for any marriage.

All of that heartache, anguish and bitterness could have been avoided had her husband not adopted the philosophy of, "Whatever you did before we met doesn't count." A person's past does count! Darma could have guarded her conscience from decay. What could she have done, and what can you do, to completely shield your conscience from being corrupted and protect yourself from losing your capacity to have normal emotions? The answers are revealed in the wisdom of God.

In the Scriptures, we are commanded to guard five vital areas. To guard means to protect from harm, danger or infection by carefully watching. It means to defend from invasion and to protect from unauthorized entry. When you guard all five of these vital areas, you will never warp your conscience or taint your emotions.

• *Guard your eyes* - In Psalm 101:3, the psalmist writes, "I will set no wicked thing before mine eyes." One of the many ways a person loses touch with humanity, is through the images they burn into their mind by looking at pornographic magazines, movies, videos and DVD's.

They lose touch by viewing illicit websites and lewd cable channels and by watching television shows that incite adultery and fornication. Another way they lose touch is by constantly watching shows that depict violence and uncontrollable anger as a normal way to express one's emotions.

With each evil image they allow to pass through their eye gates unchecked, they are one step closer to entering the dark world of a corrupt conscience. In this world, rebellion, violence and ignorance reign supreme. It is a world where one becomes entrapped in the satanic prison of promiscuity, lewdness and sexual perversion.

• *Guard your ears* - In Mark 4:24, we are commanded to, "...take heed to what we hear.." In other words, be careful of what you listen to. We were given this command because words are seeds, (see Mark 4:26-32). This is a critical spiritual law that spiritually immature men and women, to their own detriment, don't know, take lightly or just ignore. Keep this point in mind. Words are seeds. First, there are good seeds, (see Luke 8:11). Once planted, these good seeds will cause you to fulfill God's glorious plans for your life.

Then there are bad seeds, (see Genesis 3:1-5). Once you allow these seeds to pass through your ear gates, they will slowly erode your ability to discern right from wrong and good from evil. These bad seeds come packaged in many forms. You can find them hidden in the theories, philosophies and idealogies of man, (see Colossians 2:8).

Remember the bizarre beliefs of Ira Einhorn concerning love on page 44? And what about the theory Darma believed that a pregnant woman is not carrying a child in her womb, just a clump of tissue? These bad seeds are also sown through music and any other method satan can employ to use words to influence you to desecrate your own conscience. That's why you must be careful what you listen to.

• *Guard your mind* - The Word of God gives us a description of the state of a person's mind when they guard this vital area. They have a sound mind, (see II Timothy 1:7), a sober mind, (see Titus 2:6) and a ready mind, (see I Peter 5:2). When people fail to guard their minds, they can end up with any of these mindsets. An easily shaken mind, (see II Thessalonians 2:2), a weak mind, (see Hebrews 12:3), a mind that is blinded, (see II Corinthians 4:4), a despiteful mind, (see Ezekiel 36:5), an evil affected mind, (see Acts 14:2), a chafed bitter mind, (see II Samuel 17:8), a double-minded mind, (see James 1:8) and a reprobate mind, (see Romans 1:28). How does one guard his mind? By following the instructions in Romans 12:2 and in Isaiah 26:3-4.

• *Guard your heart* - In Proverbs 4:23, you are commanded to, "Keep thy heart with all diligence..." Why this command? Because you will be tempted and enticed almost everywhere you turn. The devil will see to it. He is going to send people into your life whose hidden agenda will be to lure you into the prison house of the shameful and the dishonorable. Their methods of persuasion, manipulation and coercion will be so smooth, you'll be just like Darma. You won't notice your life is on a downward spiral until your mind and your conscience look and smell like a stagnant cesspool. These messengers of satan will prey upon your natural desires, promising you pleasures, fun, excitement, riches, satisfaction and sexual freedom.

But in order to achieve their promises of fulfillment, you must agree to give control of your soul over to the kingdom of darkness. They will sway you to believe there is no God. Or, instead of believing in and obeying the one and only *true* God, through His Son, Jesus the *Christ*, they will convince you to believe in a higher power, the man upstairs or some other god conjured up by a man. You may be the nicest person in the world, but if you don't guard your heart from their tantalizing temptations and irresistible enticements, you will find yourself crying after the fact, "How could I have been so blind?"

How do you guard your heart? By following the simple instructions in Proverbs 4:20-27, Ephesians 6:10-18 and Psalm 1.

• *Guard your conscience* - Your conscience is the internal eternal gauge placed in your heart by the Lord God, to cause you to discern good from evil and to distinguish right from wrong, (see Romans 1:17 - 2:15). Your conscience is engineered with a built in radar that is *pre*-calibrated to warn you when you are about to cross the line from good to evil, from right to wrong and from righteousness to unrighteousness. If you ignore any warning, no matter how insignificant it may seem, you have just violated your conscience.

The problem with that action is manifold. First, the only way to guard your conscience is by not violating it. Secondly, when you habitually violate your conscience, you begin to lose your capacity to have normal emotions. Thirdly, once you cross the line and violate your conscience, no matter how much you'd like to, you can't go back in time and reclaim it. You cannot push a button, rewind the tape of life and magically wipe away the hurt you've caused others. Plus, you cannot flip a switch and erase any self-inflicted injuries.

Finally, each time you violate your conscience, the next time around, it becomes much easier. In many cases your actions will get progressively worse. Remember when I said that your conscience comes *pre*-calibrated? When you fail to guard your ears, eyes, mind and heart, you put your conscience through a disturbing *de*-calibration process.

Every smooth operator, whether they are a liar, adulterer, fornicator, vixen, wife beater, stalker, gold-digger, womanizer or just a plain jerk, has gone through the process of *de*-calibrating their conscience. What you want is a potential mate who has a good conscience before God, (see Acts 23:1).

Set your standard to be with a man or a woman who is committed to always guarding these five vital areas. When you find and fall in love with that person, you can always count on them to cover you with love, prayer and protection. They will never hurt you or betray you and they will never leave you crying in the dark.

On the other hand, if you detect that a potential mate has not obeyed the command to guard his or her eyes, ears, mind, heart and conscience, the only sound advice I can give you is this - watch your back! Let's do a quick recap of what we have learned in this chapter.

First, we learned that men and women are persuaded to become smooth operators through a little known but very powerful process called **influence by association**. Part of their indoctrination process is learning the tricks of the trade such as how to say, "I love you," when in fact, they don't love you.

They have been taught how to date you while secretly seeing other people, without ever getting caught and many more harmful relationship and martial tactics. We found out trainers are so brazen that they print books, stage seminars and publish teachings on the Internet, showing their trainees how to get married and afterwards sneak off and have extramarital affairs. They teach their recruits how to use various ploys and other stratagems to trick, seduce, lure, coerce or manipulate you into falling in love with them. The tactics and scams they use can only be aptly described by the legal term, "*lying in wait.*"

Throughout this book I will be revealing some of their evil hearted schemes such as (TERT), **The Engagement Ring Trick.** Ladies, you do not want to miss that one. But for now, I'm going to wrap up this first method of training smooth operators by saying this. There is a segment of society whose mission in life is to raise up the next generation of liars, vixens, womanizers, fornicators and adulterers. These immoral men and women get up in the morning and go to bed at night trying to figure out how to corrupt a person's mind and conscience.

The people who follow their teachings do so for one reason. They are intentionally trying to find ways to ruin God's glorious plan for your life. Here is the next method smooth operators use to get trained.

• *Conscience Corrupted by the Media, Music and/or Hollywood* - Our society is greatly influenced by the media, music and by Hollywood. I do not think any reasonable person will disagree with that assessment. Many of the entertainment products and messages they market to the public serve to influence, but only in a negative diabolical way. For them, it's all about two things: the almighty dollar and the glory and accolades they receive with each successful project. The fact that they are altering a person's character and influencing people to carry out immoral acts and evil deeds is irrelevant!

Take the Playstation 2 video game, "**Grand Theft Auto 3**," for instance. This game puts the player in the role of being an aspiring felon. They gain rank in the criminal society by robbing banks, committing carjackings, arsons, larceny and by carrying out other acts of violence.

Impressionable kids and others are spending hours at a time learning how to take on the spirit of a felon, conditioning their minds to scheme, connive and wreak havoc against society. The average parent wouldn't give a second thought about buying such a "game" for their child, simply classifying it as harmless entertainment.

They don't realize they're paving the way for their little kid to become a terror to humanity. It is the seemingly little things most people shrug off as insignificant that are the most dangerous.

Remember the 2002 Pepsi Cola commercial featuring Austin Powers punching Britney Spears in her face, sending her plummeting to the floor? Understand that many of the little boys who laughed when they saw that eerie commercial will be one of the next generation of adult males assaulting their wives, fiancées and girlfriends.

In your quest to find the love of your life, the issue of a potential mate's conscience being corrupted is a critical issue that you cannot ignore. Read these accounts of people whose lives and actions were influenced by the media, music and by Hollywood. (*All are real names*).

- In 1993, members of the Spur Posse Club of Lakewood High School in Lakewood, California were arrested in connection to their "sex for points" gang activities. In a long-running sexual competition, members of the Spur Posse raped and molested dozens of girls, one as young as ten years old. Each girl with whom a gang member had sex was worth one point, multiple encounters with the same girl didn't count. The group admitted to being inspired by the bolster of the basketball legend Wilt Chamberlain, who allegedly claimed to have had intercourse with 1,000 women. The boys escaped punishment.
- In 1990, 13-year-old Zacharian Hurt of St. Louis, Missouri, learned about a sex act from a porno magazine and then he carefully wrapped shoelaces around the necks of two boys, his 8-year old brother, Benjamin, and neighbor, Todd Pigg, Jr., 7, and pulled them tight, accidentally strangling them. The porn article that Zacharian told police he read dealt with cutting off the flow of blood to the brain, which was supposed to result in heightened sexual pleasure.
- In 2002, in the United Kingdom, a 15-year-old Bexleyheath schoolboy received a four year jail sentenced for raping a 13-year-old schoolgirl. Jurors heard testimony of how the teen rapist idolized rapper DMX, whose violent and explicit lyrics incite murder, illicit sex, glorifies rape and abuse, and encourages and inspires men to dehumanize and disrespect the female gender. The rapper has songs entitled: **Dogs For Life**; **Weed, Hoes, Dough**; **Murdergram**; **Money, Cash, Hoes** and **Born Loser**. During sentencing, Judge Brian Barker QC said the teen displayed "attitudes to young girls that are degrading and showed no respect or understanding." After being indoctrinated by songs and lyrics that influenced him to see females as "hoes," should we expect anything less from this teenager, or any other teenager whose idol glorifies disrespect and dishonor?
- In 2002, in Kenosha, Wisconsin, 19-year-old Micah Zoerner was arrested and charged with theft, burglary and auto theft in a crime spree involving about 100 cars. Micah told detectives that he was inspired by the video game, "**Grand Theft Auto**." He was really saying that he learned his craft from a video game!
- Certain music by Ozzy Osborne has been named to have spurred numerous suicides. In May 1986, Michael Waller put a pistol to his head and shot himself after repeatedly listening to Ozzy's **Suicide Solution**. In 1984, John McCollum's final hours were spent repeatedly listening to Ozzy Osborne's song, **Diary of a Madman** and to his album, **Speak of the Devil**, before shooting himself in the head. Are those just coincidences or influences by association? Keep reading...
- In 1994, a 14-year-old boy accused of decapitating a 13-year-old girl in Texas reportedly told police he wanted to be famous like the killers in the Oliver Stone movie "**Natural Born Killers**." In Utah, a teenager became so obsessed with the motion picture that he shaved his head and wore the same type of

distinctive glasses as the film's character Mickey. He murdered his stepmother and half sister. This particular film has been linked to influencing numerous murders from Paris, France, all the way to Atlanta, Georgia.

• In April 1992, Ronald Howard was driving a stolen automobile through Jackson County, Texas, when Officer Bill Davidson, a state trooper, stopped him for a possible traffic violation. Howard fatally shot the Officer with a nine millimeter Glock handgun. At the time of the shooting, Howard was listening to the rap album **2PacalyspeNow**. Howard said that listening to this music influenced him to shoot Officer Davidson. A jury believed him and convicted the cop killer. He was sentenced to death.

• In 1998, in Jonesboro, Arkansas, 13-year-old Mitchell Johnson warned friends that he had a lot of killing to do after he was jilted by a girl. A day later, police said, he and his 11-year-old cousin lured classmates out of the school by pulling a fire alarm, then mowed them down with gunfire. Four girls and an English teacher were killed. Eleven others, 10 students and a teacher were also wounded. After the stealth ambush, the teen told his mother that he was influenced by the violent lyrics of gangsta rap. He was infatuated with rappers Tupac and Bone Thugz n Harmony. Mitchell brought his music to school with him, listened to it on the bus, tried listening to it in class, sang the lyrics over and over at school and played a cassette in the bathroom about coming to school and killing.

• In 1997, two heavy-metal record labels, Metal Blade and Road Runner, made an out-of-court settlement with Donna Ream, who had been shot in an Oregon convenience store by four teenagers. The teens had allegedly been influenced to commit the crime after listening to the recordings of two "death metal" bands, Deicide and Cannibal Corpse.

• On September 7th, 1994, two 17-year-olds in a sniper attack on a police van, shot and killed Milwaukee Police Officer William Robertson. The triggerman, Curtis Walker, told police, a rap song called "Gangster," by Tupac, Ice-T, Spice-One and M.C.A., "geeked him up" to stalk and kill the officer.

There can be no denial of the influence the media, music and Hollywood has on mankind. People who say it isn't so are displaying a blatant rejection of undeniable and irrefutable facts. The average teenager rates their friends, music, movies and television ahead of their parents, ahead of God, ahead of the church and ahead of education as the main factors that influence them about love, sex and relationships. Do you understand what you just read? Think about it! They are being trained about love by watching shows like Elimidate, Girlfriends, The 5th Wheel, Dismissed and Sex in the City.

They are being schooled about sex by listening to lyrics that persuade them to believe females are "hoes." By the time a person repeatedly embeds these songs into their mind and conscience, their capacity for normal emotions has been seriously impaired! Through the media, music and Hollywood, teenagers and adults learn to reduce sex to being on the same level as playing sports. To them, sex is just a game, something they engage in to have their fill of fun and frolic. When the sex play is over, they numb their feelings, if they had any at all, and move on. One popular songwriter wrote lyrics stating that she never loved her boyfriend, she just used him because she was curious. Those are the type of words and attitude smooth operators drop on their soon to be *ex*-wife or *ex*-husband while their spouses are tearfully and frantically trying to figure out what they did to deserve this. They did nothing to deserve it, they just chose the wrong mate!

Many artists have made it their mission in life to introduce lyrics that convince men to view females as "hoes" and other vile, ungodly creatures. Their songs inspire, influence and persuade men to abuse and misuse women. As little boys and young men listen to these songs repeatedly, they become *pre*-conditioned to grab, slap, hit, punch, kick and rape women. Females help fuel the mindset to misuse their own gender. On any given day, sitting in your local grocery store are magazines directed at teenage girls, written by women, encouraging the teens to have sex on their second or third date. What difference does it make if she waits until the second or the thirtieth date?

Either way, she still gets used, then dumped. Certain commercials further that mentality with their slick advertisements: buy her a beer or a drink and get the *booty*. Wear this cologne and get the *booty*. Buy her a diamond ring and get the *booty*. Wear this deodorant and get the *booty*. And! If she doesn't give up the *booty*, take it! As one rapper belches, **"...don't love them hoes."** By the time they get to the age of manhood, these men have spent most of their young lives being *pre*-programmed to devalue and degrade women and treat them as if they were common prostitutes. The girls fare no better.

Just like the boys they log thousands and thousands of hours being encouraged by spiritually rebellious men and lewd females to engage in casual sex. They completely ignore all of the spiritual, emotional and physical ramifications. The devil intends on starting a person on the perilous journey of corrupting their mind and conscience as early in life as possible. Teenagers and *pre*-teens alike are constantly bombarded with distorted views of love and sex. These views are designed to leave them confused, dazed and compelled to give in to the cold relentless world of the media's sex pressure tactics.

It was announced on December 27, 2002, that America Online unit won a $6.9 million judgment against a company accused of sending more than a billion junk e-mail (*spam*) messages promoting sexually explicit Web sites to AOL customers. In that same month in Bergenfield, New Jersey, two youngsters opened a Barney the Dinosaur music book and discovered a photo of a nude man and a nude woman embracing. Under the picture was the caption, "Wilder Sex." The page also included reviews of other adult movies written in another language.

Then there are organizations such as Planned Parenthood. With a name like that, one would assume they exemplify family values. Think again! Planned Parenthood is one of the nations leading abortion providers and peddlers of immoral sex. One of their websites **www.teenwire.com** is specifically geared towards corrupting teens. On this Web site they use animated games like, **Hooray for Birth Control** and **Jim Dandy and His Very Gay Day**, to aggressively promote promiscuity and homosexuality. One page on their Web site called the **Sextionary** uses a narrator and cartoons to ask teens test questions such as: **What is a clitoral hood? What is performance anxiety? What are seminiferous tubules?**

It gets much worse. On this site they peddle articles such as **Roll It On, Slip It Off: The Art of Using a Condom, Boobs: An Owner's Manual** and **Abortion in a Pill.** A teen can click on the movies link and watch short films such as: **He said, She Said.** This is a movie about a teenage boy having sex for the first time. In the movie, a female shows him how to put on a condom and afterwards they have sex.

Throughout their website, teens are indoctrinated to believe that kissing, hugging, body rubbing, touching, and sexual intercourse is defined as *sex play...* an amusement, a sport, a game which they have a right to enjoy without interference from parents or anyone else.

Are the tactics of Planned Parenthood and other similar organizations working? Just ask the average teenager. My heart was broken when one teen confided that she had sexual intercourse with eight different boys while she was in junior high. They had sex with her and left her like thieves in the night. She was a joke to them. Just a piece of *booty* they used for bragging rights.

Those boys may never know or understand the harm they caused that little girl. They violated her innocence and left her with a spirit of depression and the spirit of suicide. Why didn't it bother their hearts? It didn't because they had become bona fide trained relationship assassins. Those boys had not even graduated from high school and already their minds and consciences had been *de*-calibrated and *re*programmed to ruin a woman's life and giggle about it.

In the spring of 1996, an outbreak of syphilis struck a group of teenagers in an affluent community in Rockdale County, Georgia. The kids were coined as the **Lost Children of Rockdale.** Epidemiologists who interviewed them, were shocked to learn that children as young as fourteen had scores of sex partners. Others told of all-night orgies.

In one interview, a young girl said, **"I get this hard front on where I'm just cold... I don't care, screw it, I'm going to go and try to ruin a guy's night or something evil like that..." "I have this anger toward guys mainly because the first guy that I loved or gave myself to, hurt me in the long run and I think I have a right to show anger toward guys."**

Those are the coldhearted words of a trained relationship assassin. Remember Olympia at the end of the last chapter, on page 39? Like this teenager, she was bitter at men. So bitter that she "laid in wait" until she found her prey named Gavin and married him. She patiently set him up for ten years before making him pay a hefty price for all the hurt she had suffered by men who had exploited her in the past.

Olympia was a cunning and patient smooth operator. Where are the next generation of marriage missiles and relationship assassins going to come from? A large portion of them are going to rise up from the training camps held by these subversive media, music and Hollywood types. Upon indoctrination and graduation, they have been trained to immediately seek to enter into a relationship with YOU!

Don't make the same mistake countless other men and women have made by not measuring the condition of your potential mate's conscience. How do you accomplish such a formidable but critically important task? By questioning and scrutinizing:

- The type of movies, videos, TV programs & cable shows they watch
- The type of music they listen to and buy, and video games they play
- The type of websites they visit
- The groups, organizations, cults and clubs they follow or have joined
- The type of friends and associates with whom they socialize
- The type of people they idolize, admire and try to emulate
- The type of books, magazines and publications they read and buy
- Their philosophies, idealogies and beliefs
- Their relationship or lack of relationship with God
- Their position on cigarettes, drugs, alcohol and addictions
- Their position on pornography, homosexuality, lesbianism
- Their position on abortion, coerced abortion and forced abortion
- Their position on teen sex, pre-marital sex, forced sex and date rape
- Their position on fornication and adultery
- Their position on living together, also known as cohabitation
- Their position on stalking, verbal, emotional, physical and sexual abuse
- Their position on marriage, separation, divorce, children and family
- Their position on keeping their word and making a commitment
- Their position on ending an engagement and halting a dating relationship

Examining these critical areas is the starting point to help you determine if your potential mate's conscience has been corrupted by the media, music or by Hollywood. Never forget this. What a person listens to, watches and reads and the people they admire and idolize directly influence the condition of their mind and conscience.

He may be an engineer, attend church, pay tithes, pray daily and boldly proclaim that he has put God first place in his life. BUT! If he enjoys listening to music that incites the spirit of violence, degrades women and promotes illicit sex, you don't have to wonder or pray about the condition of his conscience. It is corrupt! He [*or she*] may claim that it's just harmless entertainment. They may say it's just fantasy. Or, they may come back with reverse psychology and say, "If it's so bad why is everybody doing it, listening to it, watching it or reading it?"

The answer to that question is simple. It's the same reason millions of people listen to songs that promote rape, incite having sex with minors, glorify promiscuity and provoke murder and yet they treat the performers as if they were gods. Their minds and consciences have been torched!

If you interviewed wife beaters, date rapists, spousal murderers, adulterers and paternity fraud predators, you would uncover a worn out trail that ends with heartbreak, betrayal, divorce and defraud. That trail started at one or more of these three dangerous places of origin. Their minds and consciences were: (a). corrupted by immoral men and women. (b). corrupted by the media, music or Hollywood, or, (c). they were victims of circumstances.

• *Victims of Circumstances* - Some men and women become smooth operators through no fault of their own. Victims of horrific circumstances, they exit their mother's womb and enter into a dark hopeless existence that revolves around depravation, abuse and neglect. They have no one in their life to protect and nurture them and no one who cares about their well being or safety. Entangled in a harsh rigorous lifestyle riddled with lewdness, desertion and rejection, they must fend for themselves as they are repeatedly victimized by heartless predators.

After the attacks, they are left to juggle depression, flashbacks, fits of rage, nightmares, deeply embedded emotional scars, hatred, thoughts of worthlessness, feelings of revenge, suicidal tendencies, drug and alcohol abuse, eating disorders and grisly memories. They have never known *True Love* or compassion. They have only known confusion, fear, hurt and anguish.

The treatment they have been forced to endure will shock and repulse you. It has conditioned them to hurt others and to, *at times*, act without a conscience. Who subjected these individuals to such a horrendous upbringing? They are people you and I would never suspect. They are the parents, grandparents, stepparents, teachers, neighbors, priests and ministers.

They are the foster parents, aunts, uncles, cousins, nephews, nieces and other people children should have been able to trust. Do you recall what happened on November 4th, 1994? That was the day Union, South Carolina authorities confirmed that wife and mother, Susan Smith, (*real name*) had confessed to doing the unthinkable.

She killed her two young sons by strapping them in their car seats, rolling the car into the John D. Long Lake, and watching as the tightly sealed Mazda Protege bobbled peacefully on the surface of the lake, slowly filling with water and finally submerging into a murky makeshift gravesite. She violated one of humanity's most sacred bonds, the love of a mother for her children. Her actions were beyond reasoning. How could she formulate in her mind the wherewithal to commit such an atrocious act? Carefully examining the chronological breakdown of Susan's life gives us the answer to that seemingly mysterious question.

The Turbulent Life of Susan Smith

- On September 26, 1971, Susan was born into a dysfunctional home filled with bitterness and constant turmoil. When her parents got married, her mother was pregnant from a previous relationship with another man. Her dad was an alcoholic prone to violence who threatened to kill his wife, then himself.
- Both Susan and her brother were terrified at how their parents treated each other
- Before Susan entered preschool her brother tried to commit suicide by hanging himself
- After seventeen stormy years of marriage, her mother divorced her dad
- Two weeks later her mother marries a prominent businessman
- Five weeks after the divorce, Susan's biological father commits suicide, Susan was only 6 at the time
- At the age of 13, Susan attempts suicide and is diagnosed with depression
- Apparently she gets no help with her issues, no counseling, no prayer... nothing
- At the age of 15, her stepfather starts sexually molesting her
- Because of family pressure to keep things undisclosed, no charges were filed
- Her stepfather continues molesting her
- In high school Susan was involved in numerous relationships. During her senior year she got a job at a Winn Dixie Grocery Store and started secretly dating a coworker who was married, while at the same time dating another co-worker
- While dating these two men, Susan becomes friendly with David Smith, a stock clerk at the store
- She ends up getting pregnant by the married man and has an abortion
- After the abortion, the married man finds out about her other relationship and breaks up with Susan
- Depressed over the breakup, Susan attempts suicide for the second time in her life
- She spends a month in recovery. After getting out, David, who is already engaged to be married to another woman, pursues a relationship with Susan
- David & Susan had been dating about a year when he gets her pregnant. They decide to get married because they were both against her having an abortion
- By their third wedding anniversary, they had separated at least three times
- Their marriage was riddled with extra-marital affairs
- Susan obtains a job at Consco Products and while still married, gets involved in a relationship with Tom Findlay, one of the son's of the CEO of Consco
- At that time in her life, Susan was juggling sexual relations between three men: her husband, her stepfather and her new beau, Tom Findlay
- Tom ends their relationship by sending Susan a letter stating that he was not her "Mr. Right" because he didn't want the responsibility of raising another man's two

small children. In the letter he also writes, "If you want to catch a nice guy like me one day, you have to act like a nice girl." "And you know, nice girls don't sleep with married men." He was referring to an incident at a party at his house in which Susan kissed and fondled the husband of a friend while they were naked in Tom's hot tub
• Angry because she was rejected and hurt by the breakup, Susan starts to take off from work to consume alcohol, (*following in her dad's footsteps*)
• After another attempt to get Tom back had failed, Susan was furious. That was the day she murdered her two children
• She gets sentenced to life in prison. While incarcerated, Susan has sex with a prison guard, a Lieutenant, who gets arrested and fired for his indiscretions with her
• She has sex with another prison guard, a Captain. After confessing, he was arrested
• Susan ends up contracting a sexually transmitted disease
• And that is the life of Susan V. Smith...

Her life was one tragically sad story. Susan had mastered the art of seduction and was draped in promiscuity. When it came to having sex, she had no boundaries. Single or married, it didn't matter. Her track record speaks for itself. To further disrupt her own life, she attempted to commit suicide twice. She was diagnosed with depression.

She had an abortion and when a man broke up with her, she quickly went into her *self*-destruct mode. Although she married, she didn't have a clue about the sanctity or sacredness of the marriage covenant. Her marital forte was infidelity, your marriage or hers. Clearly, her mind and conscience were corrupted. How did Susan lose her capacity to have normal emotions, and what propelled her to become so self-destructive? We don't have to look far for the answers.

It was her biological father who showed her the ropes on how to become suicidal, alcoholic and depressed. It was her stepfather who introduced her to the dark world of promiscuity and sexual lewdness by molesting her. He probably didn't realize it at the time, but with each sexual encounter he was training and indoctrinating Susan to dishonor any and all marital vows, how to view people as objects of potential pleasure and how to have no capacity for normal emotions.

He was conditioning her to believe that no one would love her unless she had sex with them. She also learned firsthand how to manipulate others. There is no doubt the example set by her mother helped Susan set the foundation for her out of control sex life. Susan learned all of those things before she was 16 years of age. There was absolutely nothing innocent about her childhood.

Then came the issue of having the abortion. Once she violated her conscience and terminated her first child, numbing her conscience and terminating her other two children would not prove to be such a difficult task. She had already trained herself how to sever that maternal bond at will. Susan became a smooth operator but by no fault of her own. She was a victim of circumstances.

Born into a relationship assassin's boot camp, it was her own family who started the process of *de*-calibrating her conscience and molding and shaping her mind into the charm, disarm and harm mode. Don't misunderstand me, I'm not trying to start a movement to get Susan's sentence commuted or pardoned. She killed her two boys and for those crimes, under the laws of the land, she has to pay.

My concern is the mass number of men and women who have grown up in lewd, hostile, violent and abusive environments and just like Susan, they have yet to recover from their traumatic experiences. Let me make this clear, with the right guidance and support, victims of circumstances can recover and go on to live happy, productive lives.

With their wilted consciences restored, they are more than capable of being loving and trustworthy individuals. But this book is not about the victims of circumstances who have gotten the help they need and turned their lives around. This book is about the dangerous ones who have yet to start the healing process. It's about the ones whose minds and consciences are so far gone they don't believe they need help.

They will add your name to the divorced, betrayed, abused, date raped, stalked and spousal murder statistics without blinking an eye. This chapter is about the ones who have had no ministry or counseling to help them get on the road to recovery. To further fester their seething wounds even more, those who victimized them, have offered no apologies. From those who watched them being repeatedly victimized but refused to help, they receive more silence.

As they enter into adulthood, they bring tons of toxic baggage. Many of them are struggling with very critical issues. (*i.e., bitterness towards God, hatred of men, anger against women, rage at the world, sexual hang-ups.*) BUT! They insist on being in a relationship or marriage anyway.

They don't realize their mind and conscience is corrupted. Like Susan, they don't see how lewd, immoral and scandalous they are. They don't understand that they have no capacity for normal emotions.

As dangerous as they are, they will find someone to fall in love with them. These men and women are not rarities or abnormalities. The brutal trauma they experience happens everyday and everywhere, from Bedford Stuyvesant to Beverly Hills. Their pain and ill-treatment transcends every cultural, ethnic, social and economic dividing line. My heart goes out to every victim of circumstance.

Some of the things they have been through will bring tears to your eyes. Take the case of Terrell Peterson. In 1998, in Atlanta, Georgia, 5-year-old Terrell was finally dead. His short existence on planet earth evolved around extreme hatred, torture, starvation and then murder. He was neither killed by a kidnapper, nor was he killed by an unknown assailant. He was murdered by his grandmother, Pharina Peterson, (*real name*) and his aunt Terri Lynn Peterson, (*real name*). In court, Terrell's teenage sister testified how, while the rest of the family ate meat and vegetables, his aunt would force him to eat human feces from a toilet. She told how her aunt tied Terrell to a banister, usually naked, and how he was forced to sleep standing up. His aunt often called him "rat," because according to prosecutors, they resented taking care of him.

Terrell was beaten with coat hangers and extension cords and was hit in the head when he tried to refuse eating the human waste. That kind of treatment is one of the many ways men learn how to hate women and become wife beaters and abusers. Terrell has been laid to rest, but what about the other kids who suffer through such inhumane punishments, then grow up and enter into relationships and marriages?

And what about Terrell's siblings? Day and night they watched him being tortured. Do you realize that seeing their brother being victimized like that had to have a traumatizing effect on their minds and consciences? To constantly witness that kind of abuse day in and day out and not cry for help meant only one thing. Their grandmother and aunt had trained or coerced them to numb their emotions.

Like many other innocent children, Terrell's siblings were forced to go through the relationship assassin's boot camp. Where is the next generation of marriage missiles, wife beaters, abusers, liars, fakes and cheaters going to come from? A segment of them will arise from this group of untreated victims of circumstances.

On the surface they may seem to be the sweetest people in the world but the reality is, they have been conditioned to betray you, indoctrinated to inflict harm upon you and *pre*-programmed to rip your heart out. How do you detect if your potential mate is a victim of circumstances? Watch for these warning signs and red flags:

• They Never Knew Their Biological Father Due To Their Mother's Promiscuity, Paternity Fraud or Refusal To Let Their Father Be involved in Their Life
• Their Father Was Overbearing, Cold, Unsupportive, Non-Talkative or a Controller, Womanizer, Liar, Rollingstone or Con Artist
• They Were Neglected or Abandoned by their Mother or Father, Orphaned, Raised By The State or Raised by Reluctant Family, Friends or Relatives
• Boys Raised by Single Moms With No Stable, Strong Male Father Figure
• They Were Raised by a Domineering Mother or by a Woman Who Hates Men
• Mother Gave Birth to Them When She Was Just a Pre-Teen or Teenager
• Raised in a Household Filled With Hostility, Criticism and Ridicule, Instead of One Filled With Love, Care, Cultivation, Nurturing and Instruction
• Raised in a Home Filled With Domestic Violence or Verbal Threats
• Victim of Child Abuse, (i.e. Starvation or Other Demoralizing Punishments)

• Victim of Incest, Rape, Gang Rape, Molestation or Other Sexual Exploitation
• Adopted or raised by a Homosexual, Lesbian, Transsexual, Bisexual, Crossdresser, Transgendered or Any Other Sexually Unrestrained Person
• Parents Married - Went Separate Ways but Never Divorced
• Parents Involved in a Bitter Child Custody Battle or Child Support Dispute
• Parent(s) Addicted to Alcohol, Drugs or Other Pharmaceuticals
• Parent(s) Suicidal, Diagnosed With Depression, Bipolar Disorder, Borderline Personality Disorder or Any Other Type of Mental Illness or Psychiatric Challenge
• Siblings Suffered From Depression, Suicidal Tendencies, Addictions or Involved in Other Self-Destructive Behaviors
• Victim of a Nomadic Lifestyle – Never Had a Stable Home Life
• Parents Never Married or Did Marry But Divorced
• Parent(s) Convicted of a Crime(s) or Involved in Criminal Activity
• Parent(s) Had Children Born Out of Wedlock
• Parent(s) Promiscuous, Involved in Adultery, Fornication, Pornography or Other Illicit Sexual Practices
• They Were Never Taught Any Basic Life Skills Such As Apologizing, Forgiveness, Respecting, Appreciating or Being Sensitive To Others. They Never Learned The Proper Way To Respond When Wronged or Hurt. They Never Learned How To Handle Pressure, Stress or Setbacks. They Never Learned How To Deal With Temptations, Enticements, Loss, Sin, Anger, Wrath or Malice.

If you don't examine a potential mate for these warning signs and red flags, two things are for certain: **1). You are guilty of not guarding the door of your heart, and 2). A smooth operator will take advantage of your lapse of judgment.** When children grow up under any of those conditions, they become victims of circumstances. Gripped with shame, some of them will take their painful ordeals and riveting dark secrets to the grave.

That's why you must be responsible enough to confirm if an individual is void of a conscience and if they have no capacity for normal emotions. The one word you don't want to be part of your vocabulary when it comes to any potential mate is the word, "assume."

Never assume anything. You must ask the tough questions, the uncomfortable questions and the awkward questions and look into the deep things of their life, examine their present and scrutinize their past. Read what one of the wisest men on the earth said:

> I John 4:1 AMP [Emphasis added]
> Beloved, DO NOT put faith IN EVERY SPIRIT, but prove (test) the spirits to discover whether they proceed from God..."

That is one of the mistakes many men and women make when it comes to choosing their mate. They put their trust in untrustworthy people. Now read my special translation of that same verse.

> I John 4:1 Gillis Triplett's Relationship Translation [Emphasis added]
> Beloved, DO NOT put your trust in any POTENTIAL MATE who appears in your life, you must first TEST, EXAMINE and

I John 4:1 Gillis Triplett's Relationship Translation Continued...
DISCERN their spirit to see whether their heart is set on fulfilling God's glorious plan for your life: because many SEVERELY HARMFUL [*boyfriends*] [*girlfriends*] [*fiancés*] [*fianceés*] [*husbands*] and [*wives*] are gone out into the world.

It is crucial that you obey this command to *test, examine* and *discern* a potential mate's spirit. If you fail or refuse to do so, you might as well inscribe the words, **"Use and Abuse Me!"** on your forehead with a permanent marker because you are begging to be a primary target for liars, cheaters, fakes, users and abusers.

Demetrius assaulted his girlfriend. But in a cleverly crafted plea deal, he agreed to undergo counseling in exchange for avoiding a trial and almost certain incarceration. Read the evaluation from his court appointed counselor: **"Mr. Demetrius comes across as an extremely immature person with a history of many short-lived but overlapping relationships with women."** That counselor did what you must do with any potential mate; he tested, examined and discerned Demetrius' spirit.

Demetrius had a short fuse, he despised children and he had no respect for the female gender. None of the women he dated had tested, examined or discerned his spirit. They made assumptions about him and for their gross errors in judgment, they all paid a price. He left a number of women pregnant and alone. Afterwards, he did everything in his power to evade paying child support, even after DNA tests confirmed he was the father.

He learned that tactic from his own absentee dad. Demetrius had a history of misusing and abusing women. However, because he had mastered the art of seduction, which he learned from his mother, it wouldn't take him long before he had another ~~girlfriend~~, victim under his abrasive clutches. Then there are cases like Carina.

Carina was raised by an overbearing father who had a suitcase full of personal issues. His control over them was so harsh, that three of his five children suffered from severe depression with suicidal tendencies and two of them were alcoholics.

They were all victims of circumstances who never recovered from the trauma of living under the roof of a harsh domineering dictator. Although they looked normal, they were anything but. Their father had fried their emotions and instilled shame, fear, insecurity and a deep sense of condemnation in each of his children.

Carina left home, earned a Bachelor's degree and got married. Immediately after the wedding bells rang, she began displaying signs of mental instability. She refused to allow her husband to see her naked. If they made love, the lights had to be out and the room had to be in pitch darkness. She would not allow her husband to turn the lights back on until she was fully dressed. Carina eventually went into severe depression, attempted suicide twice and engaged in self-mutilation, picking at her scalp and refusing to wash or clean herself.

She was put in a psychiatric ward a number of times and was administered these various mind altering drugs: Zoloft, Haldol, Remeron, Effexor and Zyprexa. Although they dated about three years before they married, Carina's husband was like most people when it came to love; he just went with the flow. It never dawned on him that he was required to test, examine and discern his potential wife's spirit.

He had no clue the woman he was dating had a mind and conscience that had been warped by an overbearing dictator dad and that she was going to put whoever married her through a 24 hour living nightmare. Like Carina, most victims of circumstances are sincere in their relationship and marital aspirations. They don't intend on becoming marriage missiles or relationship assassins but because their conscience has been butchered and ransacked, they become a danger to whoever enters into a relationship with them.

Before you proceed any further, go back to page 64 & 65 and read the warning signs and red flags again. Become thoroughly familiar with them and mentally prepare yourself to be able to talk to a potential mate about these touchy issues. As I previously stated, never assume anything concerning a potential mate. Never!

When you ask them about these issues, what if their plan is to deceive you? Or what if they say they don't want to talk about their past? I'll deal with how to address those responses in later chapters. Right now, the important thing to get ingrained into your mind is knowing that you must fulfill your responsibility to test, examine and discern your potential mate's spirit.

On April 25th, 2003 in Mill Hall, Pennsylvania, Lori Ann Spangler (*real name*) walked down the aisle with Frank W. Shope II (*real name*). It should have been the start of a beautiful marital union, but hours after exchanging wedding vows they were both dead. According to crime scene investigators, the two newlyweds got into an argument at their wedding reception. Wait a minute, stop right there! They had just stood before God and vowed to love and cherish one another and then immediately turned around and became marital combatants?

Of all places, at their wedding reception? They didn't even make it to their honeymoon? From the wedding reception they continued fighting until they got home. Next, Frank pulls a gun on his newly christened bride and kills her, then commits suicide. Come on now, surely you must know that *True Love* does not behave that way.

How can we classify their whirlwind romance? There's only one possible classification. It was a murder-suicide lover's booby trap plot. Ms. Spangler fell for the bait and paid the ultimate price for choosing the wrong mate. She paid with her life! Had she known what you are going to learn about *relationship assassins and *marriage missiles, she would have detected and avoided that marital booby trap.

Here is the first set of *Booby Trap Acid Tests* you must ask yourself concerning your potential mate: [*you will need to read this book in its entirety before you can answer some of these questions*].

1. Is my potential mate a trained relationship assassin or marriage missile?
2. Has my potential mate's mind and conscience been corrupted?
3. Has my potential mate lost his or her capacity to have normal emotions?
4. Is my potential mate a victim of circumstances?
5. Has my potential mate been influenced by immoral men and women?
6. To their own detriment, has my potential mate been influenced by the media, music and/or Hollywood?
7. Does my potential mate hold any bizarre beliefs or philosophies concerning love, sex, relationships or marriage?

Over the years I have prayed for, tracked, investigated, researched and counseled literally thousands of men and women who entered into a relationship or marriage with a person who (a) **had a corrupt mind and conscience,** (b) **had no capacity for normal emotions,** or (c) **held bizarre beliefs and philosophies concerning love, sex, relationships and marriage.**

In most cases, the results have always been the same. They traveled the path of marital or relationship 'crash and burn.' Starting now I'll give you all of the ammunition you will ever need to protect yourself from choosing the wrong mate. I'll show you how to detect and avoid these smooth operating relationship assassins and marriage missiles. Get ready, make sure you're still in a quiet place and dig in...

* A **relationship assassin** is a person who finds a girlfriend, boyfriend or casual sex partner or gets engaged and then betrays, harasses, victimizes, breaks the heart of, stalks, abuses, terrorizes, murders or otherwise hurts their girlfriend, boyfriend, fiancé, fiancée, date or live-in lover.

* A **marriage missile** is a person who gets married and then presses the marital self destruct button. After they say, "I do," these men and women are going to plunge their spouses into the deep dark abyss of the dreaded marriage from hell.

- 4 -

Why Wear a Mask?

I have an illustration from the television and film industry to help you comprehend a critical truth concerning this first booby trap. First, we need to *re*-examine a statement I made back in chapter two. Get to know this powerful truth intimately.

To Avoid a Booby Trap You Must First Be Aware Of Its Existence

That statement was born from a deep spiritual truth Paul revealed to us from the Word of God.

> II Corinthians 2:11 [Emphasis added]
> Lest satan should get an advantage of us: FOR WE ARE NOT IGNORANT OF HIS DEVICES.

Most good hearted people who were duped into dating a relationship assassin or marrying a marriage missile, were victimized because they were ignorant of satan's devices. The word "devices" means: evil schemes, booby traps, diabolical plots and sophisticated trickery. We are commanded not to be ignorant of these devices.

Concerning your potential mate, being ignorant of this first booby trap is especially dangerous. From 1949 through 1957, there was a popular television show called **The Lone Ranger** which starred an actor named Clayton Moore. The focal point of the show was a masked man whose identity no one knew. After **The Lone Ranger** left a scene, the questions and debates started flying, "Who was that masked man and what is his true identity?" The only time **The Lone Ranger** took off his mask was when the plot called for him to put on some other type of disguise. **The Lone Ranger** had no visible means of support.

He had no verifiable family ties. No one knew **The Lone Ranger's** background. His place of residence was a big question mark. When he rode off into the sunset, no one knew where he was going. When he came on the scene no one knew where he came from. He was a complete mystery. In 1979, certain movie producers got a court order against

Clayton Moore's use of **The Lone Ranger** character. They forced him to remove his mask. When it comes to choosing a mate you cannot afford to wait on the judicial system or a set of bad circumstances to show you that you fell in love with a masked man or a disguised woman.

You can not depend on authorities to reveal that the person you fell in love with has used masks and disguises to hide their harmful character and destructive personality traits. Teresa was anticipating taking her life to the next level. She was a college graduate, owned her own home and had just made a major career change into the hot Information Technology industry. Although she attended church, she was spiritually immature. She had no prayer life, she didn't fellowship with sincere Christians who were strong in the Lord and none of her close friends were what you would classify as family oriented.

With her parents living in another state and no relatives living close by, Teresa needed to establish a more solid circle of true friends. By not doing so, she thrust herself into the spiritual danger zone. When Bobby coyly slipped into her life, he seemed like the answer to her half-baked prayers. He was a suave gentleman and a hopeless romantic.

Before she knew it, Bobby had mesmerized her heart. It was not long before he talked his way into moving into Teresa's peaceful home. Once he moved in, the spirit of peace that once permeated her quaint little cottage flew away like a flock of startled birds. Teresa had allowed **The Lone Ranger** to steal her heart. It was first degree theft by deception. She had fallen for a masked man. What is a mask and why wear one?

For the purpose of this teaching, a mask is a covering worn on the face to conceal one's identity. Masks are used to disguise the face by making it indistinct, unrecognizable or blurred to the senses. Oftentimes criminals use masks to conceal their identity during the commission of a crime. Bobby did just that.

He used the mask of a gentleman to disguise his true character. Instead of finding *True Love*, Teresa had wrapped her arms around a raging mad pit bull. I'll never forget the day she came to work wearing sunglasses. We sat elbow to elbow for about a year.

Teresa was one of my trainees and she knew she would have to field questions about the ugly bruise on her eye, so she tried to hide the woeful black and blue marks with dark oversized sunglasses.

Her "Knight in pining armor" now had her wearing a mask, not to conceal her identity, but to hide her painful disfiguring welts. She took a deep breath and calmly explained that she somehow bumped into a door. She then abruptly changed the subject. It was obvious. Bobby had cleverly masked the fact that he had a violent temper. He had disguised the fact that he chose physical violence to get his points across.

From the day of the first sign of abuse, Bobby's grip of control over Teresa's life began to tighten like a pair of ice-cold hydraulic vice grips. When he called her at work, it wouldn't be long before Teresa was overcome with anxiety and tensed up like a clam. Moments later, the two would be arguing. Bobby was no rookie at this. He had a way of making Teresa think the arguments and physical abuse were her fault. He led her to believe that she made him hit her. You could tell the violence was escalating when Teresa came to work one morning wearing a cast and had a noticeable limp to her walk. She was in so much pain, she could barely sit down. As before, she fielded the questions.

This time her story was, *"I was cleaning the house and accidentally tripped."* When you looked at her and listened to her explanation of how things happened, it didn't take much to figure out that her version of what happened was not the truth. Teresa had been pounced on! Bobby had worked her over really badly. Their relationship was in a vicious lifeless cycle that looked like this:

1). Bobby would start talking. 2). Teresa would tense up. 3). Bobby would yell and scream at her. 4). Teresa would get upset and cry. 5). They would argue. 6). Bobby would resort to physical violence. 7). Bobby would blame Teresa for his fits of fury. 8). Next, he would blame the stress of his job on the attack. 9). He would swear he would change as soon as they got married. 10). He would woo Teresa back into his arms. 11). The two would make up. 12). The cycle would end. 13). The cycle would start all over again.

Bobby toyed with Teresa's emotions as if she was a human yo-yo. He was her personal Dr. Jekyll-Mr. Hyde. On one hand he would melt her heart with his gentlemanly affections, on the other hand, he would remove one of his disguises, switch gears and smack the daylights out of her. I pulled Teresa aside to talk with her, to share with her the portrait of what a godly honorable man looks and acts like, but Bobby was a professional woman beater. He knew the ropes.

He knew people would get suspicious of him, especially since Teresa constantly stayed banged up since meeting him. Like any consummate smooth operator, he trained Teresa to turn a deaf ear to anyone intent on tearing apart what he claimed was *True Love*. His charm and intense sales pitch had worked. Teresa fell for the bait and now she was snared in the deadly **Lone Ranger** booby trap. How many mistakes did she make?

For starters, in her mate selection, Teresa was simple-minded. She believed everything Bobby said. To compound matters, she had no clue what *True Love* was and no idea who Bobby was. She had not interacted with any of his family or long-time friends. She knew nothing about his track record or past history except the things he told her, and she knew absolutely no one who could vouch for Bobby's character.

Truth be told, Teresa didn't know if Bobby was married or divorced. She didn't know if he had a history of shacking up with women or of sleeping around. When he convinced her to let him move into her house, he did it so smoothly, he could not have been a first timer.

Did he have any kids? Had he been arrested before? Was he on parole or on probation? Teresa did not know. What she knew about Bobby is that he had a job that called for him to travel and when he returned they had a great time together. That was until he got angry and would physically assault her. Bobby claimed he was a high-paid executive but he had nothing to show for it.

Did he have a place of residence? Teresa didn't know because she never saw where he lived. Bobby is a classic example of a masked man. Take your time and carefully examine these eight *Booby Trap Acid Tests*. Each one reveals a vital clue to detecting these relationship assassins and marriage missiles.

1. You have never seen your potential mate communicating or interacting with his or her family
2. You have not communicated or interacted with your potential mate's family
3. You have not communicated or interacted with your potential mate's long-term friends. [People they recently befriended do not count]
4. The people who vouch for your potential mate have questionable characters
5. Your potential mate shuns interaction and communication with your family
6. Your potential mate shuns interaction and communication with your friends
7. Your potential mate clams up, becomes evasive or hostile when you inquire about their past history, background, track record and family
8. Important things you should know about your potential mate are a mystery

You need to understand that as prerequisites to establishing a relationship, these traits are extremely bizarre. If you are seeing someone and you detect any of these eight (PEWS) **Primary Emergency Warning Signs**, you are being forewarned. For your sake, do not take the attitude that these signs are not as bad as they seem. They are that bad! No matter how sincere they are, do not allow anyone to talk you into disregarding these PEWS. As the Lord was dealing with my heart about why people choose the wrong mate, He shared with me this priceless four part statement concerning finding the love of your life.

Truth invites examination
Sincerity of heart does not shun it
Trustworthy people expect it
True love demands it

• *Truth invites examination* - Before you commit yourself to entering into a relationship, your potential mate must invite examination.

Be wary if they take the position that you do not need to know about their past history, family background or track record. If the sum total of your knowledge about your potential mate comes only from them, make no mistake about it, you are "in love with," dating or engaged to a **Lone Ranger**. Meditate on this next Scripture:

> II Corinthians 13:1 [Emphasis added]
> This is the third *time* I am coming to you. IN THE MOUTH OF TWO OR THREE WITNESSES SHALL EVERY WORD BE ESTABLISHED.

In every important facet of life, the rule of confirming an issue in the mouth of two or three witnesses is in effect. You see it in court room proceedings, on job applications, on lease agreements, on credit applications, in the Scriptures and on club memberships. Some applications require that you know the person at least three years in order to be considered an acceptable character reference. People who can't or won't provide bona fide character references usually don't qualify for the job. They have something to hide, or everyone who knows them has nothing good to say about them.

Truth invites examination, lies defraud, and deceit shuns examination! When a potential mate does not invite examination of who they are, you need to go to part two of this statement.

• *Sincerity of heart does not shun it* - Sincerity of heart does not shun examination. To be sincere means to present no false appearances. It means to be honest and pure. It means to stand before another without any masks, disguises, exaggerations or falsehoods. Concerning a potential mate, you must make sincerity of heart the standard.

If you accept anything less than absolute sincerity, you can be sure that insincerity will most likely come back to haunt you when you least expect it. We examined some of the glaring mistakes Teresa made with Bobby. Now let's take a brief look at the harrowing nightmare Matthew went through.

Matthew and Annette had been dating for about six months. One night as they were talking and closely embraced, Annette looked Matthew in his eyes and told him she had never had a man to treat her like he did. She told Matthew that he touched her heart and she wanted to make love to him to show him her gratitude.

Matthew was mesmerized with her offer. The thought of turning her down never crossed his mind. The two began engaging in sex. Matthew made many assumptions about Annette. These assumptions came to a frightening end the day she got painfully sick. They were headed to the mall when Annette took a quick turn for the worse.

She pleaded with Matthew to rush her to a nearby friend's house. Once they arrived, Annette ran inside and fled into the bathroom. She stayed there, door closed, agonizing in pain. Her friend, whom Matthew had never heard of until then, brought Annette some prescription medication, medicine he had no idea his girlfriend was taking. Matthew stood in the hallway talking to Annette through the door. When her unknown friend stepped outside to give the two some privacy, Annette broke the news.

She had genital herpes and she was having a painful outbreak! To inflame the matter, she informed Matthew about her many lovers and how she was careful not to have sex with him or with anyone else if she saw any lesions or felt like she was having an outbreak. The horror of Annette's confession left a gaping hole in Matthew's stomach.

He realized that he had made a great error in judgment by having sex with her. He stood there, in the hallway, frozen in time. He could no longer hear Annette's cries of pain. Matthew was in his own world.

He was now concerned about his own health, wondering if he had contracted this silent sexually transmitted disease from this woman he thought he knew. He dreaded the thought of being labeled a carrier. In a few seconds, Matthew thought about dying, storming out the door and forgetting about Annette forever. He even considered killing her.

He searched his mind to find a way to get revenge for what she had done. Matthew's emotions were running on high octane, but he kept his composure. Hours later, Annette's anguishing pain subsided. She emerged from the bathroom, drained, disheveled and in a nasty mood. She just wanted to go home and shut down but Matthew was adamant abut talking. He wanted to know why she did not tell him about having genital herpes before she so seductively gave herself to him. They rode to her abode in tense silence. Annette's lips were sealed.

When they returned to her apartment, it was only after persistent prodding that Annette finally took off more of her disguises. He discovered that she was divorced and had a child. She had never once mentioned those critical facts to Matthew. Why would a person claim to love you and not tell you they have a child?

Why would they hide the fact that they are divorced? What kind of person would talk you into having sex while withholding the fact that they have a sexually transmittable disease? The prophet Jeremiah answers those questions for us.

Jeremiah 9:5 [Emphasis added]
And they will deceive every one his neighbor, and will not speak the truth: THEY HAVE TAUGHT THEIR TONGUE TO SPEAK LIES, *and* weary themselves to commit iniquity.

They do so because they have taught their tongue to speak lies. Did you read the Scripture? These people are intent on deceiving you. When Matthew inquired about the details of her past, Annette clammed up. She refused to talk about her marriage or divorce. She did not want to talk about why her *ex*-husband obtained full custody of their child. She was evasive in discussing her family. Annette shunned examination because she was not being sincere.

She had planned to disclose certain information about herself, but only after she had snared him. The things she did tell him, he had to pry from her. What other sordid details was she hiding about her past? Had Matthew not been with her when she had that painful herpes outbreak, how long would she have kept that infectious skeleton hidden in her closet?

That is called a booby trap no matter how you look at it. Matthew had pursued **The Lone Ranger**. When people are sincere about you, they will not shun or avoid talking about their past, no matter how hard it hurts to talk about it. No matter how checkered or how stained their past may have been, being truthful with a potential mate must be the standard, (See Proverbs 6:16-19, Psalm 101:7, Ephesians 4:25).

What if telling the truth will cause the other person to decline from continuing the relationship. Then so be it! Healthy relationships and strong marriages are built on two people walking in absolute honesty with each other: no masks, no disguises, no fronts, no withholding of critical facts about their past, present, or future, no lies, no exaggerations and no half truths.

Colossians 3:9 [Emphasis added]
LIE NOT ONE TO ANOTHER, seeing that ye have put off the old man with his deeds;

• *Trustworthy people expect it* - To expect means to look forward to. Trustworthy people expect examination. To be trustworthy means you are reliable and can be trusted. It means to be upright, ethical and faithful. It earmarks you as an honorable and principled man or woman. In most major cities when the position of police chief needs to be filled, the mayor is given a list of possible candidates. Each candidate must go through a grueling examination process.

Their life, their past history and their track record will be put under the proverbial microscope. They will be scrutinized by the mayor's office, by the police department and by the public they desire to serve. Those who desire the position of police chief expect to be scrutinized. They expect a thorough examination because the position they desire requires them to be trustworthy, faithful, ethical and honorable.

Desiring to love someone or to be their spouse is a calling that also carries a tall list of responsibilities. It demands (*under God*) that you be able to safely trust your heart, emotions and physical well-being to that person. It demands (*under God*) that your potential mate be faithful, trustworthy, loyal, ethical and honorable.

It requires (*under God*) that your mate be a person of integrity, have nobleness of character and be reliable and dependable. A potential mate who is relationship ready, will expect you to examine them for the above qualities. And they also will expect your family and friends to put them under the microscope of scrutiny. Avoid any and all potential mates who shun examination!

To proceed into a relationship with such an individual, is to ask for trouble. There is a good reason they shun examination. They are not prepared to be in a relationship, engagement or marriage. Potential mates who are trustworthy expect and invite examination. They do so because they are not guessing if they meet all of the requirements of a suitable mate. They are not wondering if they are ready for love, sex, relationship and marriage. They have prepared themselves and they are ready to receive their God-given mate:

> Revelation 19:7 AMP [Emphasis added]
> Let us rejoice and shout for joy [exulting and triumphant]! Let us celebrate *and* ascribe to Him glory *and* honor, for the marriage of the Lamb [at last] has come, AND HIS BRIDE HAS PREPARED HERSELF. [And the groom himself]

• *True love demands it* - The final thing the Lord said to me is: *True Love* demands examination! To demand means to ask for urgently or firmly, leaving no chance for refusal or denial. It means to ask to be informed. It implies that one is seeking vital information. People who truly love you and sincerely care about you will demand to examine your potential mate. They will do so because they care about you and they do not want to see you get trapped into a destructive relationship or marital nightmare. They will do so because they don't want to see you marry someone with a defective character like Gregory.

Gregory was the president of a prestigious college. He met and married Marla; they stayed together for fourteen years. One day Gregory grabbed some cash and credit cards, drove his car to the airport and disappeared! He notified no one of his departure. He jumped on an airplane and left his wife, family and friends in the dust. Gregory quickly divorced Marla and found a new job. He made a new set of friends, then met and married Vanessa. He stayed married to her for seven years, and one day, this marital rollingstone jumped ship again.

Just as before, he grabbed some cash and credit cards, drove his vehicle to the airport and disappeared. Based on input from police and private investigators, Vanessa learned that her husband had pulled this stunt before. She and a friend went to the airport and found his car. By the time they tracked him down he had started a new life and showed absolutely no remorse for the people he had hurt.

He sent Vanessa some legal documents but other than that, he refused to talk to her. He claimed it was not necessary to give either of his *ex*-wives, family or his past friends any explanation.

He said his actions told the story. When he was asked about his loved ones, Gregory showed absolutely no emotions. I personally looked into his eyes and he was distant and cold as ice. That my friend, is a picture of a relationship assassin. Once Vanessa saw that Gregory had no contact with his family and no long term friends, she should have realized that she was being pursued by **The Lone Ranger**.

Immediately, she should have recognized that she was being lured into a lover's booby trap. She could have avoided the pain and drama Gregory caused her had she understood how this booby trap worked. One important key to avoiding this trap, is having the people in your life who truly love you and sincerely care about, insist on meeting and examining your potential mate. If you do not have caring people like that in your life, do you have a problem?

Are you hiding behind any masks? Do most of the people who know you have nothing good to say about you? Are you incapable of maintaining lasting relationships? Are you harboring a cantankerous attitude or mean spirited disposition? Is your motivation for getting into a relationship unpure? We'll talk about unpure motives later on.

Are you seeking to get married for selfish reasons you don't intend on disclosing until after the wedding? Are you hiding any other personality disorders like a lying spirit, a spirit of anger or a flaming temper? Are you trying to suppress the fact that you are an abuser or wife beater? Are you trying to gloss over the effects of your promiscuous or immoral lifestyle? Are you attempting to conceal any other secret sins you believe may ruin your chances of snagging someone?

Those are the tactics **Lone Rangers** employ. Are you a **Lone Ranger**? Take a moment and get brutally honest with yourself by following the instruction manual of life and pray this prayer:

Psalm 139:23-24 AMP [Emphasis added]
[23] **Search me [thoroughly], O God, and know my heart! Try me and know my thoughts!**
[24] **AND SEE IF THERE IS ANY WICKED OR HURTFUL WAY IN ME, and lead me in the way everlasting.**

Lone Rangers enter into relationships bringing with them wicked and hurtful ways. They cleverly mask their ungodly behaviors and destructive personality traits in an intentional shroud of ambiguity. They have ugly despicable things about themselves they simply do not want you to discover until it is too late. Do not wait until you are shoulder deep in a relationship crisis or neck deep in a marital meltdown before looking into your mate's background. By then, it is usually too late. Go back to page 72 and *re*-read the *Booby Trap Acid Tests* used to detect **Lone Rangers**. Get those tests drilled into your mind and do not allow anyone to persuade you to ignore those tests.

If you have not met and interacted with the family of your potential mate and their long-term friends, you could be walking "eyes wide open," into a torrential lover's hailstorm. On December 24, 2002 in Modesto, California, Laci Peterson (*real name*) was reported missing. What made her disappearance so odd was that she was eight months pregnant with her first child. It was Christmas Eve, she had strong family ties and had already made holiday plans to be with her family. Leaving without saying a word was out of character for Laci.

After she did not turn-up, police suspected foul play and began to scrutinize the last person to see her alive, her husband, Scott Peterson, (*real name*). As her disappearance garnered nationwide media attention, Scott gave television interviews claiming that he loved his wife and describing their special relationship.

Tragically, after four months of searching, Laci and her son's body were found. They had been murdered and it was Laci's husband who was arrested and charged with this incomprehensible crime. Prior to his arrest, detectives showed photographs to Laci's relatives of Scott posing with a woman with whom they believed he was having an affair.

Laci's family said that particular photograph was dated during a time Laci believed Scott was on a business trip. As news of the alleged affair made the headlines, Scott responded by calling the reports, "a bunch of lies." When Laci's stepfather asked Scott if he had a girlfriend, Scott told him, "unequivocally, NO!" A short time later, a 27-year-old single mother came forward and publicly confessed to having an affair with Laci's husband. She said, "**...I met Scott on November 20th of 2002. I was introduced to him. I was told he was unmarried. Scott told me he was not married. We did have a romantic relationship...**"

This woman fell for **The Lone Ranger** and he turned her world upside down. Whether he is convicted for murdering his wife and child remains to be seen. As to the charge of Scott Peterson being a **Lone Ranger**, how would you as a juror find him, guilty or not guilty? To the charge of being a relationship assassin, guilty or not guilty?

To the charge of being a marriage missile, guilty or not guilty and to the charge of being a smooth operator, guilty or not guilty? The evidence: he not only lied to his wife, he deceived her family and his. He defrauded the other woman and her family. The degree of Scott Perterson's deception is mind boggling. The father of Scott's mistress said he had a picture in his wallet of his daughter and Scott holding each other, smiling in front of a Christmas tree. Scott told her father that he lost his wife. Do you comprehend what you are reading?

Experts monitoring the case say, "Scott Peterson is a cold-blooded liar." Others say, "No one really knew Scott Peterson." He seemed to be a masked man to just about everyone who came in contact with him. BUT! As cunning as they say he is, the woman who had the affair with Scott could have easily avoided his deceptions. Remember our *Booby Trap Acid Tests* on page 72? She clearly failed one third of them. **1). She never saw Scott communicating or interacting with his family, 2). She never communicated or interacted with his family, and 3). Important things she should have known about Scott, such as a confirmed place of residence, were a mystery to her.**

She should have demanded those things! Had she known and implemented all eight of the *Booby Trap Acid Tests* on page 72, she would not be caught in the cross-fire of a major double homicide!

This point is so critical I must *re-emphasize* it. If a potential mate does not invite examination, put the brakes on and proceed no further! You are looking at a neon sign plainly advertising your future. That person will become a greater mystery to you, especially if the two of you join hands in holy, deceptive matrimony.

They will have you feeling as if you are a detective or a private investigator hired to spy on them. I have lost count of the number of husbands and wives I have talked to, who spend their days and nights in tears, wondering what happened to the person they married.

They had no idea their spouses would turn out to be manipulative, controlling, self-destructive or abusive, until the disguises and the masks started coming off. When they looked back and began to recall their romantic days of dating and courting, they finally woke-up and realized that all of the **Primary Emergency Warning Signs** were right in front of their faces. They either ignored them or they simply had no knowledge of what the warning signs looked or sounded like.

The glory of God that would have been revealed in their life through marriage was disrupted. Now they are finding out firsthand what it means to drink from the bitter cup of nuptial drama and what it means to eat from the sour plate of marital anguish. Never forget the priceless and powerful four part statement:

Truth invites examination
Sincerity of heart does not shun it
Trustworthy people expect it
True love demands it

What the Word of God reveals about these masked men and women is a chilling and detailed affidavit of their sinister hearts, smooth as silk conversation but cruel intentions. We looked at this Scripture before but it is so profound, you need to read it again.

> Proverbs 26:24-26 NIV [Emphasis added]
> [24] A malicious man DISGUISES HIMSELF with his lips, but in his heart he harbors deceit.
> [25] THOUGH HIS SPEECH IS CHARMING, DO NOT BELIEVE HIM, for seven abominations fill his heart.
> [26] HIS MALICE MAY BE CONCEALED BY DECEPTION but his wickedness will be exposed in the assembly.

As charming as your potential mate may appear to be, don't believe them until you have performed all of the eight *Booby Trap Acid Tests* for detecting **Lone Rangers**. These men and women know how to disguise their true intentions. The Scripture says, they conceal their malice by their deception. Here is a crucial relationship law that you must never violate or break. Inscribe this one on your heart:

If I cannot get to know your family, examine your background past history and track record, we will not have a future!

Aside from the *Booby Trap Acid Tests* on page 72, here are the other critical questions you must ask yourself. Are you participating in a secret relationship? Are you isolated from people who truly love you and sincerely care about you? Does anyone else know about this relationship? Are you sneaking around to date this person?

Does it feel like the two of you are dating or courting on a deserted or secluded island? Have you made plans to tell your family and friends about this person after you elope or after you get married? Have you or your potential mate stooped so low as to be deceptive about the relationship to your family or friends?

Have you intentionally not told your family and friends certain things about your potential mate, fearful that they may disapprove of your relationship with this person? If you answered "yes," to any of those *Booby Trap Acid Tests*, make no mistake about it, even if your intentions do not include marriage, you are being booby trapped!

- 5 -

Return To Sender: Address Undeliverable

From 1977 to 1984 there was a popular television show called Fantasy Island. The long running Hollywood show starred Ricardo Montalban as Mr. Roarke and Herve Villechaize as Tattoo, his assistant. The plot of the show was to make the fantasies of the visitors of Fantasy Island come true. You could have been flipping hamburgers and frying french fries for minimum wage. But when you called Mr. Roarke and told him that your fantasy was to eat caviar, own a Ferrari, live in South Beach, Florida and mingle with the likes of Donald Trump and super model Tyra Banks, your life was about to change.

Mr. Roarke, Tattoo and the other fine folks at Fantasy Island were prepared to accommodate your every wish, but only as long as you were living on Fantasy Island. When you left the island, you went back to flipping hamburgers and frying french fries. On the show, there were occasions when certain visitors did not want to leave Fantasy Island. They refused to go back to reality. They felt like they should have been able to live out their fantasies forever.

There are men and women who desperately desire to fall in love with you. Others passionately want to make you their spouse. The problem with them is this - they have taken up permanent residence on the Fantasy Island *in their mind* and they are going to look to you to be their Mr. Roarke. They are going to unashamedly expect you to fulfill all of their whims, no matter what the cost. Those who fall in love with individuals living on the Fantasy Island *in their mind* learn firsthand what it means to be in a dead-end relationship. Take the case of Bradford and Elayna.

Elayna grew up in Los Angeles, California, an only child. Her parents pampered and spoiled her and literally trained her to pout, whine and cry to get her way. Growing up in the city of angels, Elayna had big dreams. She saw herself in the total package: the marbled floor mansion, the three car garage with the Mercedes, the Jaguar and the Porshe. She dreamed of being adorned in Louis Vuitton and Georgio Armani, dining at the finest eateries and traveling at her whim.

Elayna couldn't wait to live the lifestyle. Bradford also had big dreams. His philosophy was simple. Pray, plan and persist. When Bradford and Elayna married, theirs seemed like a match made in heaven. They both worked. Between them at the time, they grossed about sixty thousand dollars annually. When they got married, the only debt they had were a few payments left on their automobiles.

The middle-class newlyweds couldn't ask for a better situation in which to start. Less than a year after their wedding, things started to unravel rapidly. Elayna's dream of the big life was tugging at her heart and she couldn't deny it. It was time.

She talked Bradford into going house hunting. She had picked out three sprawling subdivisions. When they arrived at the first location, Bradford thought to himself, "There's no way we can afford this house right now!" The subdivision was well beyond their financial means.

To top matters off, it was an hour's drive one way, from where they both worked, adding fuel costs plus two hours travel time daily. Ten to twelve hours a week on the road was not appealing to Bradford at all. People who purchased homes in that subdivision were grossing at least $150k a year, plus they had the luxury of telecommuting. Nevertheless, Elayna ignored those facts.

They looked at the other subdivisions, which were more expensive than the first. When they returned home, Bradford sat his wife down and explained to her that those houses were currently out of their price range. Elayna became infuriated! She lashed out at her husband in a bitter verbal attack and made it clear; if she didn't get what she wanted Bradford was going to have trouble. His wife stunned him.

Although they made up, a nasty storm was brewing within Elayna's heart. Not long after the verbal assault against her husband, Elayna noticed some changes in her body and her girlfriends advised her to purchase an **Early Pregnancy Test** kit. The test came back positive; she was pregnant. Bradford was elated about the news, but his excitement would be short lived. Against his wishes, Elayna purchased a top of the line luxury car to drive their baby around. She pridefully showed off her new wheels to family and friends whether they cared to see it or not. Her spending was completely out of control.

It was clearly evident, Elayna was living on the Fantasy Island *in her mind*. Now that their baby was due, Bradford knew they had to get their finances under control or they would be faced with financial ruin. He tried his best to get this point across to Elayna. Sorrowfully, his words fell on deaf ears. Elayna was determined to get her way even if it meant attacking and belittling Bradford's manhood. It was a tumultuous time.

Bradford called close friends and confided in them, asking them to unite with him in prayer. He would eventually spend many nights in earnest prayer for his wife, hoping she would have a change of heart. But after their baby was born Elayna became more contentious, spiteful and out of control. Bradford often rocked their baby to sleep wondering whom had he married. This was not the same woman who promised to love and cherish him. Or was it? He was perplexed and hurt. His parents had been happily married for 27 years. He had married Elayna with the intention of them spending their entire lives together.

When they married, the words divorce, separation, verbal and emotional abuse and spite were not part of Bradford's vocabulary. But now they were an integral part of his life. He thought about their infant. One thing was glaringly obvious. Elayna had rejected their little one. When it came to taking care of their baby, she refused to feed, bathe, change diapers or perform any other parental duties.

When Elayna married she assumed that her husband would fulfill all of her fantasies. When he did not, she fumed with rage and absolutely no one could talk any sense into her. Although Bradford and Elayna lived under the same roof, they were no longer sleeping together. Elayna cut Bradford off from all physical contact or sexual intimacy.

In another one of her devilish tongue lashings she told Bradford that he couldn't handle her. She told him he was not a man and informed him that she was going to find herself a real man. Her words cut his heart like a razor blade. Their condominium became unbearable to live in. Elayna attended church and was a lead singer in the choir, but she was not submitted to God by any stretch of the imagination.

After Bradford's suggestion of marital counseling which she adamantly refused, Elayna threatened her husband with promises of physical harm while he slept. Bradford braced himself and told his wife it would be best if he moved out to ease the tension and give her a chance to reevaluate things. In a cold vindictive manner, she looked at her husband and said, "Be gone!" Around others, Elayna put on a facade and acted as if all was well on her Fantasy Island. She insisted that Bradford take ~~their~~ *his* child when he left. The picture perfect couple was now separated. The time apart did not change a thing in Elayna's heart. To her, Bradford was her Mr. Roarke and he should have bent over backwards to give her what she demanded.

When the two finally divorced, Bradford was given custody of their child with Elayna being granted visitation rights. She never visited their child until about three years later. That was when she found out that Bradford was remarrying. That news so incensed Elayna, that she started demanding visits, using their child to cause discord between

Bradford and his new wife. Hours after her visitation ended, when she should have brought their daughter back, Elayna would call Bradford and insist that he come and pick her up himself. In a moment, we'll examine the *Booby Trap Acid Tests* Bradford should have performed to reveal that Elayna was living on the Fantasy Island *in her mind.* But first I need to paint a mental portrait of what a resident of Fantasy Island looks like. Words cannot express how critical it is that you be able to spot these smooth operators. I'll start by defining a fantasy. A fantasy is an imagined event or condition.

The buzz word is *imagined.* Fantasies don't really exist. People living on the Fantasy Island *in their mind* imagine a lot of things they believe are reality when they are clearly not. They insist on living as though what they imagined is real regardless of the facts, evidence or truth. All stalkers are living in a self-concocted fantasy world.

They stalk pro-athletes, movie stars and anyone who they perceive will make their fantasies come true. You read about them in the police blotters. They stalk people they have never met but they *imagined* being with. People living on Fantasy Island *in their mind* are known for frequently getting fired from jobs. Since they are living on Fantasy Island, they come to work late, leave early, go on extended breaks without permission, take days off without calling in and they do other things that blatantly jeopardize their job.

When a person is living on the Fantasy Island *in their mind*, they intentionally ignore the repercussions and consequences of their actions. Because they are impulsive people, you can find them driving cars and boats, flying airplanes, wearing clothes and taking trips they knew they could not afford when they bought them. To people living on the Fantasy Island *in their mind* - words like, lying, deceit, defraud, deception, cheat and swindle do not exist.

They will, without any discretion, roll the dice using your life savings and the things for which you worked hard, to chase after their financial pot of gold at the end of their imaginary rainbow. People living on Fantasy Island give off clues to let you know that a hurricane is slowly brewing on their imaginary island.

Here are some of those **Primary Emergency Warning Signs: 1). They regularly act on impulse 2). They often insist on having their way 3). They are inconsiderate of those they claim to love 4). They often reject sound advice and shun godly wisdom 5). Their life is about material things and the pleasures they will enjoy.** Oftentimes they boldly announce who they are by wearing clothing, necklaces, tattoos, license plates and other objects advertising that they are "Spoiled!" If a potential mate informs you they are spoiled, or that they like to be spoiled, that is your cue to be highly troubled!

You do not eat spoiled meat, spoiled vegetables or any other spoiled food! You don't drink spoiled milk or spoiled juice. If it is spoiled, you trash it! What would compel you to pursue or be pursued by a spoiled woman or man? Elayna was spoiled to the max. She told Bradford while they were dating, that he would have to spoil her. Like most men, he thought what she said was cute and took it as a challenge. He had no idea how venomous her words were. To be spoiled means to: **1). be rotten. 2). be tainted or unfit for use. 3). be in the process of decaying. 4). impair the value or quality of. 5). plunder. 6). disrupt and disturb.** When a person tells you they are spoiled, they are saying, "I am a rotten person."

Telling you they are spoiled is their way of formally announcing that they live on the Fantasy Island *in their mind.* This is one of the few warning signs that stands out like a sore thumb. Men and women who have fallen for this booby trap will wholeheartedly testify about being married to someone who lives on the Fantasy Island *in their mind.* They will tell you that you will live on a perpetual emotional, mental, physical and financial roller coaster.

Butch and Megan had been married about five years. They had three children at the time they moved to Georgia. Butch figured he could come to Atlanta and make his dreams come true. He *imagined* himself living large but because of his unstable character, Butch had spent their entire marriage bouncing from job to job and moving from apartment to apartment. Nothing about him was steady or reliable. With his lifestyle they couldn't keep a permanent telephone number.

Prior to meeting Megan, Butch joined the military but his stint was short. He came face-to-face with real men who didn't tolerate his lame excuses, lack of discipline or his contempt for authority. He was dishonorably discharged.

That was a **Primary Emergency Warning Sign** that Megan should have taken seriously but did not. Once they settled into Atlanta, Butch joined a fitness club. He loved to work out and dreamed of maybe catching someone's eye who could put him in a movie. He also dreamed of becoming a fitness trainer with his own health club, videos, and signature products. He imagined himself being a body guard for some well-known celebrity. But those were just more of his fantasies.

Butch finally talked a neighbor into getting him a job. He convinced his neighbor that he was a responsible, dependable and loving family man. During his first week on the job, Butch showed his true character; he was almost two hours late for work one day. He didn't bother to phone in. He just waltzed into the office and cracked a smile as if he was the CEO. By his second week on the job, he had lost all credibility. Less than three weeks on the job and Butch was treading on thin ice.

While that was going on, he picked up on the nightclub scene in Atlanta and he liked what he saw. Butch slipped his wedding band off his middle finger, snugly placed it in his pocket and then proceeded to live out more of his fantasies. He portrayed himself to be an elite body builder. The females in those nightclubs bought into Butch's Fantasy Island imaginations, hook, line and sinker. He convinced them he was a high roller. He fed them. Bought them drinks. Took them to the movies and had sex with many of them.

He even put some of them up in hotel rooms. For Butch, this was the life! He was living out his fantasies, but in order to continue his charade, he had to blow ALL of his paychecks.

This man refused to pay the bills in his own household. He left his wife and three kids dangling in the wind while he financed the bar tab and hotel rooms of a bunch of floozies. Megan had no way of knowing what was going on financially because they didn't have a checking account and he refused to show her his paystubs. She didn't know how much money he made and he didn't talk to her about their finances.

His response was always, "I'm taking care of things!" It was not until Megan got slapped with an eviction notice that she realized they were in deep trouble AGAIN! But Butch was one smooth operator.

He swore to his wife that he had paid the rent. He claimed the apartment management made an error and he would straighten it out. That is one of the tactical ploys used by people living on the Fantasy Island *in their mind*. **They spend their lives blaming others for their sin, poor judgment and lack of discretion.** And! For the most part they get away with it. The last day they had to pay the rent, Butch was nowhere to be found. Megan pleaded with a neighbor to use their phone to call her husband's office. She was frantic. The Sheriff had already notified her of the deadline when they would be putting their things out on the street. Megan and the kids had no place to go, no money and no clue of what to do. Men from his job raced to his wife's aid to see how they could help. When they got there, they met a befuddled, distraught, pregnant mother with three kids who was at the end of her rope.

They got over their anger towards Butch, pulled together and raised enough money to stave off the eviction for the time being. When Butch finally appeared, he showed no concern for his family. He didn't even ask if they were okay. While all of this was going on, he was out wining and dining some bimbo he had met at one of the nightclubs.

Once again, he smoothed things over by swearing that he had paid the rent.With no receipts and no proof, his famous words were, "don't you believe me baby? I love you!" Even after that ordeal, Butch continued living his fantasies as if nothing had happened.

Surprisingly, Megan was fully persuaded that Butch loved her. She would not accept the fact that all she was to him was his Mr. Roarke. To the person living on the Fantasy Island *in their mind*, their boyfriend, girlfriend, fiancé, fiancée or spouse is just a means to an end. The end is living out their fantasy and they will do and say whatever it takes to capture a potential mate and hopefully convert that person into their legally wedded husband or wife.

Through the years Butch used his skills as a pathological liar to keep Megan at his side. He needed her to pay his bills while he ran the streets and flexed his muscles at the gym. He had become a professional at pulling her strings and persuading her to believe his every word.

Megan never learned that *True Love* does not leave a pregnant wife with three kids wondering where he is. She did not understand that *True Love* is not unreliable. She did not know that *True Love* is not unfaithful and that *True Love* does not put those it cares about in harm's way. Butch's manager and assistant manager tried to talk some sense into him. He listened intently, but two months later Butch was arrested. He had rented a luxury car, paid for one week but refused to return the car when his rental agreement expired.

The manager from the car rental agency called Butch's job numerous times pleading with his fellow employees to convince him to bring the car back. Butch simply refused to comply.

He was living on the Fantasy Island *in his mind* and the thought of suffering consequences is foreign to these type of people. When he was taken into custody, he adamantly claimed it was the car rental agency that screwed up the rental agreement. More of his lies... he couldn't produce any receipts or proof to back up his claims. As usual, Butch got fired. His marriage was marked by the pain and heartache he caused his wife and family. Megan has spent their entire marriage crying, hoping and praying Butch would stand up and be a man.

In the meantime, she relegated herself to paying his bills and cleaning up after his self-inflicted damage. All the signs and red flags that Butch would act the way he did, were present while he and Megan dated. Like many men and women who are searching for love, Megan didn't know she had to sift through relationship assassins and marriage missiles before she would find *True Love*. Here are the *Booby Trap Acid Tests* she should have performed but did not.

• *Have you discovered that your potential mate has blatantly lied to you?* If you answered "yes" to this *Booby Trap Acid Test,* please note. That is not a clue. That is your cue to cut your losses and move on. When a potential mate demonstrates the capacity to lie to you while dating or courting, you must not proceed with that relationship any further.

Period! We looked at this issue briefly in the previous chapter but it demands that we take a second deeper look.

Proverbs 14:5 [Emphasis added]
A faithful witness will not lie: but a false witness will utter lies.

A faithful person will not lie to you. When a person lies to you, they are saying point blank, "Yes, I am an unfaithful person!" Is that the kind of person you want to fall in love with? While they were dating, there were numerous occasions in which Butch would tell Megan things that turned out to be untrue. But like all smooth operators, he was able to shmooze her over. What if she tells you she will call you at 7:30 tonight but you hear from her three days later? Or what if he tells you he will pick you up Saturday morning at eleven, but you do not hear from him until late Monday night?

Make no mistake about it, they just lied to you! That might not seem like a big deal when you are dating or courting, but it becomes a critical issue when it is Friday morning and your spouse says, "I'll be home by six tonight." However, they end-up creeping into the house five-thirty Sunday morning with their clothes in shambles.

Once you sanction lying, by tolerating it, you just got booby trapped! Do not let anyone convince you that their lie was an accident, a mistake or a normal thing couples go through. The only people for whom lying becomes normal are thieves, criminals, liars, cheaters, wife beaters, adulterers, gold-diggers... and the people who believe them.

• *Do you detect evidence of instability or unreliability in your potential mate?* People who live on the Fantasy Island *in their mind* frequently demonstrate the destructive character trait of instability. What **Primary Emergency Warning Signs** must you look for?

1). Always switching jobs or places of residence 2). Inability to maintain friendships 3). Always starting a new venture/business, dream, plan, project, or idea but never following through 4). Dropped out of high school and refused to continue education 5). Dishonorably discharged from the military 6). Cracking under the pressure of life's challenges or pressures 7). Gambling. 8). Using drugs or alcohol. This list includes the self described "social drinkers and casual users." All addicts and alcoholics started somewhere.

When you mix a person who is feeble minded, (*see page 49*), with a seemingly harmless marijuana joint, crack pipe or drink, you now have a self-destructive time-bomb on your hands. If you fall for this type of person your life will become a revolving door of: "I forgot to pay the bills. I can stop drinking anytime I want! I over slept again! I got fired again! My drug urinalysis test came back positive. Baby, I need you to bail me out of jail," and the biggest one - "But it wasn't my fault!"

Fall in love with this type of relationship assassin and you will in all probability become familiar with how to make a court appearance plus how to deal with police, bail bondsmen, probation and parole officers, district attorneys and public defenders. There are no words to aptly describe the stress and anguish these individuals will put you through. To avoid any of that trauma - test, examine and discern the spirit of your potential mate before proceeding forward.

• *Do you see evidence that your potential mate does not handle their finances with wisdom, discretion or with good judgment?* If talking about this critical issue with a potential mate seems uncomfortable to you, then love and marriage is not for you. You really need to consider becoming a monk or a nun, taking a lifelong missionary journey to the New Siberian Island and completely purging your mind of ever finding *True Love*.

Especially when talking about marriage, this issue must be brought to the table and dealt with well before the wedding bells ring. I will never forget the time a couple came to me seeking *pre*-marital counseling. The bride-to-be had two automobile repossessions, a judgment, all of her credit cards were in collection status and she had multiple jewelry accounts she had opened and never paid.

She exercised absolutely no discretion financially. She consistently lived beyond her means, dining at expensive restaurants, purchasing tickets to expensive plays and taking trips at her whim. With all of the bills she had accumulated, she would quit a job at the drop of a dime. This woman had the audacity to firmly believe and cheerfully claim that she was definitely ready to get married. Has your potential mate ruined their name or given themselves bad credit?

Must they use other people's names and social security numbers to get telephone, gas, electric, or other utilities? When they want to purchase or rent an automobile or a piece of property, must they resort to begging people to co-sign for them? These are all dangerous signs. When people have ruined their name, no one wants to do business with them. Therefore, smooth operators seek out potential mates with good credit so they can continue living out their fantasies. Because of their terrible credit, has your potential mate attempted to get you to sign on a business deal for them?

The young lady in the *pre*-marital counseling session disclosed to me why she had two repossessions. She had talked two previous boyfriends into co-signing car loans for her. In each case, when she broke up with them, she no longer felt that she had to pay the car notes. She ruined both of their credit profiles and neither of those men had any legal recourse. If a potential mate attempts to get you to commingle your finances with theirs prior to marriage, your answer must be an unflinching and resounding, "NO!" They may cry but their tears will dry up! However, the financial ruin they may cause you, could set you back for years. Never cosign for them. Never give them access to your bank accounts. Do not enter into any joint accounts with them. Never let them use your social security number and never sign any leases or contracts with them. There is no guarantee the two of you are going to get married. Other questions you need to ask are, "What financial preparations has this person made for the married life?" If that answer is "none," but they are claiming you are *The One*, they are definitely living on the Fantasy Island *in their mind*.

It takes preparation and money to have a stable, secure and peaceful household. Does your potential mate file taxes? Do they have any legal wranglings with the IRS? Do they have a valid driver's license? Has your potential mate filed bankruptcy? Do they have repossessions or foreclosures pending against them? Are they being sued or are they engaged in any other lawsuits? If he has children, is he paying child support? If not, he should not become involved in a relationship.

If she has a child, is she collecting child support, and are her outrageous financial demands driving the baby's daddy into financial ruin? Does she have a menacing attitude toward her baby's daddy? I have seen stunned brides and shocked grooms who didn't ask these questions. They just assumed and their assumptions caused their names to be added to the ever growing list of victims of love.

These are critical issues that you must address before you make any commitments you will regret later in life. For your sake don't wait until you've planned a wedding date or until after you've said, "I do," before getting the answers to these questions. People living on the Fantasy Island *in their mind* count on you being clueless concerning their financial condition. If your mate becomes evasive, clams up or gets upset when you bring these issues up, pack up your emotions, douse your feelings, respectfully walk away and don't ever look back.

• *Do you find yourself making excuses or alibis for this person to other people?* When loved ones who sincerely care about you meet this person and raise concerns about their character, past history or present conduct, what happens? Do you find yourself making excuses for your potential mate's indiscretions, bad judgments or sin(s)?

If you do, prepare yourself because you will have to make more excuses and in all probability even lie for them throughout the relationship. People who live on the Fantasy Island *in their mind* frequently seduce, manipulate and coerce others to cover for their bad character. They will have you singing to family, friends, employers, the public and to investigators as to what a great person they are in spite of the fact that they keep blowing their top, keep getting fired, keep quitting jobs or stay in trouble with the law. They will have you trying to persuade authorities they didn't do it when they did. They'll have you explaining to others about how much they love and care about you and how, "all the two of you had was just a normal lover's spat."

They claim every couple has these harmless arguments and quarrels and it's no big deal! Would you call slapping someone in the face, grabbing them by the neck, throwing them out of the house butt naked, pushing them out of a car or threatening to hurt or kill them, just another lover's quarrel?

That is not the picture of a healthy relationship. But people living on the Fantasy Island *in their mind* are masters at getting potential mates to blindly believe in their psychotic brand of love. They are well schooled at seducing others to look at their seedy character and somehow convince them to see a rock of Gibraltar. On June 5th, 2002, according to authorities, 14-year-old Elizabeth Smart (*real name*) was abducted from the bedroom she shared with her sister in the family's house in Salt Lake City's Federal Heights neighborhood. According to senior law enforcement officials, Richard Ricci (*real name*), a handyman once hired by the abducted girl's father, was the top potential suspect.

I want to make this clear, I am not dealing with the abduction. The kidnappers have been captured, Elizabeth is back with her family, and Ricci apparently had nothing to do with the crime. What I'm looking at is how Richard apparently convinced a woman that he was a knight in shining armor and the chain of events she experienced after she became his lawfully wedded wife.

Let's follow the timeline of Richard's life, take a brief look at his character and examine his past history and track record. During the past three decades, Ricci had repeatedly been sentenced to prison. He violated parole four times. His thirty year criminal record included convictions for burglary, aggravated robbery and attempted murder. He said his problems stemmed from using drugs. In an interview, he acknowledged that he has "an addictive personality."

Then comes the marriage. Richard and his new love were married on February 14th, Valentine's Day, 2002. They exchanged vows on the most romantic day in history. Four months later, Ricci was sent back to prison for "once again" violating the terms of his parole.

In the meantime, his newly christened bride was thrust into an extremely hot seat that no sane person would ever intentionally seek. She became Ricci's alibi. He claimed he was with his wife the day of Elizabeth Smart's abduction. Once he released those words from his mouth concerning his whereabouts, his wife was forced to face intense interrogations and endure a litany of questions, allegations and assumptions from detectives who microscopically scrutinized her every word. Forensic evidence technicians and other crime scene investigators descended upon her home and invaded her privacy looking for clues and evidence. Next, she was compelled to answer forthright to a grueling grand jury. Then shrouded in a heavy cloud of suspicion, she went on "Larry King Live" and tried to convince America that her husband of four months was a great man.

Wait a minute! Are we talking about the same man? The one with a thirty year criminal track record? The one who violated parole four times? The one who committed aggravated robbery and attempted murder? The one who burglarized homes? One reason Ricci was a top potential suspect was because the authorities confirmed that he stole from the Smart family while he worked for them. After all of that, can we honestly say that he is a great man? If so, based on what?

Am I just being cynical or do you see the entire picture? His wife got four months of marital bliss and then WHAM! Their fairytale love story came to a screeching halt. A few months after returning to prison, Ricci went into a coma and never recovered. He died the most miserable death, in prison shackles.

I'm not trying to vilify Ricci or criticize his widow. My prayers go with her. She went through hell on earth. I'm merely stating the facts. When a person lives on the Fantasy Island *in their mind*, once you get in a relationship with them, your love life goes on automatic pilot. Destination - crash and burn. What Ricci's wife went through is a portrait of some of the things you can expect if you find yourself making excuses for or trying to justify a potential mate's bad character.

• *Do you have a history of breaking up and making up with this person?* A history of breaking up and making up with a potential mate is a critical **Primary Emergency Warning Sign**. When two people are constantly breaking up and making up, this is a precursor of things to come. When you look back, do you see a string of breakups? Are any of the reasons due to cheating, verbal or physical abuse, emotional or sexual abuse, injurious arguments, lies, betrayal, signs of financial irresponsibility or immaturity, or incompatibility issues?

After the split do you end up getting back together, only to go through another ordeal? With each break up your reasoning for doing so made all the sense in the world, and each time you got back together your decision to do so made absolutely no sense at all. Some smooth operators will attempt to persuade you that getting married will somehow magically end this disruptive cycle. Friend, a wedding is not going to change that destructive pattern.

Any potential mate who tries to convince you that getting married is going to alter or altogether eliminate an erratic (*on again - off again*) love affair is living on the Fantasy Island *in their mind*. **Love-Hate, Make-up Break up** relationships only work in the movies, soap operas, romance novels and fictional books. Here's what you need to understand. When the relationship should have been terminated, smooth operators repeatedly succeed at easing their way back into a person's life.

The only way to end this dead-end cycle is by completely severing all ties except those required by law, (*i.e., visitation rights, child support, etc.*). That means terminate all phone calls. When the gifts come, return them. If you cannot return them, destroy them. Do you have any relationship mementos or keepsakes such as necklaces, bracelets, photographs or ticket stubs? Trash them! You may have to take other drastic measures, like changing your phone number and e-mail address.

If necessary, move! Whatever actions you take, be cordial but be firm and put a stop to all attempts to rekindle an erratic relationship. You have to go cold turkey with these people. Smooth operators, in an attempt to get back into your good graces, will do and say just about anything to pull you back into the spider web they've spun. They will use sex to entice you to come back.

If that doesn't work they will resort to preschool ploys such as calling you and claiming they need your help to buy a house, purchase a car or pick out a computer. Just say no, encourage them to search the Yellow Pages and politely terminate the conversation.

• *Have you noticed a pattern of them blaming others for their sin, lies, poor judgment or indiscretions?* When they talk about lost jobs, broken relationships, failed businesses, failed marriages, severed friendships, encounters with the law, do they always seem to place the blame on others? I worked for a major corporation. A fellow employee who had just started working at the company had a bad habit of coming to work late. Since he had a very likeable personality his supervisor initially talked to him "off the record" but his tardiness continued.

He was given verbal warnings and yet he still came in late. Finally, he was given a written warning. What he did next was classic smooth operator bravado. He responded by sending an e-mail to his supervisor and copying that e-mail to all the employees in the e-mail directory.

I received a copy of that e-mail. He said he was late because in the morning he had chores to complete at home, he dropped his son off at school, and then he encountered heavy traffic. He said there was no way anyone could guarantee they could be at their computer terminal every morning by 9am. He ended his e-mail by claiming someone in the company was trying to sabotage him.

What kind of a man was he? He was a man living on the Fantasy Island *in his mind*. Nothing these smooth operators do is ever their fault. They have a plausible explanation for everything. They can drink themselves into a blithering stupor, get behind the steering wheel of a car and plow into a parked school bus full of kids in broad daylight. There could be twenty eyewitnesses, but smooth operators will find a way to say it was the school bus driver's or the kid's fault, point the finger at the crossing guard, bartender or the liquor manufacturer!

They will brazenly swear they didn't do it and the only reason they were found guilty was because they had incapable legal representation. When you listen to your potential mate talk do you get the feeling that everyone else they have ever dealt with was either incompetent or was out to destroy them? When they are wrong, do they give you a list of excuses instead of owning up and taking responsibility for their actions or lack of actions? If you stay with them or God forbid, marry them, you can believe it will be just a matter of time before they are pinning all of their rebellion, failures, downfalls, sins and indiscretions directly on your shoulders. It will be your fault!

• *Do you see discrepancies in things your potential mate has told you?* A discrepancy is an inconsistency. It's a disagreement between the facts versus the claims. For example, your potential mate claims to be a Christian, but they hang out at the nightclubs, use foul language, have hatred in their heart towards others, engage in *pre*-marital sex and live their life in a manner not indicative of a true Christian. Take the case of Rupert & Drusilla. It was a fact that Rupert was divorced with two children. Like Ira Einhorn, Rupert had his own philosophy when it came to love. He thought the female gender should be in awe of him because he was in a high income bracket.

His philosophy led him to see women as his subordinates. He was clearly living on the Fantasy Island *in his mind*. After his first divorce, he quickly lassoed Drusilla into his vise-grip like clutch. She saw certain things that sent off alarms in her heart, but Rupert was so smooth he convinced her those things meant nothing. Time after time, Drusilla ignored those tell-all discrepancies. For instance, although they were divorced, Rupert's *ex*-wife slept overnight at the new house he and Drusilla had picked out to live in after they married. And! She was sleeping in the bed Druscilla bought and would be soon sleeping in!

Rupert insisted on this because he claimed their children needed to see their parents acting amicably together. What? You just dragged your wife through a hellish marital nightmare. Then you put her through a combative divorce and now you want to *appear* to be amicable? That is not the picture of a person with a rational mind.

With each incident, Rupert's children would relay what was going on behind closed doors to his new bride-to-be. They told Drusilla everything about their mom sleeping over, about their mom hanging out and frolicking around with their dad like old times, and how their mom had a key to their new house. Their mom even had clothes stashed in the new house. God was using Rupert's two children to warn Drusilla of the impending hailstorm she was going to walk into if she married this man. When she told her fiancé how devastated she was about his *ex*-wife lying in the bed she had picked out, having keys to their house and clothes in their closet, he assured her he would stop all of those things as soon as they were married. Ignoring all of the warnings, Drusilla said, "ok, honey!" After their wedding nothing changed.

Rupert let his *ex*-wife keep her keys. She still slept in the newlywed's bed when they were away. She had her own house. She had custody of the kids. Why couldn't she sleep in her own bed, at her own house? They didn't live that far from each other.

Why did she have to have her bras and panties stashed away in the newlywed's house? Your answer goes back to how smooth operators get trained. Remember how they are indoctrinated to secretly date two or more people at the same time? How to lie and how to use a person's emotional vulnerabilities against them? That's what Rupert lived for. To ruin God's glorious plan for any woman who was naive enough to fall for his bait. After five long tormenting months of marriage, the two separated. With tears in her bloodshot eyes, Drusilla pleaded with her estranged husband to attend counseling with her.

She wanted so badly for things to work out between them, but Rupert would hear nothing of it. Like many men and women in her predicament, Drusilla simply didn't get it. She had just been burned by a smooth operator. In the same manner as his first wife, she learned what a cold and conniving liar Rupert was. When you see discrepancies concerning the facts versus the claims your potential mate has made to you, don't ever ignore those **Primary Emergency Warning Signs**.

Don't add your name to the list of people who said to me about their ex *"Gillis, something told me..."* For some, the act of being betrayed was so devastating, they vented their anguish and frustration in vengeful words teeming with anger, wrath and malice. Read what they had to say after being betrayed by the one they loved. Although I do not endorse their feelings, I cannot ignore them. Their pain is real.

- I feel like God abandoned me
- I have a child by him... I hate *"that"* child
- I can't move, I can't eat, I can't sleep...
- I hate men, I hate marriage... I hate God
- She hurt me... I'm going to hurt her back
- My husband... I wish he were dead
- He ruined my life, I'll never love again
- Don't ever fall in love, it's too painful!

- My wife? No! You mean my wench!   • I was a virgin, he said he loved me... (*tears*)
- I'm going to make other women pay for what my ex did to me... you can believe that!
- For what he did to me, I hate all men; may they all burn in hell!

• ***Does your potential mate watch soap operas, read romance, erotica or other fictional novels that inspire, inflame or invoke a fantasy mentality?*** Nancy Hazle, (*real name*) loved romance novels! Apparently, following the cue of one of her fictional heroines, she poisoned her second, third, fourth and fifth husbands to death. When Tulsa, Oklahoma authorities arrested her, she told officers, *"...I'm sure I'll find my perfect mate yet..."* When a person is living on the Fantasy Island *in their mind*, not even capital murder charges will frazzle their pipe dreams. At one point during questioning, Nancy insisted that detectives allow her to keep her copy of the romantic fantasy magazine, *"Romantic Hearts."* Follow me carefully on this point...

In the process of testing and examining a person's spirit, look to see if they are drawn to this type of material. This goes back to the law of **influence by association**. If your potential mate is prone to watching soap operas or love stories, or reading materials that inspire, inflame or invoke unrealistic or destructive behaviors, you have reason to be worried. A person cannot ingest these materials into their psyche and not be affected by them spiritually, mentally, physically or emotionally.

In the end, if you fall for a person who lives on the Fantasy Island *in their mind*, when you attempt to talk some sense into them, your reply will always be: **Return to Sender: Address Undeliverable**.

You may express your feelings or deliver your thoughts, beliefs or position with scholarly wisdom, but getting through to these people is like attempting to deliver an express package to someone who swears they reside on the Bermuda Triangle. Your words and your thoughts will always be rubber stamped: **Return to Sender: Address Undeliverable**. Here is a quick recap of the eight *Booby Trap Acid Tests* used to detect if a person is living on the Fantasy Island *in their mind*.

1. Have you discovered that your potential mate has blatantly lied to you?
2. Do you detect evidence of instability or unreliability in your potential mate?
3. Do you see evidence that your potential mate does not handle their finances with wisdom, discretion, or good judgment?
4. Do you find yourself making excuses or alibis for this person to other people?
5. Do you have a history of breaking up and making up with this person?
6. Have you noticed a pattern of them blaming others for their sin, lies, poor judgment or indiscretions?
7. Do you see discrepancies in things your potential mate has told you?
8. Does your potential mate watch soap operas or read romance, erotica or other fictional novels that inspire, inflame or invoke a fantasy mentality?

- 6 -

The "Urge To Merge" Syndrome

Before we dissect this next virus like booby trap, I must define three key words that are related to its existence. It is critical that you take your time and absorb these details with the highest state of alert and give them your complete and undivided attention. Here are those three key words:

- *Urge* - 1. To drive; press; push; impel forward or onward forcefully 2. To press the mind or will of; to ply with motives, arguments, persuasion, or importunity 3. A strong restless desire 4. To stimulate or to excite to action

- *Merge* - 1. To cause to be absorbed in gradual stages 2. To combine or unite 3. To cause to be swallowed up; to immerse; to sink; to absorb

- *Syndrome* - 1. A group of signs and symptoms that collectively indicate or characterize a disease, psychological disorder, or other abnormal condition 2. A complex of symptoms indicating the existence of an undesirable condition or quality 3. A distinctive or characteristic pattern of behavior

Some smooth operators have what I have termed and coined as the Urge To Merge Syndrome. That is, they have a strong, restless desire to merge with you or with someB-O-D-Y. Any B-O-D-Y will do. Who they merge with is not the issue. The issue is them being able to find a flesh and blood physical B-O-D-Y and then merge with that B-O-D-Y. Read the definition of merge again.

They want to systematically and gradually absorb someB-O-D-Y, to swallow them up, to immerse them, to sink them into their twisted, dark and convoluted world. What method of merging do these smooth operators choose to use? Depending on their (MO), modus operandi, they are quite capable of using any of the ten methods listed below:

- Casual Sex Partner(s)
- Steady Girlfriend(s) or Boyfriend(s)
- Live-In Lover(s)
- Marriage, Serial Marriages
- Extra-Marital Affair(s)
- Forced Sex, Date Rape, Rape
- Strippers, Call Girls, Prostitutes
- Sex With Minor(s)
- Homosexuality Among Males
- Lesbianism Among Females

Whichever method of merging they choose to employ, these people have a desperate urge to merge. Just as the definition of the word "urge" describes, they are going to press you, drive you, compel you, coerce you, persuade you, stimulate or excite you or someB-O-D-Y into a relationship with them. When your path crosses any potential mate, you have to take on the mindset of a skilled physician.

Be keenly observant. Assume nothing. Ask probing questions. Look for symptoms, red flags, and warning signs. Most importantly, have loved ones who sincerely care about you examine your potential mate also. People with the **Urge To Merge Syndrome** are dangerous because they have donned (ARB) **At Risk Behaviors**. These men and women put themselves and others at risk by their blatantly abnormal, *"by any means necessary,"* behavior.

As they work to relieve their urge to merge, this cunning group will not rest until they have secured a steady, part-time or emergency sex partner to satisfy their insatiable urge to merge. They are going to be on edge until the day comes when they have moved in together with their new live-in house prize, walked down the aisle with their wedding day trophy, or until they find someone they can claim, label and crown as their boyfriend, girlfriend, homosexual or lesbian lover.

Understand this next point. Men and women who have the **Urge To Merge Syndrome** just need a physical flesh and blood B-O-D-Y! They couldn't care less about the things that come with the B-O-D-Y, such as the emotions, aspirations, physical well-being and the feelings. They are on the prowl to get it on! How you or anyone else feels about it is moot and irrelevant. Let's go to the Word of God and carefully examine a woman who had a severe case of the **Urge To Merge Syndrome.**

John 4:16-18 AMP [Emphasis added]
[16] At this, Jesus said to her, GO, CALL YOUR HUSBAND AND COME BACK HERE.
[17] The woman answered, I HAVE NO HUSBAND. Jesus said to her, You have spoken truly in saying, I HAVE NO HUSBAND.
[18] For YOU HAVE HAD FIVE HUSBANDS, and the man YOU ARE NOW LIVING WITH IS NOT YOUR HUSBAND.

This woman was married and divorced five times! Five different times she took the stroll down the aisle and made promises to love and cherish each of her husbands. On five separate occasions she said, "until death do us part." But her words meant nothing! Each of her marriages turned into unmet expectations, unfulfilled dreams and then divorce. There are so many questions we need answers to. Did she divorce each of her husbands? Did they divorce her? Did she even get divorces?

Did she defraud these men to get them to marry her? Did she have any children by these men? Did she have any abortions? Miscarriages? Could she even get pregnant? Had she contracted any sexually transmitted diseases? Was she just using these men because she was a gold-digger, ripping them off financially, taking their money and running? You and I both know that a person does not get married and divorced five times and not have some issues. To add insult to injury, per verse eighteen, this woman was shacking up with a man who was most likely on his way to becoming her sixth husband.

She had no doubt left a trail of heartbreak and disappointment behind her. But breaking the heart of others and ruining their lives never bothers the men and women who have the **Urge To Merge Syndrome**. You are about to find out just how ruthless they can be. One of the key means of detecting individuals with this dreaded disorder is clearly understanding the word "syndrome."

So let's examine this word in greater detail. A syndrome is a group of signs and symptoms that collectively indicate or characterize a disease, psychological disorder or other abnormal condition. People who have the **Urge To Merge Syndrome** give off a varying group of (PEWS) **Primary Emergency Warning Signs** and symptoms. Depending on the method they use, they each have a distinctive pattern of behavior.

It is that behavior along with those signs and symptoms that we are now going to examine. Magic Earvin Johnson, (*real name*) was addressing about 1,000 students at Cardozo High School in Washington, D.C., challenging them to responsibility.

He urged the students to put just as much energy into their academic work as they do into sports and most importantly, to save sex until after marriage. But everyone was not buying into Magic's newly launched safe sex initiative. One female student created a stir in the audience when she questioned Johnson as to why he wasn't "responsible" in his many sexual encounters with women.

His twelve year NBA career was marked by a string of one-night stands with women he met while traveling to various cities. Johnson responded by saying, "That was my mistake, I was not responsible. I didn't do what I was supposed to do... it was wrong... I can't correct that. All I can do is try and save your lives." You may recall that Magic Johnson helped the Los Angeles Lakers to five National Basketball Association championships and nine NBA finals appearances.

But on November 8, 1991, Magic stunned the world when he publicly announced that he had contracted the HIV virus, the precursor to AIDS. A few months before learning he was infected, Magic had gotten married and his new bride was pregnant with their child.

My question to you is this: How would you respond if a few months after your wedding ceremony, your spouse tested positive for the HIV virus. Imagine that... What would you do? Immediately file for divorce? Cry? Become depressed? Get angry? Contemplate suicide? Get mad at God? How would you respond? Think about it for a moment.

Just months after your wedding, instead of basking in love's overglow, you are desperately praying that your spouse has not infected you with the HIV virus. Plus, you must deal with the sobering news that if you test positively, you could infect your child.

To further intensify the matter, you learn that you can still be intimate with your spouse, you just have to spend the rest of your lives having sex on an egg shell. It is widely known that when a husband or wife is infected with the HIV virus, with each intimate contact, they run the risk of infecting their spouse. Could you live with that?

I sat down and listened to one man tell his story of contracting the HIV virus from one of his *ex*-girlfriends. He learned that he was infected soon after he had married. Six years later, he was diagnosed with full blown AIDS. He takes over twelve pills a day and can no longer hold a job because he spends most of his time in and out of hospitals fighting to stay alive. He and his wife were informed that having children was too risky a proposition because of his infection. He was also told that once his condition worsened, medical science had no other medication or treatment to help him. He realizes his death is imminent.

You must know that is not the will of God for your life! That is why we must step into the mind of someone who has the **Urge To Merge Syndrome** and take an in-depth look at three critical issues. **1)**. Their MO, **2)**. Their symptoms, and **3)**. Their patterns of behavior. In criminal investigations, police often refer to the MO or modus operandi. The MO is the method a person uses to commit a crime. Once a criminal has a MO, that information is sent to all pertinent police agencies and to the public on a need to know basis.

A modus operandi could be that a person robs convenience stores between 8pm and 11:30pm on Wednesdays. The male suspect has shoulder length blonde hair, a tattoo of a skull on his left shoulder, dons a green ski mask outside the store, enters brandishing a silver semiautomatic handgun, demands money and then flees on a metallic red motorcycle.

Imagine that you work in a convenience store and it's Wednesday at 9:30pm. You spot a man with long blonde hair pull up on a metallic red motorcycle. You can see a tattoo of a skull on his left shoulder and with his back facing you, he proceeds to pull a green ski mask over his face. Do you wait to figure out what he's going to do? Absolutely not!

You already have his MO! You know exactly what he's going to do! You hit the alarm button, dial 911, alert the customers in the store to take cover and do whatever it takes to protect yourself. Then there is the issue of symptoms. A symptom is a phenomenon experienced by an individual that is not a normal function, sensation or appearance. It gives an indication of a disorder or a disease.

If a person has a fever, chest discomfort, aches and pains, headaches and they are weak to the point of extreme exhaustion, those are usually flu-like symptoms. Those are not the normal functions of a person with a healthy body. Like someone with a medical condition, people with the **Urge To Merge Syndrome** give off symptoms to let you know they are living in the sexual danger zone.

Finally, there are the patterns of behavior. When a person is an alcoholic or is using drugs, they display undeniable patterns of behavior. No matter how hard they try to hide it, those patterns of behavior will always give them away. As an example, to determine if an adolescent is using either drugs or alcohol, a parent would look for certain patterns of behavior: a decline in schoolwork, grades slowly slipping or dropping dramatically, regularly missed curfews, money or other valuables mysteriously disappear or they have aggressive outbursts. They could also create a chaotic and hostile environment in the home.

They may become verbally flagrant toward others or refuse to do chores. They frequently appear to be depressed, agitated or sleepy. They start missing school, (*secretly skipping or "too tired" or "too sick" to go*). They develop unusual sleeping habits. They drop out of regular activities, (*hobbies, sports, after school functions, ceasing to interact with the family*). They have changes in their physical appearances, (*poor hygiene, unusual style changes*). Although that list is brief, here's the point.

When a combination of those patterns of behavior are present in a child, parents should become concerned. Let's deal with these three critical issues as they relate to people with the **Urge To Merge Syndrome**. First, we need to look at their MO.

As I stated on the bottom of page 97, people with the **Urge To Merge Syndrome** will use girlfriends, boyfriends, homosexuality, lesbianism, live-in lovers, marriages, extramarital affairs, a cache of casual sex partners, forced sex, date rape, rape, prostitutes, and sex with minors or a combination of all these methods to satisfy their urge to merge.

Let's track Silas's MO. From the observation of most females, Silas was a stable, respectable hard working man, making a mid-range five figure income who was searching for the love of his life. However, Silas had a bad case of the **Urge To Merge Syndrome**. His MO was a mixture of one-night stands, casual sex, live-in lovers and yes, even marriage.

He started the indoctrination process of becoming a smooth operator by spending hours conditioning his mind and conscience by drooling over pornographic magazines and x-rated videos. When the pornography was no longer satisfying, Silas graduated to spending a few nights a week hanging out at various strip clubs in Atlanta.

He paid for lap dances, bought table dances, dated, and had sex with the strippers. Outside of the strip club life, Silas kept a couple of girlfriends with whom he had sexual relations.

His running buddies hailed him as a player's player. His forte was women sitting in the pews. He had a penchant for seducing church girls. Silas knew all the right moves... the right words... and like most smooth operators he had mastered the art of exploitation.

Using the fact that these women were waiting on God for a husband, like a chameleon, he transformed himself to appear to be the answer to their prayers. He knew how to convince these women that he was sincerely seeking God. He'd request that they pray for him and asked them to show him their favorite Scriptures.

He'd get them to talk to him about the things of God. He'd show concerned interest in their life and ministry. Silas had an Academy Award winning act. By the time he got through, these women of God were persuaded the Lord was doing a great work in his life.

They were convinced God had sent them their husband. Their strong feelings for him, clouded their capacity to discern his true character. Silas was now in control. Getting them to hold hands with him while praying was the next act of progression.

Soon they were just holding hands without any praying and it wasn't long before Silas made his move. The gentle kiss. The warm embrace. The passionate, "I love you," and after getting into their panties, he was gone. When he met his first wife, things developed differently. She was a feisty type who didn't take no for an answer.

She was the type of female who got what she wanted. Like the other women, she fell for Silas's act, but she insisted that they get married. BUT! Marriage was never in Silas's plans. Why get married?

Between the strippers and other females, he was getting sex with zero responsibilities and no attachments. His first wife didn't know anything about smooth operators, how they got trained, or the booby traps they set. She didn't know how to determine if a man's mind and conscience was corrupted. She was just another naive female who was convinced that she could turn a man's life around with her love.

Since Silas never gave any thought to getting married, he had no idea what he was getting into. Two becoming *One Flesh*? He thought, "What does that mean? How can two people become *One Flesh*?"

He didn't get it. When he finally buckled under her pressure, and asked her hand in marriage, she assumed that he said, "Will you marry me?" That is not what he said. Silas asked her, "Will you *merry* me?" And there is a big difference! He was just using marriage to get some *booty* by any means necessary. After their wedding, his wife attempted to, as some women say, "house break" her husband.

She was going to teach him how to respect his marriage vows and communicate with his wife, things that were foreign to Silas. When he communicated with a female, he was conditioned to put $5 or $10 in her thong or g-string and order her to shake her *booty*. He was indoctrinated to take a female to dinner and a movie and then to a hotel or to the back seat of his SUV. Teaching Silas to respect his marriage vows was like trying to teach him to speak Korean.

Remember on page 43 when I talked about how a person's character is influenced by their associations? Silas had a crew of advisors influencing him who were obviously adverse to holy matrimony. His counselors were either divorced, getting divorced, in a bad marriage, or living with a lover. Since he continued going to the strip clubs, he also had a host of strippers who were telling him how to deal his wife.

What kind of advice do you think a stripper is going to give to a disgruntled husband? As you probably expected, his first wife divorced him. As with anyone taken with the **Urge To Merge Syndrome**, Silas wasted absolutely no time. He found and targeted a sweet innocent young lady named Fiona. She was another church girl not versed on smooth operators. Like a skilled vermin, Silas took his time to booby trap Fiona.

This time he used (TERT) **The Engagement Ring Trick** to make his move. That is when a man patiently pursues a woman's hand in marriage, or so it seems. During the dating or courting process he begins dropping buzz phrases in her ears like: "It would be so great to be a family, marriage is what makes a man, two are better than one," and other slick choreographed questions like, "What do you think it would be like if we were married?"

Once she takes the bait and becomes convinced he is marriage material and matrimony minded, the next phase is the presentation of the engagement ring. There are different variations of this trick. Some men infected with the **Urge To Merge Syndrome** won't sweat losing a few thousand dollars on an engagement ring if it means having sex with a hot babe. They drop that much money and more gambling.

One of the popular engagement ring tricks is when a man takes a woman to a jewelry store, allows her to pick out an engagement ring, puts the ring on a payment plan, and they both walk out of the jewelry store exhilarated.

By the time he takes her home she is on cloud nine! Love is in the air. She is telling her parents, friends, relatives and anybody else who will listen, that she is getting married, how he proposed, and how he insisted that she pick out the ring. To her, it can't get anymore real than that. While she's telling the world what a great man he is, her ~~fiancé~~, smooth operator goes back to the store and informs the jeweler that things didn't work out. He claims he and his fiancée broke up.

He cancels the engagement ring order, requests a refund and laughs to himself as he calculates his next move. While his ~~fiancée~~, victim is riding the crest, visualizing the wedding and seeing the honeymoon, her defenses are down. She trusts this man completely.

When he starts making his move to have sex, he has given her a lot to think about. She ponders them all, "I have invested a lot of time into this relationship, We are engaged, (*so she thinks*). I really love him (*there's no question about that*). He truly loves me, (*or so she thinks*). It won't hurt anything if we have sex together since we are getting married..." Against her better judgment, against what she believes morally from the Written Word of God, she gives in and begins giving herself to him sexually. Silas methodically and systematically led Fiona into sin.

She fell for the bait. She went for **The Engagement Ring Trick**. Before long, Silas was using her to relieve his urge to merge. Instead of getting married as planned, he switched gears, made up an excuse about money issues and downgraded the marriage plans to the, "let's move in together first and when we get the money issues straightened out, then we'll get married."

Once again, against her conscience, Fiona ignored the voice of the Holy Spirit and moved in with Silas, hoping and praying everything would soon straighten out. She held on to the dream Silas had so cleverly crafted in her mind. She still had no clue that days after she picked out that beautiful engagement ring and got sized, that he went back and cancelled the order.

There was never going to be a wedding. Silas didn't love her. He didn't even like her. He just wanted a B-O-D-Y to get a steady piece of booty for the time being and Fiona was it! It would be almost two years before this woman of God woke up and came to her senses.

By that time, Silas had gotten his fill of sex and had grown weary of Fiona's questions and demands. He was ready to move-on. The final time Fiona tried to talk to him about getting married, Silas used another ingenious trick employed by seasoned smooth operators.

They start a heated argument, blame their victim for not being more trusting and for ruining a good thing, and then hurriedly exit the relationship. Silas did just that.

He packed his bags and left Fiona numb, dazed, depressed and wondering what she had done wrong? She still did not have a clue that she had just been burned by a smooth operator. At some grocery stores, they ask you, "Do you want paper bags or plastic bags?" Many people respond by saying, "It doesn't matter." With certain individuals who have the **Urge To Merge Syndrome,** the method they use to merge doesn't matter. What determines their method are the circumstances.

If you talk about, imply or insist on getting married, like Silas, they will get engaged or marry you at the drop of a dime. If you settle for casual sex, they'll gladly plunder your flesh. If living together becomes the topic of discussion, they will usually have their bags packed for the occasion before determining whose name the lease is going to be in, (*usually yours*). They'll become someone's boyfriend, girlfriend, live-in lover, fiancé, fiancée, homosexual or lesbian lover, spouse or whatever it takes to get access to their B-O-D-Y. It does not matter to them!

The second issue you must come to know and understand are the symptoms and patterns of behavior that reveal when a person has taken on the deadly **Urge To Merge Syndrome.**

Before we proceed any further I need to remind you of a fundamental truth about smooth operators - their minds and consciences have been corrupted. When it comes to crossing the line and becoming perverted, depraved, queer, deviant or abnormal, they do not get it. That is why *you must* get it, to protect yourself.

Once a person takes on the, **Urge To Merge Syndrome** and dons (ARB) **At Risk Behaviors,** they become detrimental to themselves, to you and to society. Here are the symptoms and patterns of behavior you will need to examine in every potential mate. People who have the **Urge To Merge Syndrome** demonstrate these (ARB's) **At Risk Behaviors:**

Emotional, Marital and Dating Related Symptoms and Behaviors-
- Has a history of easily entering and exiting relationships and now they want to be in a relationship with you
- Has a history of always being in a relationship with someone whether (married, engaged, boyfriend, girlfriend, live-in lover, casual sex partner, etc.)
- Barely knows you but claims to love you, or claims to have fallen in love with you
- Barely knows you but claims they can't live without you
- Presently has a wife, husband, fiancé, fianceé, boyfriend, girlfriend or live-In lover but they want to be in a relationship with you
- Is separated from their spouse, is in the process of getting a divorce, or is having marital turmoil but they want to be in a relationship with you
- Has just finalized a divorce and now they are pursuing a relationship with you
- Still harboring feelings for their ex-husband or ex-wife, (whether romantic, sexual, anger, bitterness, vengeance, wrath, malice, etc.) but they still want to be in a relationship with you

• Just broke up with a girlfriend or boyfriend and has immediately set about to enter into a relationship with you

• Has *ex*-boyfriends, *ex*-girlfriends, *ex*-live-in lovers and people they were engaged to, with whom they have not doused out all of the flames and have not severed all soul, flesh or spiritual ties, but they want to be in a relationship with you anyway

Sex Related Symptoms and Behaviors-

• Has had casual sexual encounters, one-night stands, nymphomania tendencies

• Has had numerous sex partners

• Has had sex with minors

• Has initiated forced sex, raped someone or been involved in a sex crime(s)

• Has been involved in orgies, group sex or swapped sex partners

• Carries condoms in their wallet, purse, pocket, glove compartment, etc.

• Has engaged in sex with inmate(s) while incarcerated

• Is a single female who has a prescription for Birth Control Pills, IUD, Ortho Evra Patches, Lunelle Injections, Depo Provera Injections, Norplant etc. Or, she has other forms of birth control such as Morning After Pills, Foam/Cream/Jelly Suppositories, etc... (*She is advertising that she is either promiscuous or otherwise sexually active*)

• Has had live-in lovers

• Started having sex as a pre-teen or teen

• Has been married and divorced multiple times

• Has been or presently is a stripper, go-go dancer, call girl or prostitute

• Has dated or had sex with strippers, go-go dancers, call girls or prostitutes

• Has patronized strip clubs, peep shows, bathhouses or other sexually related houses of ill repute

• Has a history of sexual transgressions in the family lineage

• Has bought, sold or used Ecstasy, GHB or any other type of date rape drug

• They say they are heterosexual but they have intimate relationships with cross-dressers, transgendered, transsexuals, homosexuals, bisexuals or lesbians. They frequent establishments catering to the same, or they have engaged in sex with the same and now they are pursuing a relationship with you

• Has previously contracted any of the various types of (STDs) Sexually Transmitted Diseases

• Has been sexually active in times past - but has not tested for the HIV/AIDS virus and has not had a comprehensive exam for (STDs)

• Men and women addicted to or who enjoy any form of pornography

• Men and women who have worked in or presently work in the pornographic industry in any shape form or fashion, (appearing nude in movies, DVD's or videos, pictures on the Internet, editing, sales reps, recruiters, distributors, etc.)

• Is involved in or has been involved in deviant sexual practices such as (Partner Swapping, Pedophilia, Sado-Masochism, Bestiality, Necrophilia, etc.)

Child Related Symptoms and Behaviors-

• She has multiple children by different men

• He has multiple children by different women

• She has had an abortion or multiple abortions

• He has talked, forced, coerced, compelled or manipulated a woman into having an abortion(s)

• Has a child or children they fathered or gave birth to then abandoned them, gave them up for adoption, turned them over to the state, the state took them by force of law, or they dumped their child or children off on family members or friends
• They have previously gotten married due to an unplanned pregnancy

If your response to any of these patterns of behavior is a definite, "yes," put the brakes on! You are in relationship danger! Your potential mate might adamantly deny such an assessment, but these symptoms and patterns of behavior DO NOT lie!

To continue in a relationship with this person without wise counsel would be to blatantly risk your health, your safety, your peace of mind, your emotions, your future, and that of your family's. Your response to any of these symptoms or patterns of behavior might be:

• **It's possible**	• **I don't know**	• **I hope not**
• **I never asked**	• **I assumed not**	• **I don't think so**
• **I don't put it past them!**	• **What is that?**	• **I'm not sure**

If so, there should be great cause for alarm in your heart. I pray that you haven't engaged in sex with this person, moved-in with them, gotten engaged to them or made plans to wed them or secretly elope. These behaviors are classified as (ARB's) **At Risk Behaviors**, because they put you at the "almost certain risk of suffering harm."

Getting involved with a person who demonstrates any of these ARB's is like getting in an automobile with a person who is driving under the influence of drugs or alcohol. You have to ask yourself the question, "What are my chances of making it to my destination without getting arrested, having an accident, injuring or killing someone or destroying property?"

Rosalind started having sex when she was just a teenager. When she wasn't having sex, she experienced strong withdrawal symptoms. To alleviate that problem, she kept a boyfriend at all times. She took great pride knowing that her many lovers not only complemented her on her sexual prowess... they always came back for more.

Sexually, Rosalind knew how to please a man. To live her lifestyle, she conditioned herself to lie to the men and to her family and friends about the true nature of her relationships. Before she met her husband, Rosalind had trained herself on the rudiments of deceit, how to cheat without getting caught, and how to juggle multiple sex partners.

In her mind, the warnings about having numerous sex partners and contracting STDs were attempts by prudish people to keep her from exploring her sexuality. Sexually, Rosalind switched from one sex partner to the next without experiencing any consequences.

Rosalind got married, had two children and became a top sales representative at a midsize corporation. While running an errand one day, she bumped into one of her *ex*-lovers. Although she was now married, her MO had not changed. The two set up a romantic rendezvous, had sex and began an adulterous affair.

Rosalind's husband never suspected a thing as she began reliving the excitement of juggling multiple sex partners. Two to three months into the affair, she became lethargic and started experiencing unexplainable weight loss, extreme fatigue, fever, and other alarming flu-like symptoms. When the normal medications didn't work, she went to her doctor for a detailed examination. Rosalind was diagnosed with full-blown AIDS. Her lover was carrying the deadly HIV virus; he either didn't realize it or refused to tell her.

Once the symptoms seemed to subside, Rosalind returned to work. That was the day I started interviewing her. It didn't seem real. Her life was like a blur. Although she spoke candidly about being infected with AIDS, she couldn't bring herself to talk about the pain and shame her lifestyle caused her and her family. There were so many questions to which I wanted to get answers. Since she and her husband had sex with each other during her affair, did he get tested for the HIV/AIDS virus? If so, what were the test results?

Apparently, after receiving the news of her infection, her family shunned her. But we never got to discuss those weighty matters. Shortly after returning to work, the thing she dreaded most, happened. The symptoms returned, this time more aggressively. A few months later, Rosalind was confined to an AIDS hospice for the terminally ill. She would not survive. Prior to getting married, Rosalind had an MO and a list of ARB's that dictated this would most likely happen.

1). She had a history of easily entering and exiting relationships. **2)**. She had a track record of always being with someone romantically or sexually. **3)**. She continued harboring feelings for her *ex*-lovers. She never doused out the flames in her heart for the men to whom she had opened up her body. **4)**. She had a string of sex partners. **5)**. She started having sex when she was a teen. **6)**. She had never been tested for any sexually transmitted disease. **7)**. She barely knew these men and told many of them that she loved them.

Those behaviors clearly revealed that she had the **Urge to Merge Syndrome**. So far we have talked about the MO's and the ARB's of the people who have been infected with this deadly syndrome. What we have not discussed is their motive. In criminal investigations, once police apprehends a suspect and identifies them as the perpetrator of the crime, they start the process of deciphering their motive.

They want to answer the question, "Why did they do this?" Here are the motives why people have the **Urge to Merge Syndrome**.

- Gives Them a Sense of Power/Control
- Trying To Satisfy a Need To Feel Loved
- Getting Revenge Against An "Ex"
- Refusal To Discipline Their Sexual Urges
- Father Shopping For a Disposable Dad
- It's Their Way of Rebelling Against God
- They Were Sexually Abused
- Paternity Fraud Predator
- Trying To Mask Hurt
- A Desire To Self-Destruct
- A Feeling of Invincibility
- They Are in Self-Denial

With every individual who has the **Urge to Merge Syndrome** you can trace the reason "why" back to one or more of the above motives. With Silas, he refused to discipline his sexual urges and he derived a sense of power from controlling the women he booby trapped. With Rosalind, I never got a chance to decipher her motive(s) because she became incapacitated and died before her time. In chapter one, you learned about God's glorious plan for your life and the secret plot to destroy it.

One tactic the devil uses to wipe out your dream of a happy home is through the despair and stigma of being infected with an (STD) **Sexually Transmitted Disease**. This may be an uncomfortable issue for some people to discuss, but if you intend to find the love of your life and avoid being booby trapped into a living nightmare, you must talk to the person about their sexual history.

You need to be forewarned... some men and women have *willfully* and *deliberately* with extreme malice, set out to infect others with sexually transmitted diseases. That is the devil's sinister plot and these individuals are following his game plan to the letter.

A concerned person who contracted an STD, would advise their sex partner or potential sex partner, that they are infected. Not these men and women. If they are concerned about another person's health, they don't show it. Read how these individuals can change a person's life for the worse, sometimes with just one physical encounter.

- In December 1998, Pamela Wiser (*real name*), an HIV-positive Tennessee woman, pleaded guilty to 22 felony counts of knowingly exposing her male partners to HIV through unprotected sex. She told authorities that she had one-night stands with at least 18 men to get revenge for her *ex*-boyfriend infecting her with the HIV virus.
- On September 6, 1996, a public health official at the Chautauqua County Department of Health in western New York, informed Nushawn Williams (*real name*) that he was infected with the deadly HIV virus. He was given a stern lecture about not spreading the virus, a warning officials said he would aggressively ignore. They said Nushawn went on a sexual rampage. He boasted of having sex with about 75 females. After tracking down and testing numerous of his sex partners, health officials concluded that he directly infected at least 16 people including two women who gave birth to babies who also tested HIV positive. Nushawn was sentenced to 4 to 12 years in a state prison.

• In 1996, in the (DOC) District of Columbia, a husband sued the DOC government, alleging professional negligence and claiming damages for negligent infliction of emotional distress. **"N.O.L." vs. District of Columbia, 674 A. 2d 498 (D.C. App., 1996).** His wife was admitted to the hospital and tested positively for HIV but she told her estranged husband she tested negatively. The two reconciled and resumed sexual relations according to the record in the DOC Court of Appeals. Some time later, the husband learned his wife had tested HIV-positive in the hospital. He claimed in his suit, the hospital had the legal responsibility to inform him when it learned his wife was HIV-positive. The court disagreed.

• In October of 2001, in Brooklyn, New York, Richard Cintron (*real name*), plunged a knife into his ex-girlfriend so deeply that he couldn't pull it out. Why? He came upon the test results of her HIV/AIDS test. She had tested positively for AIDS and didn't inform him. They had been lovers for about eight months when he found the document in her possession. He later tested positively for the virus and in a furious rage, killed her.

• In March of 1998, in Fort Benning, Georgia, Raymond Humphries, a married man who is infected with the HIV virus, was sentenced to fifteen years in prison for having unprotected sex with eight women. Many of these women were single mothers, who said Humphries never told them he was married and never said he had tested positively for the HIV virus. Two of the women contracted the HIV virus after having sex with Humphries and four of the women became pregnant by him.

• In July of 2003, in Fort Laurderdale, Florida, Perdita Harris was charged with a third degree felony for knowingly spreading the HIV virus to her boyfriend. She told investigators that she kept quiet about being infected with the HIV virus because she loved her boyfriend and didn't want to lose him. According to a police report, she was infected in 1994 and married a man who later died of the disease.

I only showed you a few cases. I could show many more. Did you comprehend how these people think and act? Some are in a state of denial. Others want revenge because someone infected them, and the way they get revenge is by seducing and then infecting someone else. Others operate by the rule of reckless endangerment. They test positively for an STD, but they refuse to divulge that critical information to the person or persons with whom they are having sex. It doesn't matter... they want to have sex, even if it means infecting you to get it.

The examples I gave you are not isolated incidents. This is the type of society in which we are living. Unfortunately, these men and women have become human missiles. When a potential mate has been sexually active before they met you, there are some serious considerations you must ponder. Three in particular. **1). The effect of having pre-teen and teen sex. 2). The effect of having had multiple sex partners, and 3). The effect of having an abortion or multiple abortions.**

• *The Effect of Having Pre-Teen and Teen Sex* - When the media, parents, educators, abstinence proponents and safe sex advocates talk about teen sex, they usually talk about STD's, unwanted pregnancies, condoms and other forms of birth control. What they usually don't talk about is, how *pre*-teen and teen sex can harm a person's character and personality or about the emotional, spiritual and psychological consequences and side effects. The average teen relationship lasts about three months or less. In that span of time their experiences with the opposite sex will lead them to falsely believe they are deeply in love, believe they are going to spend the rest of their lives together, breakup, experience betrayal, lose their virginity, get pregnant, abandon their newborn, get depressed, attempt suicide, seek vengeance, have an abortion, run away, start drinking and doing drugs or get infected with a sexually transmitted disease.

The emotional consequences for them, particularly for the females, is devastating. Countless women enter into marriage covenants deeply regretting the fact that they are not virgins. They are torn because their husbands were not their first and only sexual loves. Some suffer the torment of not being truthful about their sexual history, fearing their husband-to-be or family will lose respect for them.

Many teen girls talk about how awful and painful sex was for them and why they only did it to please a boy, who eventually dumped them. To those females, *sex* becomes the much dreaded necessity of being in a relationship and the boys see *sex* as a sport. As with most sports, it's all about the score. In their maligned minds, females are reduced to points. Get sex, score points. The more sex you get, the more points you gain and the highest score always wins.

By the time they reach adulthood, they couldn't tell you the difference between *True Love* and illicit sex if you offered them a million dollars. The girls are conditioned to give sex to get love and the boys are conditioned to lie and defraud to get sex.

Many of these girls, when they gave up their virginity, also gave up their self-respect and self-esteem. Sadly, like their virginity, some of them will never *re*-gain their self-respect or recover their self-esteem. After being overexposed to the fall-in-love and break-up regimen and being jilted repeatedly, they lose all sense of moral equilibrium.

Amy was sooooo in love. For her, the sun and the moon revolved around her teen boyfriend. He was the wind beneath her wings. Hearing him say, "I love you!" made her day. When she became pregnant, Amy excitedly thought, "Wow, we're going to be a real family now!" She was clearly living on the Fantasy Island *in her mind*! As she was telling her teen lover about their forthcoming child, he turned her joy into heart wrenching emotional trauma.

He blasted her with a barrage of obscenities, threatened her with physical violence, then fled. Pregnant and alone, Amy had their child and began dating another "Knight in pining armor." In love again, she gathered her things, this time with baby in tow, and moved in with this January jeeerk of the month.

After six months of having sex, sex and more sex and nothing but sex, her fake fiancé, who had led her to believe they were going to get married, showed his true character. He threw Amy and her infant child out of his apartment in the middle of the night.

Because she was a rebellious teen and had severed her relationship with her family, she had no place to go. She and her baby slept in a park for about a week and then she did the unthinkable.

She showed how undeveloped her mind and conscience were. Amy gave her baby to a homeless couple to keep while she went begging park patrons for money. Very rarely do teen lovers comprehend the responsibilities, emotions, potential trauma or risks that come with having sex. Once a *pre*-teen or teen takes on the **Urge to Merge Syndrome**, they are subject to bring any of these ten harmful character traits into their adult relationships:

- Rage and anger over being betrayed
- Urge to "get back" at the opposite sex
- They blame God for their relationship woes
- Cannot emotionally attach or bond to children
- Unable to trust or make a commitment
- Debasement of sex
- Dehumanize sex
- Deep guilt or regret
- Depression
- Suicidal tendencies

- *The Effect of Having Had Multiple Sex Partners* - The effects of having had multiple sex partners are too many to mention. Promiscuity usually hits home when a promiscuous person decides to settle down. That's when many of them taste the bitter consequences of their past sexual history. They bring with them the memories of all of their *ex*-lovers and all of the sex acts they performed. They measure their spouse's sexual performance, penis size or vaginal tightness against one or more of their *ex*-lovers. For some infected with sexually transmitted diseases, they discover that they are infertile.

They got married thinking, "Ok, I've sown my wild oats, I've partied, now I'm ready to get married and start a family." At that point, they are advised they will never be able to have children. They find out the hard way that STD's are the leading cause of infertility. Or, when they do have a child it is born with alarming birth defects.

STD's are known causes of perinatal infections, miscarriages, premature births and still births. When a woman has sex with a man who has had multiple sex partners, she runs the risk, (*condom use or not*) of contracting (HPV) Human Papilloma Virus. With each new sex partner, she dramatically multiplies the risk of looking in the mirror and seeing her worst enemy. Some individuals don't realize until they marry, how their sexual promiscuity was an emotional, spiritual, psychological and physically unhealthy undertaking.

By then it's too late. With all of their regret, they can not go back in time and erase the effects of having a cache of *ex*-lovers. Having had multiple sex partners is one of the primary reasons certain men and women cannot experience intimacy with their spouse. Deciding to pursue a relationship with someone who has had numerous sex partners is a gravely serious matter. DO NOT take it without careful forethought.

• ***The Effect of Having an Abortion or Abortions*** - Abortion, without a doubt, is a touchy issue. Normally, if a person brings up the subject, inevitably, battle lines are drawn. I want you to be clear on my intention. I am not trying to persuade you to participate in the pro-choice versus the pro-life war. This portion of this book is designed to help you understand the potential consequences and the devastating side effects of women having abortions.

You may be a man and believe this issue does not affect you. Sir, it affects you tremendously because many of the women who have abortions enter into relationships and marriages with festering wounds.

This issue does affect you. In 1986, the Supreme Court ruled that women did not need to be informed about the potential health risks or psychological effects of having an abortion before undergoing the procedure. Once that ruling was confirmed, an army of cut throat greed driven abortionists, investors, pharmaceutical companies, doctors and other individuals with a vested interest in performing abortions, reduced themselves to creating literal blood sucking houses of horror.

Through the genius of Madison Avenue Guerilla Warfare advertising tactics, which included well thought out half-truths, covert fine print, lingo only understood by medical practitioners and the use of vivacious spokesmodels who never had abortions themselves, women were overwhelmingly convinced that abortions were safe. They brought in researchers and people with doctorate degrees to put on educational seminars targeted at women, designed to: "**Describe the safety and efficacy data of having a medical or surgical abortion.**"

They claimed that having an abortion was safer than having a normal child birth. Expert after expert gave their professional opinion, stating there is no evidence to suggest that having an abortion is a risk factor for any kind of significant emotional distress. These people had Ph.D. degrees. They were supposed to be authorities on the subject.

How could they have been so wrong? Many of the women who put their faith in the claims of these "experts," and had abortions, soon found themselves suffering severe psychological and physical trauma. Here is a partial list of the side effects which abortionists are not legally bound to inform women who are considering having an abortion.

Physically they suffer from diarrhea, fever, vomiting, abdominal tenderness, damage to the uterine lining, cervical laceration, miscarriages, permanent infertility, excessive or severe cramping, severe hemorrhaging, blood clots, infected or ruptured placenta, scar tissue that blocks fallopian tubes, potential for increased risk of breast cancer, heavy or prolonged bleeding, seizures, comas, accidental injection of saline or other medications into the mother's blood stream, infections due to body parts of the baby being left in the mother after the abortion procedure is complete, and even death.

The psychological side effects are just as severe. They suffer from flashbacks of the abortion, difficulty bonding to children, sudden uncontrollable crying, an intense desire to become pregnant again just to replace the aborted child, anniversary grief (*on the due date of the aborted child or on the date of the abortion*), inability to forgive themselves, emotional numbness, nightmares, sexual problems and depression.

Other side effects include anxiety, thoughts of suicide, eating disorders and sadness. Some women resort to drug and alcohol abuse and promiscuity to mask their guilt and regret. Others become contentious and adversarial in relationships. They harbor anger and resentment, especially if they were forced or coerced into having the abortion by their boyfriend, fiancé, husband or family. The average man will read these side effects and go, " humm." But when you have to face this issue head on, your perspective changes dramatically.

Nancy already had one child. The baby's father had abandoned her and the thought of having another child without a wedding ring on her finger did not appeal to her. Since she had the **Urge to Merge Syndrome**, she eventually found herself pregnant again. This time the child's father was a fun-loving, carefree adult male who was chronically trying to find himself. Faced with having a second child born out of wedlock, Nancy opted to have an abortion.

She terminated her pregnancy but did not terminate her **Urge to Merge**. Her flower child boyfriend got her pregnant again. After having a child out of wedlock and one abortion under her belt, Nancy had not learned. She had a second abortion and broke-up with her Fantasy Island live-in lover. Shortly thereafter, Nancy married a man she describes as a wonderful human being. Nancy became pregnant by her husband but to their horror, she had a miscarriage at twenty-two weeks.

That was the day their marital happiness came to an abrupt end. Nancy cried in the dark. She wondered if the abortions had something to do with her miscarriage. She went back and *re-*read the release form she signed at the abortion clinic. Like many women who get abortions, Nancy had not read the fine print.

She trusted the experts when they told her to "sign here." When she finally read the fine print, her heart almost froze. Below is a copy of the release of liability form Nancy had no idea she had signed.

It has been explained to me, and I am aware, that I may be sterile as a result of this operation and that I may no longer have menstrual periods, although no such result is warranted or guaranteed. I know that a sterile person is incapable of becoming a parent, and in giving consent to this operation I have in mind the probability or possibility of such a result.

Did you read that barbaric release form? Read it again! The abortionist claimed to have explained to Nancy that she could end up sterile and possibly *no longer have menstrual periods*. That was a lie! She said they never once explained to her about any possible side effects. She wanted to tell her downtrodden husband the truth to ease his pain, but she could not bring herself to do so. The truth meant exposing the fact that she had deceived him about her sexual past. That was a painful ordeal Nancy simply did not have the courage to face.

She could look into her husband's eyes and feel his pain over the loss of their child, but could not do anything to console him. Nancy elected to remain silent. Did her past abortions cause her miscarriage? Maybe, maybe not. Nancy believed they did and that was the crux of the matter. Her guilt over her abortions had literally stifled her life!

Will *every* woman who has had an abortion go through what Nancy went through? No, and I am not saying that they will! The degree of the side effects will vary with each woman. The odds of experiencing any side effects are the same as the odds of being arrested, hijacked, abducted or killed while trying to singlehandedly transport fifty kilos of cocaine from Columbia to New Jersey. Some drug traffickers will get arrested, others will get robbed, kidnapped or killed but some will arrive at their destination. The difference is, they clearly know and fully understand the risks and the consequences.

I have encountered many women who were reeling from the side effects of an abortion. I have yet to meet one who clearly understood the risks and potential consequences *prior* to aborting their child. If you are a woman who is experiencing the overwhelming guilt, pain or remorse from having an abortion, first, know this: God loves you! Secondly, no matter how you may be feeling right now, there is healing for you, (See II Chronicles 7:14-15, John 12:46, III John 2-4).

Finally, in the resources section at the back of this book, I have included a special group of people, Safe Haven Ministries. I encourage you to start the healing process by logging on to their website or by finding a local ministry in your area that understands how to minister to women who are experiencing (PAS) Post-Abortion Syndrome. I have just shared with you three areas, (*teen sex, multiple sex partners and abortion*) that have a devastating effect on our society. If you realize that your sex life is out of control, and that you are a loose cannon on a collision course with regret, sorrow and anguish, I urge you to stop now!

You will only end up hurting yourself and injuring others. You have read how people with the **Urge to Merge Syndrome** can literally ruin God's glorious plan for your life. Don't you become a snare yourself. Here are the *Booby Trap Acid Tests* you must perform to determine if a potential mate has the **Urge to Merge Syndrome**. For starters you must ask yourself this question:

Do I feel hurried, rushed, coerced, manipulated, pressured or trapped by my potential mate to:

(A) Become his girlfriend?   *(D) Fall in love?*
(B) Become her boyfriend?   *(E) Move-in together?*
(C) Have sex?   *(F) Get married?*

If your answer is "yes," you need to pull the relationship emergency brakes! Even if your answer is "no," in each case you will still need to examine your potential mate. Do they have the MO of a person with the **Urge to Merge Syndrome**? Does he have a black book filled with past and present sex partners? Does she have a list (*short or long*) of past and present male lovers? Have they had live-in lovers, a failed marriage or failed marriages? Examine how they spend their lives.

Do they use sex to ruin their bodies by turning themselves into human sex traps? Are they intentionally setting out to infect others with STD's by changing sex partners like they change clothes? Do they treat sex like it is a game or a sport? You must determine if they have an MO of a person with the **Urge to Merge Syndrome!**

Any potential mate who fails this *Booby Trap Acid Tests* and displays the MO's and ARB's is a risk. If you decide to proceed in a relationship with them, at least you now know the risks. You may ask, "Suppose they have changed or what if they go to church? What if my potential mate is an ordained minister?" Don't be naive!

Many smooth operators use the church and the pulpit as a cloak to seek out prey. Being a minister or attending a church, mosque, or synagogue does not automatically make a person trustworthy or a suitable mate. Can a person turn their life around? Sure they can, but the effect their past may have on *your* future should be your main concern. I have known numerous men who decided to settle down and get married. As soon as they got a stable address, they received a summons to appear in court and were ordered by a judge to pay child support or else! Each of these men impregnated women then fled from their responsibilities. At the time, they did not consider the consequences of their actions. After these men married, their past crept upon them like a thief in the night. By the time the court forced them to make back payments, took their tax refund checks, attached their bank accounts and garnished their wages, they could not provide for their wife and kids. Once a man thrusts himself into that system, the court gives zero consideration to his wife or family.

He has to make those child support payments first and foremost, even before he takes care of his own household. If not, (*depending on the state laws*), he faces the menacing threat of being incarcerated. God forbid that he got a female pregnant who is viciously bitter and is out for revenge. That is why you must stick to your guns and examine your potential mate for every symptom and pattern of behavior listed on pages 105 -107. As I've stated, it may be uncomfortable but you must inquire about the sexual past of your potential mate.

Men, you must ask a woman if she has ever been raped, had an abortion, miscarriage or hsyterectomy? Did she give birth and give the child up for adoption, left the child at a fire station, or otherwise give her child away? Ladies, you have to ask a man if he has gotten a woman pregnant before. If so what happened? Did he coerce or manipulate her into getting an abortion? Did he abandon his child? Does he pay child support? Is he actively involved in raising his child morally, spiritually and socially? Is he or she engaged in a heated battle with their *ex* over their child? You already know some people are going to blatantly lie when you ask them these type of questions.

I'll show you how to detect liars, fakes, and deceivers in a later chapter, but if you never ask, smooth operators are not going to divulge any crucial information. Or, they may say, "it is so," but then attempt to down play their sexual past with slick choreographed statements like, "*I can count the number of people I had sex with on one hand*."

That's when you inform them that it only takes one sexual encounter to get infected with the HIV virus. Once infected, you could easily develop full blown AIDS. You further inform them that a person could be the carrier of the HIV virus or any of the other twenty or so known STD's and have absolutely no symptoms!

Your potential mate may tell you they were always careful to use a condom and how they always practiced "safe sex." Here is where you inform and educate them that condoms are not foolproof. Even if they used them as instructed, condoms cannot protect against STD's such as herpes or HPV.

You explain that one can get infected with certain STD's by merely kissing or touching an infected area not protected by a condom. If you are considering marrying a person who has been sexually active prior to meeting you, then follow these next instructions to the letter.

WARNING! Take no shortcuts and make absolutely no exceptions! Have your potential mate submit to a comprehensive battery of tests and examinations for these sexually transmittable diseases.

- HIV/AIDS
- Hepatitis viruses
- Chlamydia
- Syphilis
- Herpes
- Gonorrhea
- Trichomoniasis
- HPV *(female)*

If a person who has been sexually active refuses to take all of the applicable tests, you need to make a note of these three facts: **1). They are not concerned about their health, 2). They are not concerned about *your* health, and 3). They are willing to put you at risk for the sake of their sexual gratification.** Armed with those facts, your next step must be to politely and respectfully wish them well, permanently exit the relationship, and don't look back... remember Lot's wife? (See Genesis 19:26).

If you fail or refuse to follow those instructions to the letter, you may regret your decision for the rest of your life! If they test negatively, you must bear in mind that some STD's have an incubation period. If they have not cleared the incubation period for that particular STD, you are still in harm's way, (*see the resource guide on STD's at the back of this book for more info on this subject*).

If they tested positively for any of these sexually transmitted diseases, what are you going to do? Will you continue dating or courting them anyway? Will you stay engaged and marry them knowing they could infect you with HIV/AIDS, HPV, herpes, Hepatitis B, (MCV) Molluscum Contagiosum, Chanchroids, Genital warts, etc?

Ladies, are you willing to chance developing **Pelvic Inflammatory Disease** by having sex with a man who has had multiple sex partners? STD's can destroy your chances of having healthy children or having children at all. Are you willing to roll the dice and take that gamble? STD's can eliminate the joy of spontaneous lovemaking with your spouse. Are you willing to deal with that? Think about it! Pray about it! Know all the potential risks and consequences. Get proper counsel.

I'll talk about how to get proper counsel later on. Ultimately the decision is yours to make, and it's going to be yours to live with. So make sure it's the right decision! Finally, if you have been sexually active in the past, you must also submit to those same battery of tests. Don't wait until it is too late. Don't take any chances. Get tested now!

(female) This test is specific to females only

- 7 -

The One Hundred Yard Dash... Now What?

The booby trap we just examined, **The Urge to Merge Syndrome,** has a lot to do with individuals who blatantly refuse to discipline their libido. For them, it starts and ends with having sex. This next booby trap deals with people who make **The One Hundred Yard Dash To The Wedding Altar.** On the surface, they may appear to race to the altar to relieve their insatiable sexual urges, but as you are going to find out, people who make **The One Hundred Yard Dash To The Wedding Altar** are not necessarily rushing into marriage with sex on the brain. Tucked away in the crevices of their hearts are other dastardly motives. Those secret motives propel these men and women to pursue ~~holy~~ rapid matrimony.

This particular booby trap is woven in extreme deception, classic sleight of hand, and disgraceful two-faced chicanery. People who have been snared into this emotionally traumatizing booby trap are not hard to spot. Many of them become bitter towards the whole concept of marriage. Their torturous marital experience has transformed them into modern day men-bashers and world-class women haters.

They didn't know it at the time, but their marriages were not matches made in heaven. The only thing God had to do with their fairytale engagements and hyperspeed weddings, was to warn them they were about to make one of the biggest mistakes of their lives. If you desire to enjoy the blessings of a glorious love story, you must see through the crafty subterfuge and identify and immediately reject these matrimonial vagabonds. The one hundred yard dash is one of the most dramatic and glamorous races in track and field.

The runners put everything on the line in a race that is over in under nine seconds flat. In this race, when the runner bursts out of the starting block, they make a fast and furious sprint to be the first one to cross the finish line. I have some facts you need to know about the one hundred yard dash. **1).** The runners only get one chance to run each race. When they run it, they have to be perfect. They can have no flaws and they can make absolutely no mistakes. **2).** If there is any inclement weather such as rain or high winds, the race is halted.

3). If the runners are confronted with debris, rocks, potholes, hurdles or other roadblocks on the track, he or she will most likely not complete that race. The conditions of the track must be pristine because the runners are not prepared to deal with obstacles. **4)**. When runners train for this race, they are indoctrinated to do one thing and one thing only, have tunnel vision for that glorious finish line. They breath, eat and sleep for the euphoria of that single moment in time.

On the opposite end of the spectrum there is another track & field race we need to briefly examine called the Cross Country race. In this race the runners prepare for contingencies. They are trained to negotiate obstacles, run over rough terrains, run through creeks and valleys, up and down steep inclines and in densely wooded areas. They are prepared to run in inclement weather: cold or hot, rain or snow.

Long distance runners have emergency plans to handle dehydration, hypothermia and muscle cramps during the race. The men and women intent on making **The One Hundred Yard Dash To The Wedding Altar,** like their track & field counterparts, have tunnel vision. They are focused on one thing and one thing only, the day they get the chance to say, "I do!" Just like the track stars, all they see is their glamorous and glitzy finish line, the wedding ceremony. Once they "tie the knot" and complete the wedding day festivities, they don't have a clue as to what is supposed to take place next.

The have made **The One Hundred Yard Dash... Now What?** From that point on, everything concerning their spouse and their matrimonial vows is a cloudy haze or a complete blur. From the very beginning, their mind was on one track and that was to make **The One Hundred Yard Dash To The Wedding Altar**. Once they have crossed that finish line, as the song says, "the thrill is gone." For many of these smooth operators, the feeling of falling in love and the euphoria of getting married is like the high a drug addict gets when they ingest crack cocaine or smoke marijuana. The instant infatuation, and the falling in love are narcotic and these smooth operators immediately become addicted.

The feeling they get when they look into someone's eyes and start hearing the violins strumming, the rockets launching and the firecrackers popping, is indescribable! Once someone has turned them on, once they can't stop thinking about a person, once they feel an attraction, and once they sense a sexual chemistry, watch out!

Just like the drug addict in need of a fix, they will scheme, lie and connive... they will use flattery, theft by deception, romance and make some of the most exaggerated promises of marital bliss your ears will ever hear. And yes, they will stoop so low as to use the name of God, Jesus, the Holy Spirit and the Bible to make the relationship seem as if it is a deep spiritual connection ordained by G-O-D! They will do or say anything to get someone to race to the altar. These marriage missiles are well versed on how to ignite a "love at first sight" whirlwind romance. They know how to turn up the kind of emotional heat that will leave a potential mate with that tingly, nervous, quivering feeling that makes them want to shout, "I'm in love!" Then comes the moment when they turn on those bedroom eyes, switch to that silky smooth voice and passionately declare, "we were meant to be; we're soul mates, twin flames, lovers for life!" Or they'll claim, "God has divinely brought us together!" Who could resist such tantalizing words of affection?

Unfortunately not many, because the next thing you will hear about is the wedding. Once the race is over and the "high" of the infatuation has waned, these honey tongued lovers are headed straight for: (a) **emergency post marital counseling,** (b) **marital therapy,** (c) **separation,** (d) **adultery,** (e) **divorce court,** (f) **domestic violence,** or a host of other lewd or despicable activities to keep that, "I'm in love (*high*) feeling."

At this point we want to examine the symptoms and patterns of behavior of people who make **The One Hundred Yard Dash To The Wedding Altar.** These men and women don't look or sound like psychos, weirdos, borderline personalities or sociopaths. Like all smooth operators, they exhibit pretty normal behavior until after the wedding ceremony.

Take the case of Della Sutorius (*real name*). Cincinnati heart surgeon Darryl Sutorius (*real name*) thought he had found the love of his life when he met and married Della Britteon.

He had no idea that this stunning looking woman had a voracious appetite for dismantling men. Della had married five times and divorced four. Her fifth marriage ended when she killed Dr. Sutorius. When a grand jury convened to indict her for murder, three of her former husbands and a former boyfriend met for the very first time.

Her third husband said, "all her husbands had seen the same thing in Mrs. Sutorius, a petite blonde." "She was very striking... eye-catching." He said. "I thought I was getting into a pretty lady, very meek. Lo and behold, Tasmanian devil." Remember how smooth operators use the media, music and Hollywood to get trained? Her third husband said that during their nine-month marriage, Della would get herself all wound up watching television talk shows and then threaten to kill him.

Shortly after she divorced him, she was convicted of threatening a boyfriend with a gun. In the police report, he stated that she told him she was pregnant and "threatened my life if she miscarried." Her fourth husband told sources that he survived their marriage only because he hid the bullets to the .44-caliber Magnum he kept in their home.

Otherwise, he said, "it would be me on the couch with a bullet to my ear." Very few of the men who crossed Della's path knew how to recognize smooth operators. On June 7, 1996, she was convicted for the murder of her fifth husband and was sentenced to life in prison.

A great place for marriage missiles to experience the exhilaration of racing to the altar and then exclaiming, "now what," is within the confines of the church walls. Like stealthy predators, these impostors ease into the sanctuaries. They use God's name as a mask, the banner of religion as a disguise and the church pews as their hunting grounds.

I put on my investigative reporter's hat and tracked down a well known wealthy businessman and minister. He has appeared on many of the religious broadcasting stations and has been tagged as a great Christian role model because of his business acumen.

This man boasts of having a deep faith in God since he was a child. He has been married three times. Paternity tests have proven that he has fathered at least eight children by various females, five of them out of wedlock. He did all of this while preaching the gospel! Each of his marriages bore his hallmark signature. They appeared as though they were ordained of God but they were not. They had one other distinctive trademark: infidelity. I tracked him as he was courting one of his *ex*-wives, whom he had met in church.

When challenged about his many infidelities and if he was truly a follower of Christ, he responded by saying, "I live my life led by the Holy Spirit; Christians aren't perfect, just forgiven!" He divorced that wife after one of his adulterous girlfriends served her with paternity papers. Take this next warning as if your life depended on it.

In your journey to find the love of your life, your path may cross potential mates who will profess to you in some form or another: "The Lord told me you were to be my wife or husband." For some people, that is all it takes. The excitement of knowing that God Himself has spoken, picked them out of a crowded room and orchestrated the love of a lifetime, is soooo heart warming. They cannot help but to immediately say, "I do!" This professed Christian businessman, convinced all of his *ex*-wives, that their marriages were GOD's idea, GOD's decision, GOD's will and GOD's orchestration!

As staggering as the damages are the statistics will never show the actual number of people who stopped serving God because they fell for one of these pew warming marriage missiles. They were convinced they had just met and fallen in love with a deeply spiritual person who had their ears tuned to the voice of the Lord. Instead of finding a divinely inspired love connection, they found themselves being jerked around, mauled and then burned by a smooth operator!

Once married, they learn by firsthand experience how people prostitute the name of the Lord, twist the Scriptures and forge God's signature to condone, downplay or completely evade their marital or sexual immorality. As painful as it is, we must expose and deal with this issue. There are too many heart torn victims to remain silent.

Take the case of a prominent pastor who leads one of the nation's mega churches. He is in the national spotlight, appearing regularly on Christian radio and television as well as being a highly celebrated Christian recording artist. He is promoted as being a bishop, a prophet and a: *"voice of authority regarding some of society's most pressing issues."*

But the bishop did something that gave many in the Body of Christ, Church Shock Syndrome. He divorced his wife of over fourteen years, then abruptly turned around and married another woman in a private ceremony, just seven days after his divorce was finalized!

In an interview, the bishop stated that God called him to preach, not to be married. Do you understand the magnitude of his words? Apparently, his divorce was because of God's calling on his life. Let's press the stop button, hit rewind and press the play button. This married man of God announced to the Body of Christ and to the world that he was no longer called to be married.

We have never seen God commit such a painful act of betrayal against one of His own daughters, by telling her husband to divorce her so he can go and preach the gospel. That command simply does not exist anywhere in the Bible! The bishop later told his wife that he did this because God showed him who his wife was supposed to be... AND! It was not the woman to whom he was already legally married.

He leads us to believe that dealing treacherously with his wife, (See Malachi 2:14-17) and his subsequent seven day ~~stroll dash~~ sprint to the wedding altar with his new bride, was GOD's idea, GOD's decision, GOD's will and GOD's orchestration.

It does not matter who the source is... they may claim to be God's anointed. They may assert themselves to be a Christian, a child of God, an apostle, a prophet, a prophetess, a pastor, a deacon, a bishop, a Sunday school teacher or a reverend. When they start expressing feelings for you or a desire to marry you because:

• They had a vision from the Lord about you
• They had a dream from heaven about you
• The Lord told them you were *"The One"*
• God commanded them to marry you
• God put you in their heart
• They claim it's the will of God
• Someone prophesied to them
• An angel told them to marry you

You need to pull the relationship emergency brakes! Do not proceed any further!

Make no mistake about it, sin is in the camp! You are not dealing with a person operating by the "Spirit of the Lord." You are either dealing with a person who is genuinely spiritually immature, (see page 48) or, with someone who is exhibiting a lying spirit, a spirit of control or a spirit of manipulation. People make passionate appeals like, *"The Lord told me you are to be my spouse... God said he wants us to be married... God is putting us together..."* as tools to pry their way into your heart.

Those statements, if you believe them, will literally stop you and people who truly love you from testing, examining and discerning that potential mate's spirit. If you accept those words as being genuinely from God, you won't question that person's character, look into their family or past history, or delve into their background.

What person in their right mind would question or defy God's will, especially if someone prophesied that you were to be their husband or wife? I know countless men and women who made **The One Hundred Yard Dash To The Wedding Altar** based solely on the belief that if they didn't marry that person, they would be rebelling against the "will," of ALMIGHTY GOD! Puhleeze... You had better thoroughly check their true motivation for wanting to get married!

When world renowned evangelist, John Jacobs (*real name*), founder of the Power Team ministry, ended his short-lived nuptials to his second wife, he gave an alarming revelation about his motive for their brief marriage. In an interview, he said his second marriage, *"was obviously a case of people who moved too quickly." "I was in a long, lonely situation and sometimes in a situation like that you move too fast."*

Those are not the words you want to hear just months after saying "I do." How do you detect a person's motive for wanting to get married? This next Scripture answers that question and gives insight on how to clear up this seemingly cloudy issue.

> Proverbs 16:2 NIV [Emphasis added]
> All a man's ways seem innocent to him, BUT MOTIVES ARE WEIGHED BY THE LORD.

You detect a person's motive for marriage by doing just like God... You weigh their motives. I must interject a sobering warning! Do not skip this critical *pre*-matrimonial process. Your failure or refusal to weigh your potential mate's motive for marriage means you are willfully signing an acceptance letter stating that you do solemnly agree to be used, misused and abused.

Since sin entered into the earth, both men and women have manufactured selfish, senseless, reckless and downright evil reasons for wanting to marry.

Their motives seemed innocent enough to them, but when the Lord weighed the true intent of their heart, it was a grim sight to behold. When the Lord weighs your motive for marriage, will your heart look like a gruesome crime scene?

Instead of your heart being stamped, *"Pure and ready for marriage,"* will you be classified by the Lord as a matrimonial vagabond? How will your potential mate's heart weigh under the scrutiny of God? Before you answer those questions, you need to examine the primary reasons why these smooth operators are so zealous about making **The One Hundred Yard Dash To The Wedding Altar**. Digest them slowly.

- Tired of Being Lonely
- Marrying for Money, Prestige or Power
- The Urge to Merge Syndrome
- The Soul Mate Syndrome
- My Mate Will Complete Me Syndrome
- The Mad Scientist Syndrome
- Need New Living Arrangements
- The Most Eligible Bachelor or Bachelorette Syndrome
- Matrimony Mania
- Living on Impulse
- Peer Pressure
- Age Desperation
- Wedding Ceremony Blues
- Tired of Being Lonely
- Getting Revenge Against an Ex

- *Tired of Being Lonely* - You read the evangelist John Jacob's statement about being lonely. Please note: marriage does not cure loneliness. Lonely people do not need to date or to get married. They need to go and get a life! If you marry a person whose motive for marriage is to cure their "I'm lonely" woes, brace yourself! Some of these people are so lonely, they will need to be attached to you 24/7.

While you are away they will pester you with a barrage of phone calls and e-mails to make certain they keep you on a short leash. Some of them will even time your errands and interrogate you on your return. They will have you in tears as they slowly suffocate the life out of you.

- *Marrying for Money, Prestige or Power* - It's no secret that some people enter into marriage for the sole purpose of obtaining money, prestige or power. Remember Della Sutorius on page 121? Donald Weber (*real name*), the attorney who represented her in three of her four divorces, said this about Della, *"...she wanted a hell of a lot more than any of the guys could give her."* Her fifth husband quickly discovered the same things as the other men in Della's life. After a brief courtship, the two made **The One Hundred Yard Dash To The Wedding Altar** in March of 1995.

By January of 1996, Dr. Sutorius was talking to an attorney about filing for divorce and getting a temporary restraining order against his new wife. He didn't move fast enough. Prosecutors said while he was asleep, Della put a gun to his head and fired. She tried to make the murder look like a suicide so she could collect her husband's one million dollar life insurance policy.

When a person's motive for marriage is money, prestige or power, and they sense or fear they are about to lose that money, prestige or power, they will usually become their spouse's worst enemy and greatest nightmare. They will do anything to protect their cash flow!

• *The Urge to Merge Syndrome* - We covered this dismal motive for marriage in the previous chapter.

• *The Soul Mate Syndrome* - On the surface, the concept of becoming soul mates can be quite alluring. "A divinely inspired chance meeting that leads to an immensely deep connection between two souls," is the stuff of which fairytales are made. There are literally a gazillion books, tapes, seminars, conferences, websites and "relationship experts," encouraging and instructing others to find their *"soul mate," "twin flame," "twin soul," "cosmic partner,"* or *"karmic partner."* With all of the information available on the subject, no one can clearly define what a soul mate is. The definition depends on who you ask. Here are a few things the experts teach about becoming soul mates:

"When soul mates first meet they sometimes feel as though they already know each other... A soul mate is someone we have known in a previous lifetime... The definition of a soul mate is a personal one... You can have more than one soul mate in a lifetime... Soul mate love is an inextinguishable force. It arrives when it wants and departs when it pleases... Twin Flames, on the other hand, are very different and very rare. Twin flames are two people in two separate bodies that share the same "soul." Twin flames meet each other in their first incarnation... They also have a very strong bond and often have telepathy with each other..."

You've known this person in a previous lifetime? Soul mate love arrives when it wants and departs when it pleases? You met each other in the first incarnation? You share the same soul, HUH? They have telepathy with each other? How do you have telepathy with someone?

The people who make up this stuff are the same people who write books, hold seminars and teach classes on leprechauns, mermaids, vampires, flying saucers, and aliens from another planet.

There is one common thread amongst people who have the soul mate syndrome. They believe in that chance meeting with a person and it instantly feels as if they've known each other all of their lives.

Once they get that feeling, they set out to make **The One Hundred Yard Dash To The Wedding Altar**. People infected with the soul mate syndrome have doomed themselves for failure because they are chasing after that magical feeling that lasts twenty-four hours a day, seven days a week, four weeks out of the month... you get the picture?

When the high of that tingly sensation subsides, you can pretty much kiss that marriage good bye. I consistently see *ex* soul mates in the divorce and family courts fighting against each other like mortal enemies. Clearly, these men and women never understood *True Love.*

• *My Mate Will Complete Me Syndrome* - These people define themselves as being diamonds in the rough who need a spouse to smooth out their jagged edges. Once they secure a husband or wife, they expect their spouse to bring them out of their state of depression, free them from their drug, alcohol or pornographic addictions, propel them to keep a steady job, cause them to stop lying and cheating, or help them clear up their other emotional, mental, financial, social or psychological defects. Their motivation for racing to the wedding altar is clear.

The sooner they get married, the sooner their spouse can begin turning their life around. In their mind, their bride or groom becomes their saviour, their deliverer and their crutch. When their spouse cannot deliver them or make them whole, or fails to bear the weight of their defective character, these marriages quickly slam into the jagged rocks.

• *The Mad Scientist Syndrome* - In 1999, the makers of the much touted weight loss drug **Fen-Phen** resolved one of the largest product liability cases at that time. They agreed to pay $3.75 billion dollars to settle claims that their product caused dangerous heart valve problems. **Fen-Phen** was another scientific experiment destined to fail. To know why, you have to understand the definition of an experiment. It means to: **1). Demonstrate a known truth 2). Examine the validity of a hypothesis 3). determine the effectiveness of something previously untried**.

When the scientists claimed **Fen-Phen** was a safe and effective weight loss drug, they were not demonstrating a known truth. They were examining the validity of a hypothesis. They were trying to determine the effectiveness of something unproven. It took years before the FDA, medical science and the public figured out that **Fen-Phen** was a failed experiment. The men and women who create and market such harmful products can only be aptly classified as *mad scientists*.

When it comes to marriage, there are individuals who with great zeal and excitement race to the wedding altar. Sadly, they are just like the mad scientists who created **Fen-Phen**. With them, marriage is just an experiment. Their concept of marriage is an unproven hypothesis and a theory. What they believe about love, sex, relationships and marriage is not based upon a known truth.

They wait until they marry before deciding that they want to pursue a career and they cannot be hampered by a spouse or a child. They may pull a Prince Charles. When Prince Charles married Princess Diana, according to sources, he still had the hots for Camilla Parker-Bowles. BUT! He decided to give it a *try* with Diana anyway. That is called a marital experiment! When these smooth operators look their mates in the eyes and say "I do," they know in their hearts that for them, this is just an experiment.

They are using matrimony to conduct an exploratory probe to see whether this person might possibly be *The One*. They may be experimenting to see if their attraction to the opposite sex is stronger than their attraction to the same sex, or, if they are even cut out for marriage. As with most trial experiments, their marital experiment is bound to end with the rubber stamp: *failed*.

• *Wedding Ceremony Blues* - Anything can set off this affliction: the announcement of a friend, stranger or family member getting married, seeing a husband and his wife strolling in the park, a bridal magazine in the grocery store, or a movie about a love story. It hits like a ton of bricks. They start singing the blues. "How come I'm not married? When will I be loved? When is it going to be my turn? Seems like everyone is getting married but me!"

Next, they come up with a bright idea on how to cure their wedding ceremony blues. Find someBODY... anyBODY and get married, as soon as possible. From that moment on, they develop a severe case of tunnel vision. That glistening wedding altar is all they can see. Like all smooth operators who make that sprint, their marriage has nothing to do with the person they marry.

This is about *them* and what *they* feel they rightfully deserve. In their minds, their spouses usually do not even qualify as an afterthought. You don't have to have a genius IQ to figure out where these marriages are headed.

• *Getting Revenge Against An "Ex"* - Remember Olympia and Gavin on pages 39 and 40? Olympia took out revenge against her *ex*-boyfriends on an innocent man named Gavin. She used ~~holy~~ rapid matrimony, ten years of marriage, two children and then an ugly unjustifiable divorce. What she did to Gavin was the exact same thing her *ex*-lovers had done to her. They claimed to love her, led her on, stole her virginity and then they left her in the dust. On page 59, you saw the attitude of the teenager who felt jilted by a boy to whom she gave her virginity.

You read this before but you need to read it again. She was so bitter that she made this chilling declaration: **"I don't care, screw it, I'm going to go and try to ruin a guy's night or something evil like that, I have this anger towards guys mainly because the first guy that I loved or gave myself to, hurt me..." "I think I have a right to show anger towards guys."** Their "ex," hurt them, they are fuming mad and now, using marriage as their whipping stick, they seek revenge!

• *Need New Living Arrangements* - Roman had pursued Hanna's hand in marriage from the moment he said hello. Five months later, they were husband & wife. Friends say it was a lovely whirlwind fairytale romance. Just before they were about to exchange wedding vows,

Hanna discovered Roman was hiding a checkered past. He had been previously married and had a daughter he said nothing about. At that point, Hanna should have terminated the relationship. Astonished and upset about the startling revelation of his *ex*-wife and child, Hanna confronted her nightmare in pining armor but she was no match for the quick-witted, smooth talker. With the finesse of a master manipulator, Roman softened Hanna's heart with a passionate apology.

The two married in a bland courtroom ceremony. Then Hanna rented an apartment for them, in her name, using her social security number. Contrary to what he had promised, Roman brought nothing with him: no furniture, no appliances, no pots or pans, no forks or spoons, no artificial plants, not even a roll of toilet paper.

He brought a few clothes, a toothbrush, a stick of deodorant and a few other personal items. When Roman met Hanna, he found a quick shortcut to the comfortable life. She had a good job, good credit, money in the bank and a car. Roman had no proof that he had any of these things. Once they moved in, their marriage took an accelerated nose dive. Roman wasted no time showing his true colors.

Using his hands as a nightstick, he whipped Hanna as though she was a violent criminal resisting arrest. The police responded to the couple's war zone apartment. Unfortunately, like many women who find themselves in the unfamiliar and unchartered territory of being booby trapped by a resourceful and cunning wife beater, Hanna declined to press charges that night. Her family said she did not want to see her husband go to jail on her account.

The way the domestic violence laws were written in her state, the officers could not arrest Roman unless Hanna pressed charges because she had no visible marks. The next day, Hanna had a change of mind and went to court seeking a restraining order. But she made another fatal mistake. She told her violence prone, short fused husband of her intentions to leave him. Shhhh... get real quiet... listen...

Do you hear that? Listen carefully... that's the sound of me desperately pleading with women like Hanna who find themselves hiding swollen eyes and making up absurd explanations for the burn marks, bruises, cuts and welts on their body. That's the sound of me urgently begging women who have been choked, kicked, slapped, punched or stabbed by a man who claims to love them. You know who you are! Remember the horrors to which he has subjected you.

He has put a gun to your face, put a knife to your throat, threatened you, dared you not to leave him, swore he would kill your family or said he would make your children disappear. He's pushed you down the stairs, locked you in the closet for hours, broken your bones, caused you to get stitches, pulled the telephone out of the wall to keep you from calling the police. Listen to me... you may not get another chance to leave. For your sake and for the sake of your family and loved ones, take it NOW! Don't try to explain to him why. There's no explanation needed. You were booby trapped into a relationship from HELL!

Almost assuredly, if you stay, you will suffer greater harm. You want him to seek help? Haven't you noticed? He's already getting help. He gets therapy every time he punches you in the kidneys, spits on you, grabs you by the neck, twists your legs and screams obscenities and threats at you. You need to contact the appropriate agencies, (*I've listed them in the Resource Guide*), get a plan together and then depart.

When Hanna informed Roman that she was leaving, he told a friend, *"I'm madly in love with her and if she can't be with me, she can't be with anybody."* That same week, the newlyweds were found dead in their apartment. Crime scene investigators determined that Roman ended their **11-day marriage** by killing his wife and then committing suicide. If that was not a satanic plot to ruin her life, what was it? Could what happened to Hanna have been the will of God? A thousand times, NO! What happened to Hanna is that she got booby trapped. She was snared by a seasoned marriage missile.

Some people will make that mad dash to the altar just to get away from their parents. Others decide for various reasons that marriage is the best option for them to file a change of address form with the United States Post Office. That's why it is so critical for you to perform all of the *Booby Trap Acid Tests* before you say "I do."

We have just examined some deplorable motives smooth operators use to make **The One Hundred Yard Dash To The Wedding Altar**. Before we proceed, I need to warn you about a harmful phenomena created by these individuals. Since 1980, statistics reveal that one of every two first marriages, will end in divorce and about eighty percent of those divorcees will eventually remarry. Many will divorce, remarry and divorce again and continue repeating this destructive cycle

This era of a series of marriages has given rise to a category of men and women classified as **Serial Spouses**. A serial spouse is a person who has had three or more marriages. No one knows what is going through the minds of these individuals. However, we can clearly see the damaging effect their actions have on our society.

With their string of divorces they: (a) **help fuel the staggering high rate of divorce,** (b) **raise children and step children who come to expect divorce,** (c) **raise children and step children who devalue marriage,** (d) **convince others that marriage does not work, and** (e) **unwittingly influence others to adopt the spousal replacement mentality.**

Here are few examples of men and women who have had multiple divorces. Carefully read their accounts...

• Former U.S. House Speaker, Newt Gingrich (*real name*), known as a staunch family values conservative, is now in his third marriage to a woman with whom he admitted to having a six year extramarital affair. In response to questions about his marital infidelity, Gingrich once said in an interview: "In the 1970s, things happened - period. That's the most I'll ever say.... I start with an assumption that all human beings sin. So all I'll say is that I've led a human life."

• Billy Bob Thornton, (*real name*) the Academy Award winning writer, actor and director has been married and divorced five times.

• Zsa Zsa Gabor (*real name*) wrote a book entitled: **How to Catch a Man, How to Keep a Man, How to Get Rid of a Man**. Apparently she followed her own advice. She was married nine times.

• Melanie Griffith (*real name*), a well known actress, has been married and divorced four times with a child by each of her three husbands. She married and divorced one of her husbands twice.

• Relationship expert Barbara De Angelis, PhD, (*real name*) has sold millions of books, tapes and videos on how to make relationships work. Many view her philosophies on love, sex and relationships as if they are infallible. Some of her followers swear by her beliefs and teachings.

Read how the media describes Barbara: (a) **One of North America's leading relationship therapists,** (b) **America's foremost expert on relationships and personal growth,** (c) **An internationally recognized expert on human relations,** (d) **Barbara's award-winning television infomercial, *Making Love Work*, is the most successful relationship program of its kind**.

A reporter for Cox News Service said, "Barbara De Angelis is the last person you would expect to be an expert on relationships." He reported Barbara as being married five times. Am I criticizing any of these individuals? A thousand times no!

Their examples reflect what other people believe about marriage. You must face this fact. There is a segment of our society that has a cavalier attitude towards matrimony. They will become your spouse at the drop of a dime and just as quickly, serve you with divorce papers, leave you crying in the dark, and think nothing of it.

You have read their words, some of them are so spiritually disjointed, that after becoming matrimonial dropouts, they will try to persuade you that marrying you and divorcing you was not their idea at all. According to them, it was GOD's idea, GOD's decision, GOD's will and GOD's orchestration. Some marriage missiles are so brazen they have created their own brands of matrimony called: **practice; icebreaker; training; trial** and **starter marriages**.

No matter how they classify their marriages, these unions always end the same way. Startled spouses are rammed through the divorce court automated heart grinding machine. After their divorces, they experience varying degrees of heartbreak, emotional pain and financial damage. Plus, their names may be added to the growing list of divorcees who are bitter at God, hostile towards the opposite sex, and who now vehemently oppose marriage altogether.

If they do decide to remarry, they must face the fact that some people and their families classify divorcees as damaged or used goods and would not talk to or touch them. Those are just some of the reasons why you must detect and avoid matrimonial vagabonds at all costs. The bottom line is this - do not become their first, second, third, fourth or fifth spouse. Don't add your name to their list of *ex's*. Here are the other motives marriage missiles use to snare a spouse.

• **The Most Eligible Bachelor or Bachelorette Syndrome** - These men and women have deluded themselves into believing they are the most eligible bachelor or bachelorette. They have compared themselves to the competition and they are IT! When they look in the mirror, they see pure perfection. They love themselves more than anything or anybody in the world. They love themselves more than God.

To best describe these relationship assassins we are forced to use words such as: vain, narcissistic, attractive nuisances, self-centered, self-absorbed, conceited and self-worshipping.

As they are enroute to making **The One Hundred Yard Dash To The Wedding Altar**, they are savvy enough to use the skills of a licensed tummy tuck surgeon to temporarily hide their glaring defects.

Instead of using anesthesia and scalpels, they use fraudulent affection, irresistible romance, and fake "I love you's." Their primary targets are people who are desperate, naive, spiritually immature, easily influenced or quickly impressed.

• *Matrimony Mania* - To understand this absurd motive for marriage, you must first understand the word, "mania." Mania means to have an exaggerated or unreasonable desire or enthusiasm for something. It is the female gender who is most guilty of this matrimonial crime.

Once a woman acquires the mania, she will spend almost every waking moment fantasizing, dreaming, scheming, plotting, and getting hyped up for *her* wedding ceremony. She will go to every bridal show. She will accept every bridal shower invitation. She will read every bridal magazine and attend every wedding ceremony that she can.

She has already chosen her wedding invitations, gown, cake and stretch limousine. She has selected her honeymoon destination, picked her neighborhood and decided how her husband is going to act.

As soon as she finds a man and seduces, lures, traps or tricks him into popping the big question, she will put her plan into full swing. Let's pause right here and clear the air. These females are not looking for genuine love or true matrimony. Oooh noooo! They are desperately seeking a flesh and blood robot. Their enthusiastic foot race to the altar is all about and only about fulfilling their wedding ceremony fantasies. They are residents of the notorious Fantasy Island *in their mind.* What they conjured up in their minds is not a plan but a plot.

Their plot has transformed the sacredness of the marriage covenant into another hyped-up gala social event and matrimonial circus - a nuptial exhibition from which they will obtain their forty-five minutes of wedded bliss fame.

The men who crossed paths with these type of females knew before they said, "I do" that they should have backed out of her circus. But they got caught up in the pressure of the moment and followed after the tradition of other spineless men: Adam (see Genesis 2:7 thru 3:17), Ahab, (see I Kings 21:1-25) and Barak (see Judges 4:1-9).

The couples who do not get an immediate annulment or divorce, usually require emergency marital counseling or therapy. Others stay together but their years are spent bickering and fighting until one of them finally pulls the divorce trigger.

• *Living on Impulse* - Remember Samson on page 28? If you recall, it took Samson one look and BAM! He was hooked. Judges 14:1-2 [Emphasis added] "And Samson went down to Timnath, and SAW A WOMAN... And he came up, and told his father and his mother, and said, I HAVE SEEN A WOMAN... ...now therefore GET HER FOR ME TO WIFE." Samson's motive for marriage: he was living on impulse.

Although he was a judge, he was not marriage material. Had he chosen a good wife, he would have broken her heart. All it takes for these type of smooth operators is a small temptation, a minimal test of their integrity, a feather weight pressure, or a little inclement weather in their life. At that point, their lack of discipline, lack of commitment, and refusal to honor their marital vows will become apparent to all.

• *Peer Pressure* - These people feel pressure to get married from family, relatives, friends, church members and potential mates. One day they just crack! They cannot take it anymore. The gossip, the questions, the whispers, and the pressure were all too unbearable.

So they quickly find a BODY, anyB-O-D-Y, and make **The One Hundred Yard Dash To The Wedding Altar.** Their ill-advised decision thrusts an entire new list of marital and spousal issues and pressures into their laps which they are ill-prepared to handle. As the new pressure mounts, just as before, they crumble. Now what?

• *Age Desperation* - Age desperation can take place at any age. A sixteen year old can experience this mental lapse as well as someone who is thirty or forty years of age. The premise of the men and women infected with age desperation is that, unless they get married before they reach a certain age, their life is ruined. They make that false assertion based on peer pressure, media stereotypes, the infamous, "*my biological clock is ticking*" and various other reasons.

They become so enshrouded in their desire to exchange nuptials that they break every fundamental rule that governs entering into a healthy marriage. Like others who raced to the wedding altar with unpure motives, these spouses eventually find themselves scratching their heads and licking their wounds in the divorce courts.

This below list covers more unpure hidden motives used by marriage missiles to make **The One Hundred Yard Dash To The Wedding Altar.**

- To Obtain a Father or Mother For Their Child
- They Feel Guilty About Being Single
- A Burning Desire To Have Children
- To Obtain Social, Professional or Peer Approval
- To Obtain a Sense of Security
- Need An Adult To Structure Their Life, (*i.e. Momma's Boys and Spoiled Females*)
- She's Pregnant
- To Obtain Citizenship
- Trying To Mask Hurt
- Just Released From Prison
- They Made a Bet

As I have stated, weighing your potential mate's motive(s) for marriage is an imperative necessity. For your safety, sanity, security and well-being, you must take all of the motives I have shared with you, line them up next to your potential mate and examine their reasoning for wanting to marry you.

This is the part of being in a relationship when you put on your reseacher's and investigator's hats and ask probing questions. Do you see any red flags? Has your potential mate expressed a displeasure with being lonely? Are they showing any signs of peer pressure, wedding ceremony blues, age desperation, matrimony mania or marrying on impulse? Are they unhappy with their current living arrangements? Are they in a profession or position in which they are expected to be married? (*i.e., politics, ministry, certain corporations, etc.*).

On the surface, such reasons for marriage may seem harmless, but marriages established on wrong motives will eventually crumble. Here are the *Booby Trap Acid Tests* you'll need to perform to assist you in determining if a person is using this fast paced booby trap to snare you into a marital booby trap.

1. Did they start things off by trying to "get married" as opposed to getting to know you and you getting to know them?
2. Have they tried to whisk you off to the altar in a private ceremony?

3. Have they tried the, "It's love at first sight," let's get married routine?
4. Have they tried to convince you, "The Lord told them you were to be their wife or husband?" Have they tried to persuade you that the Lord gave them a vision or dream about marrying you?
5. Have they received any prophecies that they were going to get married? [Especially prophesies declaring they would be married by thus and such date?]
6. Has your potential mate tried to convince you that the two of you should get married because you are soul mates, twin souls, twin flames, cosmic partners or karmic partners?
7. Do you feel compelled, pressured, forced, manipulated, coerced, rushed or cajoled into getting married by your potential mate? By their family or yours? By a church?
8. Is your potential mate being guided or led into marriage by a horoscope or a psychic reading, astrology, a lucky charm, a bet, a pact or a dare?
9. Is she pressing you to marry her because she says she is pregnant?
10. Have they used any of these lines on you?

- "I don't feel like it takes that long to get to know a person"
- "When you're in love there's no reason to take your time"
- "I know we don't know each other that well, but..."
- "The sooner we get married, the sooner we can..."
- "When you are soul mates, things will always work themselves out"
- "I know you have concerns, but things will change once we're married"
- "If you don't marry me, my life will fall apart, and I might as well die..."
- "Sometimes you just have to go for "it" [*marriage*].

Another area to be examined is the attempt by your potential mate to use her physical beauty or sex to entice you to make **The One Hundred Yard Dash To The Wedding Altar**. This ploy is commonly used by females shopping for disposable dads, gold-diggers, paternity fraud predators and females looking to exact revenge against the male gender.

Has your potential mate flaunted signs of wealth or power to lure you into marriage? Have they attempted to lavish you with expensive gifts? Smooth operators commonly use the bait of (*glistening jewelry, fancy trips, fine cars, five-star restaurants, etc.*) to buy their way into holy, unholy matrimony. When a man must flaunt wealth or power to win a woman's heart, that is a sure sign that he has some serious character flaws.

The question arises, "How long should I date or court a person before getting married?" It will vary. Some people believe in the two year or three year rule. Be warned - there are many patient marriage missiles and nonchalant relationship assassins who are willing to trek two, three or more years of their time just to ruin your life. The two or three year rule then becomes a moot rule.

Quite frankly, something is amiss anytime a person needs to date or court a person for two or more years before they make up their mind if he or she is *The One*. I would want to question what exactly were those two people doing during that time?

Did they spend their time making googly eyes at each other as opposed to testing, examining and appraising each other? Did they not talk about each other's intentions and about their future together? Is one or both of them not suitable marriage partners? Are they compatible with each other? Are they trying to force a relationship that was not meant to be? Are they together because someone is afraid of saying, "It's not going to work!"

Why have they spent all of this time together but still are not sure if he or she is *The One*? Is the glue that has kept them together sexual contact? Is this a case of emotional defraud? Is one of them reluctant to get married? Is one of them already married? Is he just using her as his part time playmate? Is she just using him to supplement her income? These are questions that must be addressed!

When considering a person as a possible marriage partner, your first and foremost priority must be to examine your potential mate's motive for marriage. I have shown you the wrong motives for marriage, so what are the right motives?

For a man, his motive for marriage must be that he is ready, willing and able to be a husband, true friend, leader, father, protector, cultivator, gentleman, effective communicator and provider. Do you have to badger, cajole or prod a man into accepting any of these husbandly duties prior to marriage? If so, eventually, he will most likely make you regret your decision. If he has not made the decision to be those things before he met you, realize that you are marrying a man who is ill-prepared for marriage. After you cross the wedding line, your marriage will become a nuptial blur.

For a woman, her motive for marriage must be that she is ready willing and able to be a: wife, helpmeet, sounding board, safe haven, nurturer, true friend, mother, comforter and household manager. Has your potential mate accepted these as her wifely duties? If not, I can guarantee you that after your honeymoon phase is over, you won't be happy with your choice of a wife. She will most likely make both of your lives miserable.

It is an undeniable fact, men and women who get married but who do not understand their husbandly and wifely duties prior to their wedding day, often become distasteful and unbearable spouses. Your second priority must be to perform each and every *Booby Trap Acid Test* in this book. Locked within these tests are fail-safe measures designed to protect you from ending up in a marital nightmare.

8

Antacids Can't Cure Lover's Heart Burn

Erica is the daughter of a very prominent and well beloved pastor. She was raised in a godly Christ centered home and had blossomed into a beautiful woman of God. When you looked at Erica, you were looking at a perfect portrait of a Proverbs 31 woman. Verse by verse, she had all of the qualities. Erica was the type of woman men who earnestly prayed for a wife desired to have. She had not been in and out of relationships. She had not allowed and would not allow any man to toy with her emotions or use or misuse her physical body.

She walked humbly before the Lord and was fully committed to serving Him. Erica's mother had set an exemplary example of what it meant to be a true helpmeet. With a servant's heart, Erica graciously followed in her mother's footsteps. She had a sweet and gentle spirit. She exuded kindness and was quite beautiful. She was truly a diamond in the rough.

Rick was a college graduate on the corporate fast track, a mover and a shaker. When he saw Erica, his mind was made up. She was *The One*. Rick put a plan in motion and started his pursuit to win Erica's heart. While he was courting her, Erica did not detect anything indicating that trouble could be looming in his life. In her thoughts, she often toiled over the question, 'Is he really *The One?*" She called out to the Lord in prayer about Rick, shuffling everything about him around in her mind. It really looked like he was *The One*. Erica's parents however, were not impressed by the superficial things they saw in Rick. Although they couldn't quite describe their reservations, they sensed by the Holy Spirit that Rick was not *The One* for their daughter.

As loving parents they never tried to impose what they sensed in their hearts upon their daughter. They never criticized her about believing in Rick and they did not speak distasteful words to her concerning him. They walked in love and earnestly prayed for Erica. They gave her godly counsel by sharing with her in a loving manner what they sensed. It was to no avail. Erica had already been smitten. She had been snared by a smooth operator.

They were married long enough to have two children before the nuptial trauma hit with a deafening blow. Rick had broken his marriage vows. It turns out he had never stopped living his college lifestyle of casual sexual romps. He just kept his activities secret while he pursued Erica. If this heart breaking tragedy should not have happened to any one person, it should not have happened to Erica. What warning signs did she overlook? What did she miss about Rick?

We will answer those questions in just a moment, but first let's examine another case. Emerson was a minister in a small church who was elected as the new pastor. When he took over the reigns, the church starting growing by leaps and bounds. A single man at the time, Pastor Emerson greatly desired a wife. But between working a full time job and doing the work of the ministry, he had no time left for romantic pursuits. In her usual manner, Miriam made her way to a front seat in the sanctuary. She knew she had caught Pastor Emerson's eye and she made it a point to be in the church every time the doors were opened. She seemed to listen intently to his every word.

After observing her over a period of time, Emerson made his move. They had delightful conversations. Miriam told Pastor Emerson that she put God first in her life. Since she was always in the church, who could argue? Miriam also expressed to Pastor Emerson that she was a virgin and would be the best friend, wife, lover, and helpmeet he could ever pray for. He recalled seeing her worshipping the Lord in the sanctuary and thought he was in heaven. Pastor Emerson had seen enough. He was convinced God had sent him his *True Love.*

He got an engagement ring and asked Miriam to marry him. Miriam immediately accepted! As a single pastor of a growing and close knit church, it was only natural for the pastor and groom-to-be to introduce his bride-to-be to the congregation. The word got out and there was excitement in the air. The atmosphere was a buzz with romance. Everyone would finally get a chance to meet the woman who won Pastor Emerson's heart. When he introduced his bride-to-be, the atmosphere rapidly changed from excited anticipation to alarm, jaw dropping shock and stunned disbelief!

The men and women who knew Miriam personally, described her to be a wild and loose one night stand who had a cache of sex partners. What was she doing trying to become a pastor's wife? The answer goes back to what you learned in chapter 1. She was being used by the devil to destroy God's glorious plan for Pastor Emerson's life. Miriam's skeletons came blasting out of the closet like a Tomahawk cruise missile. The identity of Pastor Emerson's fiancée spread through the church and community like wildfire.

Their impending marriage had become one comedian's punch line. *"The pastor of that church is marrying a hoochie mamma!"* Church members, family, and friends who truly loved and sincerely cared about Pastor Emerson, urgently and passionately advised him to cancel the wedding and to dump this wild and rebellious girl. They shared with him cold hard undeniable facts about his immoral bride-to-be.

Instead of taking heed and breaking off the engagement, Emerson talked to his fiancée. She claimed that the devil was trying to break them up and Pastor Emerson believed her, so they bumped up the wedding date and made **The One Hundred Yard Dash To The Wedding Altar.**

What in the world was Pastor Emerson thinking? Did he not realize that he was a man of God and a pastor of a church? Did he not understand the consequences and perceive the repercussions of marrying a woman like Miriam? The last thing any true minister would ever want is a wife who was mocking God by playing church. After the honeymoon, Emerson finally got to see the real Miriam. Life with his new bride was so unnerving that his hair turned grey almost overnight. The young Pastor Emerson was now looking like an old man.

His wife was hanging out at night clubs and coming home in the wee hours of the morning. At one point she had completely stopped going to church. Word of her illicit lifestyle was getting back to the congregation and some of the members were furious. Concerned family members, friends, and parishioners pulled Miriam aside and pleaded with her. They reminded her that she was married to a man of God.

They tried to convince her not to embarrass the ministry. They attempted to persuade her that she needed to act and carry herself like the first lady of the church. Talking to her was like talking to a hardened criminal. Miriam just wanted to get those church folk off her back. Their best hope was that her wanton ways wouldn't come back to hurt Pastor Emerson or bring reproach upon the ministry. Both Erica and Pastor Emerson chose the wrong mate because they failed this critical *Booby Trap Acid Test*. Read it carefully.

Have You Ignored Any Wise Counsel From People Who Truly Love You And Sincerely Care About You?

I wish I could tell you that even though a man disregards this *Booby Trap Acid Test* and marries a woman like Miriam, that God will eventually change her heart through his fervent prayer and fasting. I wish I could tell you that when a woman ignores this *Booby Trap Acid Test* and marries a man like Rick, all she has to do is seek God and He will move on her husband's heart, but I cannot tell you that.

I wish that I could tell you her husband will repent, humbly seek her forgiveness and all of the hurt, pain and betrayal will be forgiven and forgotten. But I cannot tell you that. No one can! If they could, people who went to church would never get divorced, never end up in tense child support or child custody cases, never have their names splashed on the domestic violence court dockets, and they would never need marriage counselors or therapists.

Furthermore, men of God like myself would never get calls from teary eyed spouses wondering what in the name of God they should do. When people in your life who **Truly Love You and Sincerely Care About You** give you godly counsel concerning a potential mate, please listen intently and take to heart what they have to say. Let's go to the Word of God to find out why this *Booby Trap Acid Test* is so critical.

> Proverbs 13:10 AMP [Emphasis added]
> By pride *and* insolence comes only contention, BUT WITH THE WELL-ADVISED IS SKILLFUL *AND* GODLY WISDOM.

> Proverbs 11:14 [Emphasis added]
> Where no counsel *is*, the people fall: BUT IN THE MULTITUDE OF COUNSELLORS *THERE IS* SAFETY.

> Proverbs 20:18 NIV [Emphasis added]
> MAKE PLANS BY SEEKING ADVICE; if you wage war, obtain guidance.

Read that first Scripture again. Notice what comes to those who are *well-advised* - skillful and godly wisdom. The second Scripture reveals another reason why one of every two marriages ends in divorce. They didn't have proper counsel prior to getting married. Did you notice what happens to those who have a multitude of counsellors?

They live in safety! In the third Scripture, we are instructed to make marital plans, by seeking advice. If you ignore those commands, here are your replacement instructions: **1). Put a marriage counselor or therapist on standby, 2). Get the phone number to a 24 hour prayer hotline, 3). Put a divorce attorney on retainer, and 4). Get the phone number to the Excedrin P.M. Headache Resource Center** - in all probability you will need them all.

Remember Erica's parents? Through prayer they discerned that Rick was not *The One*. However, they were unable to give Erica a specific reason because there were no smoking guns. There was no lipstick on his collar, no panties in his back seat, and no pestering calls on his cell phone. What Erica's parents sensed was precipitated by the Holy Spirit. He sees all and knows all. Jesus said of the Holy Spirit, in (John 16:13) "...he will show you things to come."

The Lord showed Erica's parents things to come when He planted that uneasiness in their hearts about Rick. "Why didn't the Lord just tell Erica?" He did! He told her through people who **Truly Loved Her and Sincerely Cared About Her**. Let us return to the Scriptures...

Proverbs 15:22 NIV [Emphasis added]
PLANS FAIL FOR LACK OF COUNSEL, but with many advisers they succeed.

The reasons why so many relationships end up looking like a car wreck scene should be clearer to you by now. For your sake, do not ever let this next Scripture describe you.

Proverbs 15:12 NIV [Emphasis added]
A mocker resents correction; HE WILL NOT CONSULT WITH THE WISE.

Never reject, resent, take lightly or ignore advice that comes from people who **Truly Love You and Sincerely Care About You**. Never let it be said you would not consult with wise people concerning a potential mate. How many advisers or counselors should you have? There are no set rules. At least two to three but no more than five, (See II Corinthians 13:1, Matthew 18:16). The primary qualifiers for someone to give you godly counsel and advice concerning a potential mate is that you must be able to answer "yes," to all five of these questions:

1. Does this person truly love you and sincerely care about you?
2. Will this person earnestly pray for you and with you about this matter?
3. Does this person have your best interest at heart at all times?
4. Can you share things with this person in total confidentiality?
5. Does this person exemplify integrity, godly morals, and sound judgment?

If you do not already have people in your life from whom you can seek advice and guidance, you need to put the brakes on your love life and find them right now! You read the Scripture, only a mocker will not consult with the wise. Is that what you are, another hardheaded mocker bent on doing things your way? Do not take the road most traveled, by deluding yourself into believing that you are intelligent and savvy enough to figure out love on your own.

Do not become part of the countless number of men and women who have found themselves on a *virtual* deserted island called "Love," shipwrecked with a masked man or a disguised woman. When you refuse or neglect to obtain advice from wise advisors concerning a potential mate, you end up in a relationship on a deserted island.

The problem is... there are only two ways to get off a deserted island: by death or someone has to rescue you. I need to stop right here and reiterate what I said about your selection of people from whom you receive counsel. They must meet all of the qualifications. It does not matter if the person is your father, mother, brother, sister, friend or an ordained minister. If you cannot answer "yes," to all of the qualifications, I strongly advise against receiving guidance or counsel from that person concerning the selection of a mate or marriage.

The bottom line is this, there are certain people who simply are not qualified to give *pre*-marital advice. They may give advice on other issues, but when it comes to issues of love, sex, relationships and marriage, you need to be concerned about these groups.

- Singles
- Newlyweds
- Troubled Couples
- The Divorced
- Those Who Cohabit
- Impudent Ministers

• *Singles* - The average modern day single has no clue about God's glorious plan for their love life or the devil's secret plot to destroy it. They know nothing about smooth operators or the nine deadly booby traps. There are some exceptions, but they are rare. When it comes to choosing a mate, most singles are concerned about: *"What kind of car he drives? Is he handsome? How does she look? Is she fine?"* They do not know the critical questions to ask, or the warning signs and red flags.

They know how to have candlelight dinners, go to the movies and enjoy other forms of entertainment together. Yet, when it comes to measuring a person's character, knowing the qualities that make up a well-rounded spouse, they have a bad case of the "head in the clouds." They habitually opt for the superficial things that fade away after the aura of the honeymoon has fizzled out. That is one reason so many newlyweds get divorced before they reach their second year of marriage.

• *Newlyweds* - On the surface, it would seem as though newlyweds would be the perfect choice for relationship and *pre*-marital advice. As a matter of fact some newlyweds falsely christen themselves as *"love gurus."* Upon returning from their honeymoon, they start pairing their friends together. You must avoid the temptation of allowing enthusiastic newlyweds to play "advisor" with your love life.

When a person joins the United States Armed Forces or gets drafted into the National Football League, they are called new recruits and rookies for good reason. A new recruit or rookie is a person who: **1)**. lacks knowledge gained only from training and experience, and **2)**. has not yet demonstrated the skills or expertise to prove proficiency. That's exactly what newlyweds are - Matrimonial Rookies! Although their intentions are most noble, they have not yet proven that they have what it takes to sustain a healthy marriage. As newlyweds, what they have is high expectations. Have they mastered the art of communicating? Do they have the proper knowledge and skills to meet the demands, pass the tests, handle the challenges and reject the temptations that come to married people. Are they even willing?

We simply do not know the answers to those questions and only time will tell. Before they start dispensing advice in this area, they need to first: 1). gain the knowledge that comes only from experience and training, and 2). demonstrate that they have developed the skills necessary to have a healthy and blessed marriage. Until then, they're just marital freshmen and excited newlyweds.

• *Troubled Couples* - This includes spouses involved in abusive relationships, ones dealing with drug or alcohol issues, those separated, those in need of or receiving marital counseling, those abandoned by their spouses, those in unhappy marriages, or those involved in combative disputes with their spouses concerning, legal, moral, spiritual, family, financial or religious issues. It should be pretty obvious why you should not seek advice from these individuals. I'll clarify those reasons along with the divorced.

• *The Divorced* - Being divorced or in a bad marriage can create some pretty warped beliefs about marriage, cynical feelings toward the opposite sex and plant seeds of mutiny against God. Through **influence by association**, some divorcees use their bad experiences, ill-feelings and animosities to corrode the sanctity of marriage, mock sexual purity and introduce philosophies concerning love, sex, relationships and marriage that directly conflict with the marital directives established by God.

Here are some examples: living together first and then getting married, living together instead of getting married, signing prenuptials, alternatives to marriage and starter marriages are some of the schemes born out of the minds and hearts of men and women who suffered heartbreak from terrible relationships, bad marriages and bitter divorces. They created from their pain and hurt what they believed would be better ways of finding love and experiencing companionship.

They did not realize their beliefs and methods only serve to morally weaken and corrupt others. Are all divorcees holding grudges, harboring animosities or giving bad advice concerning these issues? No, and I am not declaring that! I am making you aware of what many divorcees go through and how they influence others through their pain. I'm sorry for what they had to endure and I pray for their recovery. Their pain touches my heart, but when it comes to obtaining dating, courting and *pre*-marital advice you must seek counsel from seasoned couples.

You must seek advice from couples with healthy marriages. Look for those who understand what it takes to develop marital harmony.

• *Those Who Cohabit* - Seeking relationship advice from cohabiters is like seeking health advice from people who sell french fries and jelly filled donuts. Such people have no regard for your health. Those who cohabit display no regard for the sacredness of the marriage covenant, (*You'll learn why later*). You cannot trust the opinion of people who have taken such a position concerning this serious issue.

• *Impudent Ministers* - The word impudent means: to have a bold contempt or disregard for, or to casually disrespect. Sadly, there are numerous ministers who are ordained, have licenses to preach, seminary degrees and Bible college diplomas and yet, they have a high degree of contempt and disregard for the Word of God. It is brazen sin for someone who declares they are a minister of the gospel to perform a wedding ceremony for: (a) **two people and one of them is not born again,** (b) **two people and both are not born again,** or (c) **people who are cohabiting.**

A true minister of God would absolutely refuse to perform such wedding ceremonies. It is his duty under God. This is just another reason the divorce rate is so high. These impudent ministers casually disrespect their ministerial duties and perform these ceremonies when they should: **1). strongly rebuke those Christians seeking to be married to an unsaved person, and 2). inform the unsaved person that God forbids His ministers from joining a unsaved person to a Christian in matrimony,** (see II Corinthians 6:14-18). God gives His ministers zero authorization to marry nonbelievers. To do so would cause them to violate the Written Word of God. Finally, some ministers are not true shepherds.

They are what Jesus described as hirelings, (See John 10:13). To them the ministry is just a J-O-B, another dismal nine to five! Pastor Kilborn treated the ministry that way. When Danny & Darlene requested that he marry them, he quickly obliged. He never once sat down and questioned or counseled the two. He took their money and put the ill-advised ceremony date on his preaching calendar.

On their wedding day, Danny showed up thoroughly intoxicated and barely able to stand up. Pastor Kilborn did not blink an eye. He patted the drunken groom on the back, gave him a smirky little smile and hurriedly married the boozer to his startled bride. Pastor Kilborn grossly derelicted his pastoral duties. He should have said, "Not today, folks," and cancelled that wedding ceremony fiasco. But hirelings will not stand up and put their foot down when they are required to because they are just hirelings. After all, it's just another J-O-B! Avoid these ministers and churches like the plague! After the wedding, Danny could not keep a job due to his drinking and other childish behaviors.

What happened? Danny's mother pampered him, fed him, bought and washed his clothes, and housed him until her grown boy found a woman that he could sweet talk into taking over his mommy's job. Sometimes a minister is the last line of defense to protect a person from being booby trapped into a marriage destined for the divorce dumpster. What if the couple gets upset and rushes off to Las Vegas, the courthouse or to one of the drive through marriage mills? Let them GO! They won't be the first or the last to rebel against the Truth! Once again, here is your million dollar *Booby Trap Acid Test...*

Have You Ignored Any Wise Counsel From People Who Truly Love You And Sincerely Care About You?

If you answered "yes," you just failed a critical *Booby Trap Acid Test.* If you failed, for your sake, please say "no" to marriage until you get wise counsel. If you shun what the Written Word of God says concerning obtaining godly counsel... if you reject those Scriptures on obtaining advice... if you disobediently walk down the aisle, say "I do," and then defiantly sign that marriage license... I hate to be the one to tell you, but I must. At that point, concerning marriage, *"You are on your own!"* You say, "but Brother Triplett, God will never leave me nor forsake me." I did not say that God would leave you. The Scriptures make it very clear, He will never leave us nor forsake us, (See Hebrews 13:5, Joshua 1:5). I said you were on your own! Read the chilling consequences of not seeking godly advice concerning a potential mate.

> Proverbs 1:30-31 NIV [Emphasis added]
> [30] SINCE THEY WOULD NOT ACCEPT MY ADVICE and spurned my rebuke,
> [31] THEY WILL EAT THE FRUIT OF THEIR WAYS and be filled with the fruit of their schemes.

Did you read that passage of Scripture carefully? Read it again! He [*God*] said in verse 30, "Since they would not accept my [God's] advice..." Whose advice? God's advice! Not Gillis Triplett's advice.

God was the one who advised you to make plans by seeking advice and obtaining guidance. God was the one who declared that your love life, your dreams of having a happy home and your marital plans would *fail* without His counsel. God was the one who classified those who neglected, ignored or refused His advice as mockers.

What is a mocker? A mocker is a person who laughs at or ridicules the Word of God. They do not take what God says seriously. In verse 31, He [*God*] said, "they will eat the fruit of their ways..." In other words, ignore His advise and you are on your own!

He goes on in that same verse to call their godless relationship and marital plans, not plans at all, but a bunch of schemes. Remember Pastor Emerson? He did not accept God's advice. He rejected the counsel of his family, friends, and parishioners who **Truly Loved Him and Sincerely Cared About Him.** Soon after their wedding ceremony he started having sleepless nights. Do you really think he was going to get a good night's sleep knowing his wife was out partying and having sex with any man she pleased? His hair turned grey because he was worried about his wife's sexual romps and all-night parties.

Concerning marriage, Pastor Emerson was on his own. What could God do? Force his wanton wife to walk straight? Make his rebellious wife go to church? Coerce her to be a true woman of God? The answer to those questions is, NO! Read this next Scripture very slowly:

Proverbs 1:33 NIV [Emphasis added]
BUT WHOEVER LISTENS TO ME will live in safety and be at ease, without fear of harm."

Did you get that? Listening to the advice of God will cause you to live in the safety of a healthy, vibrant and blessed marriage without fear. The flip side of that verse is this, if you do not listen to His advice, the odds are stacked against you. At some point in your life, you are probably going to experience lover's heartburn. This is the excruciating pain caused by knowing that had you listened to people who truly love and sincerely care about you, your love life would not be in shambles. There is no antacid to cure that type of heartburn. I earnestly pray that you never go through such trauma.

Imagine the heartburn Erica must have felt while telling her parents how her adulterous two-timing husband ripped her heart out and took the wind from beneath their children's wings. Virtually everyone in her family had a sense of uneasiness about her plans to marry Rick. If only she had listened, she would have avoided that tense moment in time when she had to inform their children that mommy and daddy were getting a divorce. She would have avoided joining the ranks of the multitude of broken hearted *ex*-wives who are forced to raise their children by themselves. If only she had listened... Once again, here is your invaluable, *Booby Trap Acid Test...*

Have You Ignored Any Wise Counsel From People
Who Truly Love You And Sincerely Care About You?

9

The Red Flagged Relationship Resume

You are about to learn *one of* the most clever booby traps ever employed by relationship assassins. The tactic of persuading others to ignore their ungodly behaviors and turn their heads to their destructive personality traits. How they pull off this booby trap, will send chills up your spine. Take the case of Richard SaintCalle (*real name*). August 15, 2002 was a grim day for the Germain family.

Prosecutors say that about an hour after 32-year-old Keymhare Germain (*real name*), told her *ex*-boyfriend, 36 year-old Boeing engineer, Richard SaintCalle, that she was engaged to marry another man, her "*ex*" brought her life to an abrupt halt. In a brutally vicious attack, SaintCalle blew the lock off the door to Germain's apartment with a shotgun, stormed in and opened fire. The blast hit her in the heart and head, killing her and critically wounding their daughter.

The couple's son narrowly escaped injury during the mayhem, but only because his gun-wielding father (*for some reason*), warned him to leave if he valued his life. SaintCalle then fled the scene of the slaying and was spotted by police near the home of his estranged wife, whom they believe he was on his way to hurt or kill, (*she had a restraining order against him*). When authorities arrested him, they found nine shotgun shells in his pocket and several other loaded weapons in his 2000 BMW.

Let's scan Richard SaintCalle's horrific love life to learn how he persuaded people to ignore his ungodly behaviors and turn their heads away from his destructive personality traits.

Court documents revealed that SaintCalle had a history of domestic violence which included assaults and threats to kill his: (a). **First wife and their daughter**, (b). **His current estranged wife, and** (c). **His *ex*-girlfriend who had a protective order against him when he murdered her.** Deputy Prosecutor Adam Levin (*real name*), said that Germain had the first of her two children with SaintCalle when she was fourteen. He said the couple had *"a long and violent relationship"* dating back to when she was thirteen. In most states that is statutory rape, but SaintCalle was never charged. Wait a minute? He gets a minor pregnant and nothing happens to him: no grand jury, no charges, no arrest, no trial, nothing? Where was this little girl's parents or guardians? What about the doctor who delivered the baby? Everyone should have been screaming rape at the top of their lungs! This incident was the first record we have of SaintCalle succeeding at getting others to turn their heads to his destructive personality. Next, he somehow cleverly covers up his crime of impregnating a minor and then slips into another relationship.

He booby traps that woman into becoming his first wife. Mrs. SaintCalle finds herself married to a poster boy for domestic violence. Their union, like all of his reported relationships, involved assaults and threats. As you would expect, their marriage ended in divorce.

Undaunted, SaintCalle snares another woman into ~~holy~~ unholy matrimony. The results are the same. He abuses and threatens her. The second Mrs. SaintCalle, like the first, finds herself booby trapped in a marriage ordained from hell. She became *One Flesh* with a consummate wife beater. His record testifies to his destructive personality, with prior arrests for malicious mischief related to domestic violence, stalking, as well as a conviction for harassment.

Three different women became victims of SaintCalle's warped definition of love. Each woman either unintentionally or intentionally, ignored SaintCalle's ungodly behaviors and turned their heads to his destructive personality traits.

How could they have known he was so dangerous? We will answer that question momentarily. First, this next incident will help you understand how people ignore ungodly behaviors and turn their heads away from destructive personality traits. In the early morning hours of January 16th, 2002, Letonika Griffin, (*real name*) drove to her boyfriend's apartment with a .38 caliber revolver in her lap. When she arrived, she saw a car in the parking lot belonging to a woman with whom her boyfriend had been or currently was involved. Press pause for a moment... you confirm that the person you have developed feelings for is seeing someone else behind your back. What do you do?

(a) confront them and demand an apology
(b) confront them and get into an argument
(c) confront them and demand that they respect you
(d) make them choose between you and their secret lover
(e) confront them, forgive them and give them another chance
(f) forgive them, forget them, walk away and get on with your life

Tough call? Not if you respect yourself! Not if you have any self dignity! And not if you have been paying attention. On page 46, you learned that one of the underhanded tricks of smooth operators is to secretly date two or more people at once. Think this through clearly ...

In order to pull that feat off, your boyfriend, girlfriend or potential mate has to be a proficient, *"I will look straight in your eyes and bold face lie,"* type of liar. Such an incident is your cue to cut your losses and move on. If you decide to persuade the two-timer to dump their secret lover and stay with you, don't forget to inscribe the words *"slap me here,"* on your face, *"kick me here,"* on your buttocks and *"lie to me,"* across your heart. The answer is (f)! You forgive them, forget them and move on with your life. Miss Griffin said she was hurt by her boyfriend's apparent indiscretion, so she chose (b) and decided to confront him.

An argument ensued. Remember the gun in her lap? She moved it to her hand, pulled the trigger and fired, killing him. She immediately added her boyfriend's name to the long list of men and women murdered in a domestic dispute by the person who claimed to love them.

Press the stop button, hit rewind and then press play again. Prior to that deadly incident the couple had a telling history. Miss Griffin had admitted to several previous fits of rage which included: (a) **slapping her boyfriend during an argument,** (b) **slashing his mattress with a knife, and** (c) **hitting his motorcycle with her car.** The first time a potential mate displays any such behavior, it is time to terminate that relationship and move on with your life. As you are about to find out, those are not the behaviors of a person you can trust with your life.

AND! If you cannot trust a potential mate with your life, do not, I repeat, DO NOT become their boyfriend, girlfriend, fiancé, fiancée or spouse. Miss Griffin's boyfriend and all the women who crossed SaintCalle's path, either ignored or did not know this critical *Booby Trap Acid Test.* Concerning your potential mate...

Have You Ignored Any Ungodly Behaviors Or Turned Your Head Away From Any Destructive Personality Traits

I need to define ungodly behaviors and destructive personality traits. An ungodly behavior is when a person acts, reacts, responds or conducts themselves in a manner that does not reverence God. Here is a short list of some of the more prominent ungodly behaviors:

> Colossians 3:8-9 AMP [Emphasis added]
> [8] But now put away *and* rid yourselves [completely] of all these things; ANGER, RAGE, BAD FEELINGS TOWARDS OTHERS, CURSES *and* SLANDER, and FOULMOUTHED ABUSE *and* SHAMEFUL UTTERANCES from your lips!
> [9] DO NOT LIE to one another..."

In verse eight, we were commanded to rid ourselves of these behaviors. Notice how we are told to do it, not halfheartedly or partially.

The crucial point you must remember is this - these people mock the Word of God. What God has said is a big joke to them. They reject His Word and opt to have foul, dirty mouths. They will effortlessly curse you out, curse God and use other verbally offensive and abrasive language. They are champions when it comes to holding grudges, keeping animosity stirred and harboring ill-feelings toward others. Did you closely examine their list of ungodly behaviors? Read them again.

This bunch is subject to blow up in a fit of rage or anger at the flip of a switch. When they get upset, pressured, ticked of, hurt, scared, stressed, depressed, angry or mad - watch out! They will resort to slamming doors, punching holes in the wall, slashing mattresses with knives, brandishing firearms, hurling furniture and breaking dishes. They will crack your windshield, key your car, slit your tires, put sugar in your gas tank, threaten you and try to set your clothes on fire.

After committing any of those criminal offenses against you, some of them will passionately look you in the eyes and start singing the ballad by Lou Rawls, "You'll Never Find Another Love Like Mine..."

Some defense attorneys have made astronomical incomes trying to convince jurors these men and women did what they did because they were temporarily insane. Others tell us that people who display such behaviors are good people who just "lost it," for a split second. Smooth operators want us to believe they really did not mean to do it or say it. If they curse you out, threaten you, or hurt you, according to them, it was a completely uncontrollable act brought about due to *sudden passion*. If they did not love you so much, it never would have happened or, it was simply a mistake or, it was no big deal.

They try to persuade us that such behavior is typical. They say every couple has fights and arguments where they end up screaming at each other. They claim it is normal for a man to punch, slap or kick his wife or girlfriend when he gets upset. They say it is reasonable for a woman to stab her husband or boyfriend if he makes her really angry.

Who is telling the truth? What is the real reason these individuals display such behaviors? To get the "Truth," we must go to the unfailing and never changing Word of the Living God.

> Colossians 3:5-7 AMP [Emphasis added]
> [5] So kill (deaden, deprive of power) the EVIL DESIRE LURKING IN YOUR MEMBERS [those ANIMAL IMPULSES and all that is earthly in you that IS EMPLOYED IN SIN]: sexual vice, impurity, sensual appetites, unholy desires, and all greed and covetousness, for that is idolatry (the deifying of self and other created things instead of God).
> [6] It is on account of these [VERY SINS] that the [holy] anger of God is ever coming upon the SONS OF DISOBEDIENCE (those

Colossians 3:5-7 AMP [Emphasis added] continued...
who are OBSTINATELY OPPOSED TO THE DIVINE WILL),
⁷ Among whom you also once walked, when you were LIVING
IN AND ADDICTED TO [SUCH PRACTICES].

Verse five reveals three key points. 1). These people have evil desires lurking in their members [*or flesh*]. Their actions have nothing to do with temporary insanity, a chemical imbalance in their brain or an act of sudden or uncontrollable passion.

Their behaviors have to do with the evil intent *they* planted in their heart, which *they* chose to express through their flesh, (See Mark 7:20-23). 2). They are described as behaving like lowly animals, living and acting on impulse. 3). Lastly, their flesh is classified as being employed in SIN! In verse six, because they refuse to completely rid themselves of these behaviors, God calls them sons [*and daughters*] of disobedience. He goes on further to say in that same verse, they are, "...obstinately opposed to the divine will..."

Obstinately means: (a). stubbornly adhering to an attitude, opinion, or course of action, (b). difficult to manage, control or subdue, (c). difficult to alleviate or cure. Remember Saintcalle? He stubbornly adhered to his attitude of hating women. Even after being arrested and convicted, he stuck to his course of action of seducing, then threatening, abusing and controlling women. You can talk to, pray for and preach to these men and women until you are blue in the face. Some of them will even go as far as to agree with you and say, "Amen!" Yet, in their hearts, they vehemently oppose the will of God.

These relationship assassins will gleefully go to church and sing the songs of Zion, give offerings, teach Sunday school, play the role of deacon, prophetess, pastor or preacher. Meanwhile, they have live-in lovers, make and respond to booty calls, smoke dope, and pass the Courvoisier. They live just like a rank and file sinner. Why? Because they are obstinately opposed to the divine will of God. In their opinion, there is nothing wrong with their behavior. Their list of ungodly behaviors continues in the book of Galatians.

Galatians 5:19-21 NIV [Emphasis added]
¹⁹ The acts of the sinful nature are obvious: SEXUAL IMMORALITY, IMPURITY and DEBAUCHERY;
²⁰ IDOLATRY and WITCHCRAFT; HATRED, DISCORD, JEALOUSY, FITS OF RAGE, SELFISH AMBITION, DISSENSIONS, FACTIONS
²¹ and ENVY; DRUNKENNESS, ORGIES, and the like. I warn you, as I did before, that those who live like this will not inherit the kingdom of God.

The question becomes... "What type of behavior must a potential mate display to indicate they are ready to be in a relationship?" Here is the list with the instructions included:

Colossians 3:12 AMP [Emphasis added]
[12] Clothe yourselves therefore, as God's own chosen ones (His own picked representatives), [who are] purified and holy and well-beloved [by God Himself, BY PUTTING ON BEHAVIOR MARKED BY]..." Press pause. In verse 5, we were "commanded" to completely rid ourselves of the ungodly set of behaviors and now we are "commanded" to put on these behaviors...

Colossians 3:12 NIV [Emphasis added]
[12] "...compassion, kindness, humility, gentleness and patience. [To settle the questions, "Are arguments healthy? How should we deal with disagreements and disputes?" We are further commanded to...]

Colossians 3:13 AMP [Emphasis added]
BE GENTLE AND FORBEARING WITH ONE ANOTHER and, if one has a difference (a grievance or complaint) against another, readily pardoning each other; even as the Lord has [freely] forgiven you, so must you also [forgive]. [The next verse tells us how these behaviors are bound together to bring absolute harmony]

Colossians 3:14 AMP [Emphasis added]
[14] And above all these [PUT ON] LOVE and enfold yourselves with the bond of perfectness [WHICH BINDS EVERYTHING TOGETHER COMPLETELY IN IDEAL HARMONY].

Did you notice what is missing when you seek out a potential mate who holds firm to God's standard for entering a relationship? There is no cursing, yelling or screaming at each other. There is no bickering, fighting, hitting, kicking or slamming of doors, no restraining orders, and no court enforced anger management courses.

There are no verbal threats, no domestic violence, no frantic 911 emergency calls, no police, judicial or penal system intervention. What you get instead is harmony and oneness. When a potential mate has not obeyed the command to completely rid themselves of all ungodly behaviors and *put on* the godly behaviors, they are not qualified to be in a relationship with you or with anyone else. You read the Scriptures... God classifies them as sons and daughters of disobedience.

If you allow yourself to fall for a man or woman who displays any of the ungodly behaviors you read in the book of Colossians or Galatians, that is exactly what you have. Is that the type of person with whom you want to be in a relationship: a son or daughter of disobedience, or a person employed in sin? Here is where it gets really dangerous.

Ungodly behaviors are the seeds to destructive personality traits. Once a person takes on any ungodly behavior, they have planted the seeds necessary to bring forth a destructive personality. A destructive personality is when a person (*through their behaviors*) hurts, damages or destroys their relationships with others.

The persons affected could be a potential mate, their husband or wife, their parents, their children or their employer or employee. Sooner or later, they will make you cup your face in between your hands and cry, "Oh noooo, my God, why Lord, why?" We read and hear about the jaw-dropping acts of these men and women everyday, (*all real names*).

- **Paul Harrington** – killed his wife and two kids, pleaded insanity, received 60 days of psychiatric treatment and walked away a free man. DETROIT, MI, 1975
- **Paul Harrington** – remarries and 24 years later he goes on another rampage, kills his second wife and their son and once again pleads insanity. DETROIT, MI, 1999
- **James Ferree** – told detectives he became angry because the pet cats had strewn garbage all over the kitchen. Police said his anger intensified right after he learned that his live-in girlfriend's infant child had soiled in his diaper. Upset over the two incidents, in a fit of rage, he reportedly beat her child to death. MCKEESPORT, PA, 2002
- **Michael Antonio Glass** – authorities say he had a history of assaulting women at the time he beat his girlfriend because she refused to get an abortion. She was pregnant with twins and both of the babies died because of the attack. FAYETTE, GA, 2002
- **Ruthmae Bethel** – investigators say Ruthmae had a problem with breaking up with men. In early 2000, she refused a boyfriend's desire to break up, making threats, forcing him to file a restraining order against her. Three years later, when a new boyfriend, and father of her three month old child, decided their relationship was not going to work, investigators say Ruthmae got depressed, then drove her vehicle into Biscayne Bay, killing herself and daughter. Her other child was put on life support. MIAMI, FL, 2002
- **Dernell Stinson** – two weeks before this Cincinnati Reds outfielder was kidnapped and brutally murdered, he had received this death threat by text message to his cell phone from an ex-girlfriend, *"U better pray I never see U again. I swear Dernell U R worth a Murder charge 4 & that is all U R worth."* Phoeniz, AZ, 2003
- **DeKelvin Martin** – confessed to attacking his live-in girlfriend and her family. In the end, he killed her father and stabbed to death her 12-year-old son as the child tried to protect his mother from her violent, knife wielding lover. ATLANTA, GA, 2002
- **Kanita Thomas** – murdered her boyfriend because he objected to her going out with one of her friends. They got into an argument that escalated to violence when Kanita wielded a knife and stabbed him to death. ST. LOUIS, MO, 2003
- **Patricia Lynn Rorrer** – consumed with jealousy, kidnapped her *ex*-boyfriend's wife and infant, murdered and buried them in a shallow grave. BETHLEHEM, PA, 1994
- **Warren Lee Mace** – police say he had been drinking heavily and at some point turned against his wife and stepson and viciously attacked them with a knife. Investigators described the crime scene as, "very bloody." WINSTON, GA, 2002
- **Roberto Campos** – had two children by his ex-girlfriend. After they split-up she got married, had two more kids and got on with her life. But not Roberto. He kidnapped his *ex*-girlfriend, killed her and then committed suicide. RALEIGH, NC, 2002
- **Sandra Jonas** – prosecutors say Sandra was furious when she learned that her ex-husband was going to remarry. She was so angry that she shot and killed his fiancée, and then decapitated her body. BURLEY, ID, 1999

• **Doctor Maynard Muntzing** – confessed to spiking Cytotec, a miscarriage inducing drug into his pregnant girlfriend's beverages. Their child died. When the detective asked him "why?," he said he wanted to get rid of the problem. DAYTON, OH, 2000

• **Dionne Baugh** – Prosecutors say this wife and mother was having an adulterous affair with Atlanta businessman, Lance Herndon. They say when Lance became weary of Dionne's controlling obsessive behavior and had planned to end their fling, Dionne became furious. They say she was so enraged with being let go that she bludgeoned Lance to death with a wrench as he was dosing off to sleep, probably right after having sex with her. They said she cleaned the crime scene, stole his laptop computer and one of his credit cards and charged a $3000 cabinet for her home. ATLANTA, GA, 1996

• **Paula Bode** – devastated over the breakup with her child's father, shot and killed their 5-year-old daughter, then committed suicide. DENVER, CO 1999

• **Gavin Pellew** – told cops about his wife, "She got me crazy." In a jealous rage he stabbed her in the chest. She fell from the car and while people watched in horror, he beat her and stabbed her twice more before fleeing the scene. BROOKLYN, NY 2003

In each of these incidents, the common denominator that brought about the pain and tragedy was a person who yielded themselves to ungodly behaviors. As you have read, these individuals displayed everything from fits of rage, jealousy, temper tantrums, fornication, adultery, hatred and drunkenness... to bad feelings which ended in physical violence against the person they claimed to love.

With some individuals you will detect or observe a tendency to have yelling and screaming matches, heated fights and inflamed arguments. Those ungodly behaviors are part of their persona. They thrive on that type of drama, bedlam, and chaos. Here is the list of the ten most destructive personality traits:

• Men Meandering Manhood
• Individuals Suffering From Depression
• People Who Threatened or Attempted Suicide
• Mental Illness/Psychiatric Issues
• Angry/Temperamental Men and Women

• Contentious Women
• Alcohol or Drug Addictions
• Abusers - Male or Female
• Pornography Addictions
• Jealous Men and Women

When you see any of these traits in your boyfriend, girlfriend, fiancé, fiancée or potential mate, make no mistake about it, they have thrust you into the relationship danger zone. Read how God commands us to deal with these destructive personalities:

Proverbs 22:24-25 NIV [Emphasis added]
²⁴ DO NOT make friends with a hot-tempered man, [*or woman*]
DO NOT associate with one easily angered,
²⁵ OR YOU MAY LEARN HIS WAYS and get yourself ensnared.

Proverbs 29:22 NIV [Emphasis added]
AN ANGRY MAN [*or woman*] stirs up dissension, and a HOT-TEMPERED one commits many sins.

Proverbs 14:17 NIV [Emphasis added]
A QUICK-TEMPERED MAN [*or woman*] does foolish things..."

Proverbs 14:7 NIV [Emphasis added]
STAY AWAY FROM A FOOLISH MAN, [*or woman*]..."

Proverbs 21:19 NIV [Emphasis added]
BETTER TO LIVE IN A DESERT than with a QUARRELSOME
and ILL-TEMPERED wife.

Some relationship experts will advise you to go to counseling with your potential mate, to help them manage or control their temper tantrums, anger or poisonous personalities. But did you read how God ordered you to handle them? He commands you NOT to make friends with angry or hot tempered persons, because you may learn their ways.

We are further instructed to stay away from these men and women: **1). A GREEDY MAN brings TROUBLE to his FAMILY...**" See Proverbs 15:27 NIV [Emphasis added]. **2). WINE IS A MOCKER and BEER a brawler; WHOEVER is led astray by them IS NOT WISE.** See Proverbs 20:1 NIV [Emphasis added] **3). Like a gold ring in a pig's snout is a BEAUTIFUL WOMAN who shows no discretion.** See Proverbs 11:22 NIV [Emphasis added]. **4). LAZY HANDS MAKE A POOR MAN...**" See Proverbs 10:4 NIV [Emphasis added].

Is this sinking in yet? We are instructed to avoid greedy men, women with no discretion, sluggards and people who have been led astray by drugs and alcohol. Take note of this next critical insight.

Proverbs 22:3 NIV [Emphasis added]
A prudent man [*or woman*] sees **danger** and takes **refuge**, but the
SIMPLE KEEP GOING and SUFFER FOR IT.

When a person decides to continue in a relationship with an individual who has displayed ungodly behaviors or destructive personality traits, God classifies that person as being simple. Simple-minded men and women regularly ignore the commands to *stay away from* and *do not make friends with*. Like the Scripture says, the simple see the danger signs but choose to proceed in the relationship anyway.

Because of their decision to stay, they or their family will most likely suffer hurt, harm or destruction. To understand why they stay, you must understand what it means to be simple. To be simple-minded means: **1). to make silly decisions, 2). to subject oneself to exploitation, corruption or cruel treatment, 3). to be easily enticed, seduced, flattered, persuaded or deceived, 4). to be gullible, naive or immature, and 5). to lack the fortitude necessary to make critical life saving decisions or judgments.** As far as God is concerned being simple-minded, naive or gullible is totally unacceptable.

He requires you to be prudent. He demands that you make a quality decision concerning the person with whom you fall in love. He expects you to carefully examine a potential mate's character and measure their morals and values or lack thereof. He expects you to examine and know their background and past history.

Proverbs 14:15 [Emphasis added]
THE SIMPLE BELIEVETH EVERY WORD: but THE PRUDENT *man* [*or woman*] looketh well to his [*or her*] going.

A prudent person looks well into their goings. Being prudent is the exact opposite of being simple-minded. A prudent person exercises good judgment and common sense. They are not easily seduced, enticed, flattered, persuaded or deceived into relationships. They do not subject themselves to exploitation or ill-treatment.

They do not make bad decisions like marrying a man who grabbed or punched them or marrying a woman who has threatened them. They do not gamble with their life by continuing to date or court an individual who has temper tantrums or who is prone to violence, suicide, homicide or depression. They do not take chances with men and women who are law breakers or who are caught up in the penal system. When it comes to falling in love, they follow these instructions...

Proverbs 12:26 NIV [Emphasis added]
A RIGHTEOUS MAN [*or woman*] IS CAUTIOUS IN FRIENDSHIP, but the way of the wicked leads them astray.

Proverbs 13:16 [Emphasis added]
Every prudent *man* dealeth with knowledge..."

A prudent person understands that our society is filled with smooth operating relationship assassins and marriage missiles who are on the prowl and will ruin your life at the drop of a dime. That is why they obey the Word of God and enter into a relationship with caution.

They ask the tough and uncomfortable questions and they do not avoid or beat around the bush concerning critical issues relating to their safety, sanity, or peace of mind. They do not squint their eyes at discrepancies. They seek out the facts. They check out and confirm things. They make sure things add up.

Remember the victims of SaintCalle? Had any of those women understood these rules and irrefutable laws and (*tested, examined and discerned*) his spirit, SaintCalle's abusive history would have been revealed. They would have seen that his relationship resumé was red-flagged with brightly lit, danger signs.

When you meet a potential mate, you need to immediately think in terms of, "What does this person's relationship resumé look like?" When a person applies for a job they usually start the process by sending the employer a resumé. A resumé is a brief account of a person's work history, professional experience and qualifications. Every individual has a relationship resume.

The Red Flagged Relationship Resumé

Some relationship resumés are replete with red flags and brightly lit warning signs that read, **STOP! Danger ahead - DO NOT ENTER.** Proceeding into a relationship or marriage with this person is dangerous for your emotions, physical health, financial outlook, well-being and your sanity. **Warning! Proceed no further! Turn around now!**

People who ignore relationship resumé red flags pay a dear price. Some will lose their life or subject their family members to physical harm. Rarely does a person to ignore this next set of *Booby Trap Acid Tests* and come out of the relationship or marriage unscathed.

You perform this next set of *Booby Trap Acid Tests* before becoming emotionally attached, before saying, "I love you," or before making any type of verbal commitment. If you wait until after the fact to detect these relationship resumé red flags, you may have waited too late.

1). Does my potential mate currently have or previously had a restraining order or a stay away order filed against them? - If your answer is "yes," accept the fact that you are walking on thin ice. Has your potential mate somehow convinced you to proceed forward in the relationship in spite of their past or present abusive or violent tendencies? You need to follow the same instructions I am going to give you when your potential mate has been arrested or convicted of domestic violence, domestic stalking, kidnapping or harassment.

2). Has my potential mate been arrested or convicted of domestic violence? Domestic stalking, kidnapping or harassment? - If the answer is "yes," you need to terminate that relationship immediately. If your potential mate says they didn't do it, and you think they may be telling the truth, you have a serious judgment call to make. To do so you need to follow these instructions to the letter: (a) *read the actual warrant or arrest report, (b) talk to the arresting officer, the detective, the District Attorney, and the victim, (c) if they were convicted, also read that report along with the victim's impact statement, and (d) immediately notify those who truly love you and sincerely care about you to get their input about the red flag on your potential mate's relationship resumé. *(To find out how to obtain that information see the resources guide).*

If you are not willing to take all of those crucial steps before committing yourself to such a person, you are being simple-minded.

3). Has my potential mate had to file a restraining order? - If the answer is "yes," you need the actual details. Has their *ex* threatened bodily harm? Has your potential mate's *ex* intimidated, brow beaten, coerced or warned them not to leave? Have they made death threats, harassed, stalked, mentioned suicide, or otherwise indicated they were not going to let their *ex* walk out of their life? If so, take those threats seriously.

Your potential mate has a ticking time-bomb on their hands and you could be jeopardizing your own physical safety by continuing in a relationship with this person. The graves are filled with men and women who were gunned down, stabbed, ambushed or attacked by a disgruntled *ex*. This is not a game and you are not a super hero. If you decide to proceed in this relationship, understand the risks. You are subjecting yourself to a possible domestic related ambush or attack.

4). Does my potential mate have a criminal record? - When a person has a criminal record they now have a long list of very serious disadvantages you or they cannot ignore. For the most part, they are rejected by society. In some circles, they are classified as sub-human.

Their criminal record prevents them from applying for certain jobs or getting certain licenses. Depending on the crime they committed, the law can forbid them from being around certain people without court appointed supervision.

When they do apply for a job and their criminal record pops up, some employers will treat them as if they were an accomplice to the serial killer, Ted Bundy. They also lose the right to vote. There are other considerations such as recidivism. Recidivism means to fall back into or relapse into prior criminal habits, especially after conviction and punishment. Any person who studies or tracks people convicted of crimes will tell you that the recidivism rate is around seventy percent.

That means more than half the men and women who become incarcerated will eventually return to jail or prison. When a potential mate has a criminal record, you cannot ignore or take that issue lightly.

5). Has my potential mate served time in prison or in jail? - If your potential mate has been imprisoned, you need to know the cold hard brutal facts about their time of incarceration. Behind those concrete walls, barbed wire razor fences, and steel bars is a world that can only be described as depraved. The term "hardened criminal" exists for a reason. Once a person is thrust into the penal system, they enter a lewd, emotionless, conscienceless, dysfunctional and predatorial culture. Incarceration literally forces each inmate to torch their moral compasses, deaden their emotions and numb their consciences in order to survive.

What I am presenting about the prison culture refers to the men's jails and prisons. My information stems from my experiences in ministering to inmates and from the many jailers and officers that I know. I cannot speak on the condition of women's jails or prisons because of my current lack of knowledge on the subject. If a female has been incarcerated, you must use heightened caution as well.

The men are faced with witnessing other inmates getting beaten, assaulted or raped on a daily basis. They see men engage in lewd sexual acts with and against one another. They observe men lose their minds as they spend years cramped in cells with rapists, murderers, serial killers, pedophiles, armed robbers, kidnappers and other unrepentant violent men. When an inmate *re-enters* society, many of them have either become: (a) **institutionalized** - meaning they no longer have the capacity to function on their own, (*They need someone to tell them when and what to eat, when to get up and what to wear*), (b) **a hardened criminal** - meaning that the habitual exposure to that obscene culture has made them incapable of functioning as an honorable law abiding citizen, or (c) **psychologically, physically, emotionally or mentally marred.**

Certain prisoners are targeted for exploitation the moment they enter a penal facility. Their age, looks, size, lack of physical strength, lack of a gang affiliation, nonaggressive behavior and other characteristics marks them as prime candidates for sexual, physical and mental abuse. This abuse leaves them physically, mentally and emotionally scarred for life. Here is a sampling of the lifestyle and language the men must adapt to while incarcerated.

Catch A Square = you better get ready to fight
Catcher = a sexually passive or submissive inmate victimized by other inmates
Chin Check = To hit someone in the jaw to see if he will stand up for himself
Dressed Out = To be assaulted with urine, feces or some other liquid mixture
Getting Rec = attacking or harming someone for no reason
Pruno = a potent fermented concoction made by inmates to get or stay intoxicated
Shank = a homemade knife used to attack guards and other inmates
Stay Down = to engage in a fight to prove one's manhood

If your potential mate has been incarcerated, it is virtually impossible for them to have escaped that depraved world while behind bars. Do not ignore that fact. The majority of men and women who leave the penal system, exit with some type of psychological, mental, physical, sexual or emotional damage. But remember, the penal system culture has trained them to deaden their emotions and hide the damage.

6). Is my potential mate on parole or probation? - If so, the same rules apply for those who have been incarcerated or who have a criminal record.

7). Does my potential mate have any warrants for their arrest? Are they under investigation by the police, DEA, ATF, FBI, FTC, CIA, IRS, INS, USPI or any other law enforcement agency? - You need to know that some smooth operators enter into marriages and romantic relationships knowing they are about to be arrested or incarcerated. They have destroyed all of their relationships with loved ones, so they target someone simple-minded enough to fall in love with them. They exploit their new found love or newly christened spouse, using them as a false alibi, to post bail, to evade authorities, to provide transportation, to send them money while incarcerated, to provide a place to stay, or to receive conjugal visits.

8). Has my potential mate brandished any of these ungodly behaviors or displayed any of these destructive personality traits?

• Depression	• Gambling Addiction	• Temper Tantrums
• Suicidal	• Alcoholic Addiction	• Psychiatric Issues
• Jealousy	• Drug Addiction	• Hatefulness
• Mental Illness	• Pornographic Addiction	• Abusive/Contentious
• Food Addiction	• Foul Mouthed, Curser	• Lazy-Sluggard
• Liar/Deceiver/Con	• Spirit Of Control	• Fits of Rage
• Self-Destructive	• Perpetual Victim Mentality	• Verbal Abuser
• Short Fuse	• Disrespects Authority	• Magnet For Trouble

9). Does my potential mate use aliases or has my potential mate had their name changed? - Relationship assassins and marriage missiles use the subterfuge of multiple aliases and a mixture of legal or illegal name changes to hide their true identity and to cover their tracks. If they have changed their name, why did they? Are they trying to evade authorities? Are they avoiding bill collectors? Name changes and aliases on a person's relationship resumé is a glaring red flag.

Do they switch their first name with their middle name? Does she use an assortment of maiden or married names? Red flag them! Do not allow yourself to be lured into a relationship with a person you know by their nickname, street name, alias, pseudo name or "everybody calls me," name. You need to know their legal birth name, the one on their birth certificate, the one attached to their legal social security number. No other name will suffice! If they cannot provide that, you need to make a rapid exit from that person's presence.

Remember - it is your responsibility to know the difference between godly and ungodly behaviors, to detect relationship resumé red flags and to weed-out potential mates who have destructive personalities. Here is your critical *Booby Trap Acid Test*...

Have You Ignored Any Ungodly Behaviors Or Turned Your Head Away From Any Destructive Personality Traits

10

True Love, Tru Luv, or True Lust?

"...I love you!" "I love you to..." Those words combined are probably the most heart touching words in any language. To hear someone say, "I love you," can be an awesome experience, one that affects you to the very core of your being. What is *True Love*? How do we define it? How do we measure it? Who sets the standard for it? Without knowing the answers to those vital questions you become a prime target for fakes, liars, cheaters, users and abusers. When a person says to you, "I love you!," or you decide to express your heartfelt love to someone, if you do not know what *True Love* is, you may end up making one of the worst mistakes of your entire life. Those three words grouped together have changed the course of the lives of multitudes.

If you asked the average couple, "Why are you dating? Why are you living together? Why did you get married?" The majority of them will usually respond by saying, "Because we love each other." But with over half of all marriages ending in divorce and with one in four dating relationships involving some type of abuse, it is obvious most men and women do not know nor understand what "*True Love*" is.

We will be answering the following questions, "What is *True Love*? How do you measure *True Love*? How can you know when you have *True Love*? Who sets the standards and guidelines for *True Love*?" Let's examine how the majority of men and women learn about love. Here's a comprehensive list. Check all the ones that apply to you:

[] *By going to the movies*	[] *Rap/rock/country/R&B music or videos*
[] *By listening to love songs*	[] *From television, radio or other media*
[] *From high school class mates*	[] *From reading various magazines*
[] *From sexual experiences*	[] *By making up your own rules about love*
[] *By talking to parent(s), family, friends*	[] *From conferences and seminars on love*
[] *By watching other couples*	[] *From pornographic magazines, movies...*
[] *By marriage, living together or dating*	[] *By attending parties, clubs, bars...*
[] *From psychics, tarot cards, black magic...*	[] *From astrology, zodiac signs, horoscopes...*
[] *Watching soap operas, love stories...*	[] *While living in a college dormitory*
[] *Psychology, therapy, symposiums...*	[] *While incarcerated*
[] *From romance novels, fiction books...*	[] *By daydreaming, fantasizing*
[] *Various websites, chat rooms...*	[] *From relationship experts*
[] *Other_____*	[] *I never learned about true love*

After going through one or more of those training venues, pay close attention to what people say, believe and feel about the subject:

- Love will make you do wrong
- Love is blind
- Love is hard to define
- True love makes your life stressful
- Love is sooo confusing
- Arguments, fights... are all part of love
- Love makes you do crazy things
- More than anything, love is a gamble
- "If I can't have her, nobody can," is the strongest kind of love a man can have
- Love doesn't mean you have to be committed to just one person!
- True love is when your emotions are under the control of the person you adore
- When you harm or hurt a person but they stay with you anyway; that's true love
- Love is that indescribable feeling that eventually fades
- Love is whatever two people who believe they are in love "agree on"
- True love is when you place your happiness in the happiness of another
- The truth is, I only say, "I love you," because that's what "women" want to hear
- When you feel there's no reason to live unless you have that person, that's love
- Love is painful; I have felt it's pain and my heart is forever scarred
- Love is that feeling aroused by a magnetic animal kind of attraction
- When you really love a person, how they behave or treat you doesn't matter
- True love makes you angry... it makes you lose your control and composure
- Love is different for everyone and no one can tell you what love is to you
- It's that awesome feeling two people experience when they share ...sexual love
- True love is when nothing they say or do irritates or bothers you
- When you think about a person every second of every day, that's true love
- Love is a game people play, sometimes you win and sometimes you lose
- Love comes and goes... it's fleeting... no marriage was meant to last forever
- When I give myself to a man sexually, that is the purest highest kind of love
- Love is when you eat the same foods, like the same people, places and things
- Love is when you are prepared to die rather than for her to be with anyone else
- True love is that warm embrace and gentle kiss that leaves your knees buckling
- Love can mean one thing but then it can mean something completely different
- It's not true love until you are willing to cross the line for the person you adore
- True love is when you can't stand the thought of them being with anyone else
- Cheating greatly intensifies the love you have for the person you cherish
- Love can be as sweet as honey or as bitter as horseradish
- True love is when you break up with a person but you keep getting back together
- Love is when you sigh each and every time you look at his/her picture
- When a person does something illegal but you stay by their side, that's real love
- When you don't know why you love them, that's true love
- You can only define love through your own experiences, whether good or bad
- I can't explain it; I "fall in love" and after a while, I "fall out of love." It's weird?
- True love is when, 'if we can't be together, then we will die together...'
- I provide for her and she obeys me and does what I say, that's true love

The average individual has his or her own interpretation of what they think love is. **Real love is when, 'if we can't be together, then we will die together...'** Did you read this one, **Love is when a person controls your emotion?** Where did they get such outlandish beliefs? Some by devouring romance novels, watching soap operas, love stories, television shows and movies, and by adoring songs filled with warped psychologically damaging lyrics. These varying sources helped them form unhealthy views about love. Some follow the advice of self described relationship experts who have repeatedly failed at love and marriage. Still others take on the beliefs of their *mis*-informed parents or scripturally illiterate ministers.

Whatever method they use to find out about love, one thing is crystal clear; their beliefs are dead wrong! When they say, "I love you," it could mean a variety of things. As you have read, some of it is down right evil. Take the case of Gregory Ware, (*real name*). In April 2003 in Augusta, Georgia, while Deputy Jason Rogers, (*real name*) was responding to a domestic call, he heard a woman's cry for help. After he kicked in the door, he found Gregory sitting on top of a woman with a box cutter in his right hand.

The woman was bleeding from the neck. Deputy Rogers drew his gun and ordered Mr. Ware to stop the attack. Gregory's *ex*-girlfriend was probably seconds away from death. At the hospital she gave this chilling account of the attack.

"I arrived at my apartment and realized my ex-boyfriend was hiding behind the door. I tried to run back outside, but he caught me and dragged me inside by my hair. He threw me down on the living room floor and got on top of me. He said he was going to kill me. He said if he couldn't have me, no one would. He told me to say my prayers. He began cutting my neck with the box cutter, slicing me four times as I jerked my neck to avoid the blade. I screamed frantically..."

Now read the disturbing note found at the crime scene police say was handwritten by Mr. Ware:

"To Whom It May Concern:
"Today is the day I made the gravest decision of my life.
"Today is the day that I will kill my would-be wife.
"Sad and tragic, yes this is true.
"But you don't know me and I don't know you."

Get this point drilled into your mind; the people who harbor these bizarre brands of love in their hearts are not a small minority. Ladies, you need to know - there are multitudes of men who believe in this satanically inspired fatalistic brand of love. In this brand of love, the rule is to completely control and thoroughly dominate a woman.

She becomes a man's possession. She does what he says and goes where he tells her to go; she eats when he tells her to eat and wears what he tells her to wear. When she cannot take it anymore and tries to leave his dictatorship, he has been trained to murder her and then take his life. I wish that I did not have to be the bearer of bad news.

However, if a women gets booby trapped into a relationship or marriage by one of these human torpedoes, she will either end up dead or he will attempt to kill her. This happens more often than you have been led to believe. Read these police blotters, (*all real names*).

- **Brett L. Studdard** tracked his ex-girlfriend down, shot her in the back, killing her and then committed suicide. ROSWELL, GA, October 2003
- **Gary Clugston** fired ten rounds into his wife with an AK-47 assault rifle, then shot himself in the head. CHESTNUT RIDGE, NY, January 2003
- **Purnell Rick Cauley** was having an affair... when his wife and mistress decided they had had enough, he wrote a suicide letter, killed them both, murdered his three children, then committed suicide. HOUSTON, TX, February 2003
- **Alan Booker** killed his wife and himself in broad daylight, right after she dropped their child off to the doctor's office. STONE MOUNTAIN, GA, January 2003
- **Albert Guardo** ended his seven year relationship by strangling his girlfriend then committing suicide. BALTIMORE, MD, May 2003
- **Tom Newell** shot his wife, then killed himself, they had a history of marital discord. HOMOSASSA, FL, May 2003
- **Anthony Ferrara** attacked his ex-girlfriend's mother, then killed himself; Burlington. NJ, March 2003
- **Clarence Shumate** shot his long time live-in girlfriend then killed himself. AUGUSTA, GA , May 2003
- **Barry L. Tkachik** shot his wife and her sister before killing himself. OTIS, IN, February 2003
- **Daniel Jantzen** murdered his ex-girlfriend, her daughter, and her daughter's male companion. VALLEY CITY, ND, April 2003
- **Pastor Mike Tabb** brutally beat his wife to death then attempted to commit suicide the day he was due in court to plead guilty. TYLER, TX, May 2003

These are just a few of the bizarre love murder-suicides that took place between January and October of 2003. There were many more. Let's get one thing clear. There are certain issues in life you simply cannot debate or argue and win. For instance, who founded the Microsoft Corporation? When the light on a traffic signal is red, what does the law require you to do? Can goldfish live outside of water?

Concerning the answers to those questions, everyone comes to the same conclusions. Before we proceed any further, we must come to some irrefutable conclusions about love. First of all, no man or woman created love. Secondly, since we did not create love, we are not qualified to set our own standards as to what love is and what love is not. Thirdly, if a person sincerely wants to know and understand what love is, they must ask the inventor of love.

No sane owner of a $780,000 dollar custom Bentley Azure, calls a Chevrolet dealer to inquire about their automobile. If they want a proper diagnosis they call Bentley. Since we need to know what *True Love* is, it is imperative that we shun and reject the advice, opinions, beliefs and theories of all others and consult with the Creator of love. Here is where love was conceived: I John 4:7 [Emphasis added] Beloved, let us love one another: FOR LOVE IS OF GOD..." Get that point settled in your mind and heart. Love originated with God. He is the inventor and creator of love. Read the Scripture again! Love did not start with relationship experts, romance novelists, therapists, or psychologists.

Love was not invented by people with Ph.D.'s, MA's, M.Ed.'s or L.P.C.'s. Love started with God. He alone created love, defined love and set its boundaries. The second sequence of events concerning love is when love flowed from the heart of God to the heart of mankind: I John 4:19 [Emphasis added] We love him, BECAUSE HE FIRST LOVED US.

Focus your attention on the word "first." He loved us first. After God created love, He took the initiative and bestowed His tender love upon us. Read what He commanded us to do with our new found love.

> John 15:9, 12 [Emphasis added]
> ⁹ AS THE FATHER HATH LOVED ME, SO HAVE I LOVED YOU:
> continue ye in my love.
> ¹² This is my commandment, THAT YE LOVE ONE ANOTHER,
> AS I HAVE LOVED YOU.

We are commanded to love one another in the exact same manner in which God loved Christ and Christ loved us, and to continue in that love. Those two commands present us with a vital requirement. Before you can truly love anyone or vice versa, you both must know how the Father loved His Son and how His Son loves us. Here is how God planned for us to find out about *True Love*.

> I Thessalonians 4:9 NIV [Emphasis added]
> Now about brotherly love we do not need to write to you, for you yourselves have been TAUGHT BY GOD TO LOVE EACH OTHER.

Until a man or woman has been taught to love by God, it is not possible for them to know what *True Love* is. If you fall for a person who is loving you with a brand of love other than the love of God, you are taking a tremendous chance. This may seem like a basic question but, some people might not know the answer. "How is God going to teach us how to love?" Is an angel going to pull us to the side and talk to us? Are we going to hear a voice from heaven? Is God going to appear to us in a vision or a dream? The next question is, "What exactly is He going to teach us?" How to pick up women? The rules of flirting? The art of seduction? Dating tricks that work? I am not trying to be comical. He said He would teach us how to love one another.

When it comes to falling in love, sex, relationships and marriage, we need to know two things: **1)**. What God is going to teach us, and **2)**. How He is going to teach it to us. If you found out about love by any other means except what you are about to learn from God, you are probably one of the millions of men and women who have falsely convinced themselves into believing they know what *True Love* is.

You just read God's foolproof plan of how to learn about love. There is no other way to fully understand or comprehend *True Love* except through God. My assignment is to open up the Scriptures to you, so that you will be able to discern, express and receive *True Love* and reject all substitutes and counterfeits. If a potential mate is not going to love you with the love of God, they need to be gone! You cannot afford to have them in your life. By the time you are through with this chapter, you will know beyond a shadow of a doubt what *True Love* is.

The Four Facets of True Love

The first thing you need to understand about *True Love* is that it is made up of four facets. To help you understand these four facets, I need to give you a brief course on diamonds. In the diamond industry, a diamond's value is measured by what is called the Four *"C's."* **Cut, Clarity, Carat** and **Color**. Every skilled jeweler and diamond expert uses the four C's to establish the value of a diamond. The "C" that we want to focus our attention on is the **Cut**. A skilled jeweler takes a rough uncut diamond with its blemished and unpolished surface and by *cutting* it, transforms it into a radiant breathtaking masterpiece.

A diamond with a good **Cut** *will* speak to you! It will be bright, fiery, symmetrical and it will glisten in the light. Each **Cut** produces a flat polished surface called a facet. The facets reflect the light and cause a diamond to have its brilliant sparkle. Left uncut and unpolished, a diamond cannot reflect light. It has no sparkle. You could not even tell it was a diamond. What about you? As a potential mate are you a diamond in the rough, one that has no sparkle, are you uncut, unpolished, or are you cut and polished and able to discern and radiate all four facets of *True Love*? What about your potential mate?

Before you can answer those questions, you must first discover what *True Love* is. You must first see what the Scriptures say about you being properly cut and polished and reflecting all four facets of *True Love*. Here is what you need to know before we start the cutting process. The Written Word of God is the razor sharp cutting instrument, (See Hebrews 4:12). The Holy Spirit is the polishing cloth, (See I Corinthians 2:13) and I am like the jeweler, the Lord has sent me with the Sword of the Spirit to cut away your rough parts and places, and to see to it that you are properly polished, (See Ephesians 4:11-16) so that all of your *facets* are reflecting and radiating *True Love* from the light of God's Word, (SeeMatthew 5:14-16 and Ephesians 5:8).

When you are properly cut and smoothly polished, here is what your completed four facets of *True Love* will look like. The foundational facet of *True love* is **Agape love**. The second facet is **Phileo love**. The third facet is **Storge love** and the forth and final facet is **Eros love**.

Eros love is the physical attraction and sexual love

Sadly, most people get involved in relationships or get married based solely on **Eros** love, the physical attraction and sexual love, but **Eros** love is only one facet of *True Love*. As you are going to find out, if you have **Eros** love without the other three facets of *True Love*, your relationship is completely worthless.

In the jewelry industry, some companies sell costume, imitation, fake and counterfeit diamonds. On the surface, these man-made stones look like the real thing but they have numerous flaws. **1)**. They are worthless! You can purchase a 5.5 carat Cubic Zirconia Solitaire for a measly fifteen dollars. **2)**. Eventually, imitation diamonds get cloudy and they discolor. **3)**. Common things such as rain, faucet water and household products like dishwashing liquids that cannot harm real diamonds will destroy imitation diamonds. **4)**. Fake diamonds cannot reflect light like real diamonds. Relationships that do not reflect all four facets of *True Love* are just like imitation diamonds.

They cannot stand up to the common pressures of life so they eventually corrode. I want to remind you of our present objective. We are in the process of defining what *True Love* is. I am going to start with **Eros** love and work my way up to **Agape** love. We can find **Eros** love throughout the Scriptures.

Solomon 1:2
Let him kiss me with the kisses of his mouth: for thy love *is* better than wine.

Proverbs 5:19
Let her be as the loving hind and pleasant roe; let her breasts satisfy thee at all times; and be thou ravished always with her love.

Proverbs 7:18 NIV
Come, let's drink deep of love till morning; let's enjoy ourselves with love!

These are all descriptions of *Eros* love, the physical attraction and sexual love, (See also Genesis 4:1 and Song of Solomon 5:10-16). Write this next statement down and do not ever forget it. A person can have *Eros* love towards you and not love you with *True Love*. A classic example of this critical point is the *Eros* love Shechem expressed towards Dinah.

> Genesis 34:2-4 [Emphasis added]
> ² And when Shechem the son of Hamor the Hivite, prince of the country, SAW HER, HE TOOK HER, AND LAY WITH HER, AND DEFILED HER.
> ³ And his soul clave unto Dinah the daughter of Jacob, AND HE LOVED THE DAMSEL, AND SPAKE KINDLY UNTO THE DAMSEL.
> ⁴ And Shechem spake unto his father Hamor, saying, Get me this damsel to wife.

On the surface Shechem's love toward Dinah seemed passionately heart warming, but this wasn't *True Love* because the other three facets of love were missing. When Shechem saw Dinah, the only thing stirred up in his loins was *Eros* love. His sole motivation was to accomplish one goal: get into Dinah's panties by any means necessary!

The fact that he wanted to marry her after having sex, is a moot and irrevelant point. Just because two people have great sex does not guarantee that if they marry, their marriage is going to be great. I consistently meet men and women who married a person because they were excited about being sexually compatible. They did just like Shechem, they confused *Eros* love with *True Love*. After the wedding bells faded, these couples found out that the sex was great, but they were incompatible in just about every other area!

The fact of the matter is, Shechem was a smooth operator. Verse 3, states that he used "kindly" words. He used flattery and seduction to entice her. The vivacious and carefree Dinah probably figured that she had the catch of the century. Shechem was nobody's slob. He was the prince of an entire country, (See Genesis 34:2). AND! He was expressing tantalizing romantic overtures toward Dinah. How often does a woman get a prince to pursue her and sweep her off her feet?

All their relationship had to stand on was one thing. The *Eros* love they had was both earth shattering and knee buckling! Having sex with Dinah was so arousing that Shechem developed a severe case of the **urge to merge syndrome**. He was in so much sexual heat that he insisted on marrying her, (See Genesis 34:4). The average person looking at these chain of events, would pat him on his back for desiring to take Dinah's hand in matrimony. But Shechem's actions were not the acts of an honorable man. Did you pay close attention to Genesis 34:2?

Read it again. The Word of God says that Shechem **DEFILED** Dinah. Did you get that? It is no secret that in our modern day society many people think just like Shechem. They will be the first to tell you, they don't see anything wrong with a little bump-and-grind.

They will tell you no one has the right to judge them, and if God did not want them to enjoy casual or *pre*-marital sex, He would not have put a burning desire in their loins to get it on.

They will tell you that they have a right to express their sexual freedom and frankly, after they have had their fill of *Eros* love, God is not going to strike them with lightning. So what is the problem? To understand, you first have to read this warning:

> Hebrews 13:4 AMP [Emphasis added]
> LET MARRIAGE BE HELD IN HONOR (esteemed worthy, precious, of great price, and especially dear) in all things. And thus LET THE MARRIAGE BED BE UNDEFILED (kept undishonored); FOR GOD WILL JUDGE and punish the unchaste [all guilty of sexual vice] and adulterous.

God commands the marriage bed to be undefiled. To defile means to dishonor, to contaminate, to pollute, and to make unclean. When a man engages in *Eros* love with a woman who is not his wife, they have defiled each other. Even if they both happily consented to having sex with each other, they have dishonored themselves before God. That is why *Eros* love without the other three facets of love is so dangerous.

You need to know that *Eros* love, the physical attraction and sexual love, is *one of* the most beautiful experiences a man and a woman have together. *Eros* love is pure ecstasy on earth! *Eros* love is exhilarating, sexy, sensual, and romantic. BUT! Outside of the marriage covenant, *Eros* love becomes dirty and repulsive in the eyes of God. Read the admonition Solomon's bride gave to the daughters of Jerusalem.

> Solomon 3:5 NIV [Emphasis added]
> Daughters of Jerusalem, I charge you by the gazelles and by the does of the field: DO NOT AROUSE OR AWAKEN [Eros] LOVE UNTIL IT SO DESIRES.

Three times she pleaded with these women not to awaken or arouse *Eros* love until its proper time, (See Song of Solomon 2:7 and 8:4). If having *Eros* love will cause you to be defiled, it is never the proper time. Never awaken *Eros* love until the other three facets of *True Love* are in place and until you are in a marriage covenant.

Phileo love is the friendship love

Mere words crafted by the most prolific authors cannot completely define *Phileo* love, but we are not trusting in men. We are going to the source! You will come to understand and comprehend this awesome facet of *True Love. Phileo* love defines and sets the standard for true heartfelt friendship. I hate to be the bearer of bad news but the truth is, most couples have never experienced *Phileo* love. Why not?

They have never been taught what *Phileo* love is, or how to walk together in it. Now is a good time to put away all of the preconceived ideas you have about friendship and take an in-depth journey with me into *Phileo* love. This is guaranteed to change your heart forever. The Greek word *"Phileo"* means "I love."

The Phileo love between a husband and wife is the mysterious unseen glue that fuses the two together into a permanent bond

Phileo love describes a person who you know intimately, [*the type of intimacy that can only come through Phileo* love]. *Phileo* love describes a person whom you love dearly and trust completely. *Phileo* love means someone who is always mindful of you: a wellwisher, one whose friendly feelings toward you never wane, someone who shows you favor and who promotes you, a trusted and unwavering confidante, one who always bears good will towards you. *Phileo* love means the two of you are closer than close. *Phileo* love never ends up in the divorce court, separated or spewing bitterness, because *Phileo* love is never, ever hostile towards a friend. When a man or woman has engrafted *Phileo* love in their heart, it is impossible for them to ever be your foe or your enemy.

Phileo love has no capacity to hate, to display unfriendliness, opposition, nastiness or contrariness. *Phileo* love will never harm you or hurt you. Every day, multitudes of men and women file for divorce citing irreconcilable differences.

Phileo love is incapable of experiencing irreconcilable differences because *Phileo* love is a devoted friendship, a firm friendship, a tried friendship, a staunch friendship, an intimate friendship, a cordial friendship, a sincere friendship, a lasting friendship, a warm friendship, an ardent friendship, and a harmonious friendship. *Phileo* love is tenderhearted and warmhearted where you are concerned.

Phileo love means to be at home with, to be hand in glove, to be two peas in a pod, arm in arm, and hand in hand. It means to receive with open arms and gently embrace.

Phileo love means to be on good terms with, on friendly terms, on amicable terms, on good footing, on speaking terms and in one's good graces. *Phileo* love means you are your friend's companion and comrade and *Phileo* love implies absolute solidarity with your friend.

Phileo love is of God. The secret to engrafting *Phileo* love in your heart is revealed in the Scriptures. One must first be a friend of God before he or she can ever fully express *Phileo* love:

> James 2:23 AMP [Emphasis added]
> And [so] the Scripture was fulfilled that says, Abraham believed in (adhered to, trusted in, and relied on) God, and this was accounted to him as righteousness (as conformity to God's will in thought and deed), AND HE WAS CALLED GOD'S FRIEND.

Did you read that verse of Scripture? Think about this for a moment, suppose you were a close personal friend of Bill Gates? I mean close enough that you had his home phone number, address, personal e-mail, cellular phone number, and the two of you ate together often.

What if you had that type of friendship with the Sultan of Brunei or with Steve Jobs? Who are these men? They are some of the wealthiest men on earth. Can you imagine the benefits you would gain if any of these men esteemed you as one of their best friends? Abraham had a much better Friend!

He was in the glorious position to be called God's Friend. That meant that he was always on God's mind, (See Psalm 115:11-14). It meant the Lord always had Abraham's back, (See Hebrews 13:5-6). It meant that God was Abraham's very present help in the time of trouble, (See Psalm 91:14-15). When you become a friend of God's, He becomes your Healer, (See Exodus 15:26). He becomes your Provider, (See Genesis 22:14). He becomes your Wonderful Counsellor, your Mighty God, your Everlasting Father and your Prince of Peace, (See Isaiah 9:6).

You say, "But Brother Triplett, how can I experience becoming God's Friend?" To find out how, you need to read the requirements from life's easy to follow instructional manual.

> John 15:13-15 [Emphasis added]
> [13] Greater love hath no man than this, that a man lay down his life for his friends.
> [14] YE ARE MY FRIENDS, IF YOU DO WHATSOEVER I COMMAND YOU.
> [15] Henceforth I call you not servants; for servants knoweth not what his lord doeth: BUT I HAVE CALLED YOU FRIENDS; for all things that I have heard of my Father I have made known unto you.

In verse 14, Jesus reveals a simple but stunning truth. This truth has the capacity to transform your life forever but only if you fully yield to it, (See James 1:22-25). He declares that the way for you to become God's friend is by obeying His Word.

That is the only pathway to becoming His friend. A true friendship takes time to develop. Trust has to be formed. Sensitivity to one another has to be developed. Loyalty has to be firmly established. Respect has to be earned. Your friendship with the Father is no different, but once you commit yourself to obeying His Word, you get a Friend who will...

1). Love you at all times, (See Proverbs 17:17). **2).** Lay down His life for you, (See John 15:13). **3).** Speak to you forthright, (See Proverbs 27:6). **4)..** Confide in you face to face, (See Exodus 33:11). **5).** Be your Friend forever, (See II Chronicles 20:7). **6).** Never do you wrong, (See Matthew 20:13). **7).** Be there for you at all times, (See Luke 11:5-13). **8).** Sharpen you in every aspect of life, (See Proverbs 27:17) and, **9).** Stick closer to you than your natural family, (See Proverbs 18:24).

Only the *Phileo* love you experience through friendship with the Father can prepare you to express *Phileo* love to your mate. Men and women who have not developed a firm friendship with God will struggle with having a staunch, ardent, devoted, everlasting friendship with their mate. Without *Phileo* love, what you have is a superficial friendship.

Storge love is the affectionate love

There is a difference between loving a person and being "in love." *Storge* love is the facet of *True love* that puts the "in love" in a relationship. Here's what the Word of God says about *Storge* love.

Romans 12:10 [Emphasis added]
BE KINDLY AFFECTIONED ONE TO ANOTHER with brotherly love; in honour preferring one another;

We are commanded to be kindly affectioned [*to have storge love*] one to another. This is not an option or a possible choice between two or three alternatives. This is a command that a friend of God and a good potential mate will always obey. When a bride and groom have submitted themselves to this command prior to their wedding day, the cankerworms of divorce, separation and hostility towards each other will never find a way to erode their marriage.

In most homes that have a modern heating and air conditioning system, the temperature is controlled by a thermostat. When the thermostat is S-E-T to the specified temperature, the heating system automatically comes on if the house drops below the S-E-T temperature. If the house rises above the S-E-T temperature, the air conditioning unit comes on. Just as you S-E-T a thermostat for a house, we are commanded to S-E-T our affections: Colossians 3:2 [Emphasis added] SET YOUR AFFECTION [*storge love*] on things above, not on things on the earth.

What is the temperature setting of *Storge* love? *Storge* love is S-E-T to be affectionate, (See Romans 12:10). *Storge* love never strays away from home, never commits adultery and never deceives. *Storge* love never abandons a spouse or children. *Storge* love will not slam the door on you, curse you out or slam the phone in your ears. *Storge* love will not slash your tires, scratch the paint on your car, stalk, harass or pressure you. *Storge* love will never do those things because *Storge* love is S-E-T to be sensitive to your feelings, (See Ephesians 4:32). *Storge* love is S-E-T to insure that you prosper, remain in health and are at peace, (See III John 2). *Storge* love is S-E-T to be fond of you, courteous towards you, and compassionate towards you, (See I Peter 3:8).

Storge love is S-E-T to have an intense yearning for you and to long to be with you, (See Romans 1:11 and Philippians 1:8). *Storge* love is S-E-T to cherish, protect, and nourish you, (See Ephesians 5:29). *Storge* love is S-E-T and has made you the apple of its eye, (See Zechariah 2:8).

Storge love is S-E-T to have a kindred spirit with you, to genuinely care about you and your interests and to be devoted to you, (See Philippians 2:20 in the Amplified Bible). *Storge* love is S-E-T to be pleasant and peaceful towards you, (See Proverbs 3:17). *Storge* love is S-E-T to express sentiment for you, to be pleased with and delighted in you. *Storge* love is S-E-T to smile upon you and show you favor, (See Esther 2:15). *Storge* love is S-E-T to send you a billet-doux and blow you a kiss. *Storge* love is S-E-T to be concerned for your welfare (See Genesis 43:27).

How does a man and woman find out about this kind of love? Remember our Scripture in I Thessalonians 4:9? They must be "...taught by God to love each other." No one can learn about *True Love* by happenstance or through osmosis. The only way to learn about *True Love* is by fully submitting yourself to the Word of God.

Agape love is the God kind of love

Agape love is the sole foundation of *True Love* and as you are going to learn, a relationship established upon *Agape* love cannot fail.

Song of Solomon 8:6-7 AMP [Emphasis added]
6 Set me like a seal upon your heart, like a seal upon your arm: for LOVE IS AS STRONG AS DEATH, jealousy is as hard and cruel as Sheol (the place of the dead). Its flashes are flashes of fire, a most vehement flame [the very flame of the Lord]! 7 MANY WATERS CANNOT QUENCH LOVE, NEITHER CAN FLOODS DROWN IT. If a man would OFFER ALL THE GOODS OF HIS HOUSE FOR LOVE, he would be utterly scorned and despised.

That passage of Scripture reveals five golden nuggets concerning **Agape** love. On the previous page, I said that **Agape** love is the sole foundation of *True Love*. Having said that, these five golden nuggets are the prefabrication of the foundation. They are the mortar, the rebarb, the fasteners, the structural support and the load bearing walls of **Agape** love. These five golden nuggets are what set **Agape** love apart from all of the wishy-washy and bizarre brands of love created by men.

1). Verse 6, **Agape love sets a seal upon your heart** - That word "seal" means a signet ring. In the western world most couples signify their marital union by wearing wedding rings. Some pay tens of thousands of dollars for these dazzling rings, yet they do not have the signet ring of **Agape** love for each other sealed upon their hearts. Inside this ring you will find the inscription: *"I will never leave you nor forsake you."*

2). Verse 6, **Agape love is stronger than death** - On Wednesday, June 29, 1983, Joe Delaney (*real name*) was enjoying a quiet afternoon at Chennault Park in Monroe, Louisiana, when he heard cries for help.

Three boys were drowning in a nearby lake. Even though he could not swim, without hesitation or reservation, Mr. Delaney jumped into the lake to attempt to rescue the boys. He managed to pull one boy from the rough waters to safety. He returned to the lake for the other two boys, but was unable to save them. In the process, Joe Delaney drowned. He sacrificed his life for the lives of three boys he had never met. Joe demonstrated the power of **Agape** love.

Death is a powerful force, but **Agape** love is much greater. To save mankind, Jesus had to make a solemn decision: face death or you and I would die in our sins. His **Agape** love for us propelled him to choose to face death so that we may live. Of His heroic act, these words are recorded in John 15:13, Greater love hath no man than this, that a man lay down his life for his friends. **Agape** love will lay down its life for you.

3). Verse 7, **Many waters cannot quench Agape love** - The right amount of water can put out any fire but many waters cannot quench the fire of **Agape** love. **Agape** love is quenchless and indestructible. **Agape** love cannot be put out or torn asunder... it never grows cold, wanes or dies.

4). Verse 7, **Floods cannot overcome Agape love** - In 2002, heavy rains across Central and Eastern Europe caused catastrophic flooding conditions that ravaged historic city centres in Germany and the Czech Republic. In 1999, Mexico experienced flooding which President Ernesto Zedillo classified as the country's worst disaster of the decade. Entire towns were buried in mud. Floods are a powerful and destructive force. They can destroy everything in their path. As powerful as floods are, their strength is no comparison to the strength of **Agape** love. The Scripture reveals: "...neither can floods drown it [**Agape** love]..."

5) Verse 7. *Money cannot buy Agape love* - It is one thing to learn about *Agape* love by reading about it. It is a completely different thing to actually love someone, or to be loved by someone with this level of passion and power. What causes a man to want to love a woman with such esprit, commitment, and affection that her knees melt and her heart flutters just thinking about his *Agape* love? What inspires a woman to want to love a man with such kindness and devotion that he safely trusts her with all of his heart? The Word of God reveals there is only one way for a man or woman to get *Agape* love infused into their heart.

> Romans 5:5 NIV [Emphasis added]
> And hope does not disappoint us, BECAUSE GOD HAS POURED OUT HIS [*Agape*] LOVE INTO OUR HEARTS BY THE HOLY SPIRIT, whom He has given us.

God has to pour or infuse His *Agape* love into a person's heart by the Holy Spirit through the new birth, (See Ezekiel 11:19-20). Until that transaction takes place in a person's heart, they are not capable of loving you with *Agape* love. *Agape* love cannot be bought with roses, perfume, candlelight dinners, candy, expensive gifts, Valentine cards or romantic getaways. *Agape* love cannot be purchased with $60,000 wedding ceremonies, diamond rings or luxurious honeymoons. Do not misunderstand me, those things are nice if a person can afford them, but they are not a confirmation or a validation of *Agape* love.

A relationship between a man and woman can only be certified as *True Love* when all four facets of God's love, *Agape*, *Phileo*, *Storge* and *Eros* love are reflected in their relationship. In certain areas, when a builder builds a foundation he has to include earthquake foundation reinforcement, termite protection, waterproofing sealants, and mildew control protectants. These following attributes of *Agape* love are the waterproofing, termite protection and earthquake reinforcement. They are what make *Agape* love so indestructible.

> I Corinthians 13:4-8 NIV [Emphasis added]
> [4] Love is patient, love is kind. It does not envy, it does not boast, it is not proud.
> [5] It is not rude, it is not self-seeking, it is not easily angered, it keeps no record of wrongs.
> [6] Love does not delight in evil but rejoices with the truth.
> [7] It always protects, always trusts, always hopes, always perseveres.
> [8] Love never fails...

Paul by the Holy Spirit lists sixteen powerful chemical ingredients and support beams infused into *Agape* love. Let's review each of them:

1. **Agape love is patient** - It calmly deals with life's challenges and situations without acting hastily, rashly or impulsively. It stays cool under stress and pressure. It undergoes tests, trials, and temptations without murmuring, complaining, or being fretful.

2. **Agape love is kind** - It is friendly, generous, and warmhearted. It shows sympathy and displays understanding. It is agreeable, considerate, and forbearing.

3. **Agape love does not envy** - To envy means to be jealous. To have a jealous spirit. It means to begrudge or to show malice or ill-will towards someone because of their good fortune or success. It means to strongly desire or covet something or someone to whom you have no right. (*like someone's spouse, fiancé, fiancée, car, house, job, etc.*)

4. **Agape love does not boast** - To boast means to glorify oneself in speech. To talk about yourself in a self-admiring way, leaning towards being narcissistic. Agape love demonstrates humility with no airs, no trumpets, and no ticker-tape parades.

5. **Agape love is not proud** - To be proud means to have an inflated ego. It means to have a disdain for others because you consider them inferior. To be proud means to be arrogant and conceited. It means to have an inordinate self-esteem.

6. **Agape love is not rude** - To be rude means to be abrupt with, to snap at, and to be impolite. It means to be ill-mannered, snobbish and discourteous. It means to display socially improper behaviors like being unpleasantly forceful, curt, harsh and uncivil.

7. **Agape love is not self-seeking** - To be self-seeking means to make decisions without regarding or being concerned for others. It means to be interested only in oneself, to be self-absorbed. It means a person insists on having their perceived rights, and having their way to the detriment of the relationship, or to the hurt of others.

8. **Agape love is not easily angered** - To be easily angered means to be easily enticed, induced, roused or provoked to outbursts, anger, rage, fits of fury, wrath, indignation, malice, resentment or temper tantrums. It means to be easily irritated, infuriated or inflamed.

9. **Agape love keeps no record of wrongs** - To keep records of wrongs means to be reluctant, unable or refusing to forgive someone. It means to be unwilling or unable to show mercy. It means to hold resentment, grudges or hard feelings against others. Agape love is empowered and infused to forgive and move on.

10. **Agape love does not delight in evil** - To delight in evil means to seek revenge against, to get back at, to retaliate, to get even with, to be spiteful against, to hit back, to hope or wish pain, shame, loss, failure, hurt or embarrassment on someone.

11. **Agape love rejoices with the truth** - To rejoice with the truth means to receive satisfaction when justice, fairness, honesty, impartiality, and integrity prevail. Agape love takes no pleasure in sin or iniquity.

12. **Agape love always protects** - To protect means to cover or shield from danger, to defend, to guard and to preserve. It means to keep from being damaged. It means to defend from abuse, attacks, destruction, theft, loss, hurt, or injury. Agape love does not protect someone on a part time basis. Agape love protects all of the time. When a person has allowed God to pour His Agape love into their heart by the Holy Spirit, domestic violence will never be named among them because Agape love will NEVER hurt you.

13. **Agape love always trusts** - To trust means to place confidence in, to rely on, to confide and to put faith in. It means to give credence to and to believe in. This is not blind trust. This trust includes prudence, quality decision making, and good judgment. This trust is established over time. A person must earn this trust by proving they are trustworthy, reliable, dependable, and truthful. Liars, deceivers, defrauders, cheaters, users, misusers, abusers, exaggerators, and manipulators do not qualify to receive this type of trust.

14. **Agape love always hopes** - In Proverbs 13:12, in the Living Translation of the Bible, the Scripture reveals that: **Hope deferred makes the heart sick; but when dreams come true at last, there is life and joy.** There will be times in a relationship

when you will face insurmountable challenges. In the natural, there will be no hope. But there is a supernatural hope that only comes from standing on the promises of God and fervent prayer. Agape love, because it always hopes in that hope, always triumphs.

15. **Agape love always perseveres** - To persevere means to persist or remain constant to a purpose, idea, or task in the face of obstacles or discouragement. Agape love does not fluctuate. Agape love remains constant in all circumstances and situations. It is the wishy-washy love created by men that wanes, grows cold, and falls out of love.

16. **Agape love never fails** - To fail means to decline, as in strength or effectiveness, to cease functioning properly, to become bankrupt or insolvent, to deteriorate, to disappoint or prove undependable. It means to come to an end. Everyday we hear about couples breaking up, separating and divorcing, and after their relationships crumble, many of them claim how much they still love each other in spite of the breakup. They may love each other but their love is the flimsy man-made love that eventually fails. Their love was not the Agape love infused into a person's heart by the Holy Spirit. Agape love never ends. Agape love never fails. Agape love never comes to separation. Agape love never ends in divorce. Agape love never ceases to function properly because it is born of God.

Two things should be pretty obvious to you by now: **1)**. *True Love* is much deeper than most men and women have been led to believe. **2)**. Some of the most dangerous people on planet earth are the men and women who do not know, do not understand or who have rejected the four facets of *True Love,* yet still insist on dating, courting and getting married. What *Booby Trap Acid Tests* must you perform to detect and avoid these relationship assassins?

1). Do you know and understand what true love is? - Your answer to that question should be YES! If not, go back and read this chapter again. Remember this - when it comes to the four facets of *True Love*, [*Agape, Phileo, Storge and Eros love*] accept no substitutes.

2). Does your potential mate know and understand what true love is? - If the answer to this booby trap acid test question is, "No," you must face the cold hard facts. Your potential mate has placed you in the relationship danger zone... they have put you at risk!

3). Has your potential mate created their own brand of love? - If they do not know or understand what *True Love* is, and if they have not submitted themselves to God's four-faceted brand of *True Love*, the answer to this test question is, "Yes!" They have created their own variety of love. Remember the various brands of love from page 162? Are you willing to subjugate yourself to such brazen insanity?

4). Is it true love or true lust? - The easy way to make that determination is by answering these questions: are you engaging in *pre*-marital sex, casual sex or other sexual activities? Remember the **urge to merge syndrome**? Remember Shechem? Once you throw sex into the equation without marriage, it's never *True Love*, it is always lust. For your sake do not deceive or lie to yourself; what you have is not *True Love*.

Contrary to what the relationship experts are telling you and contrary to what your lover might be claiming, what you have is pure lust! *True Love* will never put you in a position where you are violating your conscience or doing what you know is morally wrong. *True Love* will never seduce, coerce, or force you to violate your values. *True Love* never makes you feel dirty, sinful, regretful, ashamed, condemned or guilty. *True Love* will always protect you - spiritually, mentally, physically, financially and socially.

5). Is it true love or misplaced trust? - Misplaced trust is when you bestow (*trust, confidence or belief*) in an unsuitable or unworthy individual. If your potential mate cannot successfully pass all nine of the *Booby Trap Acid Tests*, what you have is misplaced trust, not *True Love*.

6). Is it true love or obsession? - To be obsessed means to have an unhealthy occupation for. Are you or your potential mate obsessed with the idea of getting married, having a boyfriend, girlfriend or live-in lover? In other words, if you don't get one or the other, you or your potential mate is going to fall apart, blowup, go crazy, have a nervous break down or become suicidal? Obviously, that is not *True Love*.

7). Is it true love or infatuation? - When you first laid your eyes on this person, there was an undeniable attraction. You became two peas in a pod. You could not stand being apart, but honestly, your relationship has no substance, no depth and no foundation. It is all about puppy love and about the schoolboy-schoolgirl crush, that is not *True love* and it will eventually fade.

8). Is it true love or true luv? - "I luv you!" Smooth operators use those three words to keep their true intentions enshrouded in deception. In their twisted minds, they feel less guilty if they say, "I luv you," instead of saying, "I love you."

Don't ask me why, but it is a game that they play. If you look up the acronyms for "Luv," here is what you will find: Light Utility Vehicle, Linux Users of Victoria, Lisp Users and Vendors Conference, and Luv is also the NYSE stock symbol for Southwest Airlines. When these people say, "I luv you," they could be saying anything!

9). Is it true love or love's addiction? - As you have learned, some people are in love with the idea of being "in love." In their mind, life is utterly meaningless unless they are saying and hearing the three magical words, "I love you!" They are addicted to being "in love." But once the high of that "in love" feeling wanes, it is time for them to move on. I have shown you what *True Love* is, and I have said this before but it bears repetition... when it comes to *True Love*:

Accept no substitutes!

- 11 -

"Honey, Will You 'Merry' Me?"

We just examined the booby trap, **True Love, True Luv, or True Lust?** As you have learned, it is easy for a relationship assassin to snare someone using this booby trap. There are only two prerequisites. **1)**. Find someone who does not know or understand what *True Love* is, and **2)**. Use any one of the counterfeit man-made brands of love to lure them into a lover's nightmare. This next booby trap is also based on your lack of knowledge. I must advise you, I have some extremely good news and some very bad news. First the bad news. Our society is filled with marriage missiles, literally millions of them. On page 68, I defined a marriage missile as **a person who gets married and then presses the marital self destruct button**. I will to add to that definition by saying:

A marriage missile is any potential mate who desires to marry but who does not know, understand, or respect the sacredness of the marriage covenant.

In this booby trap, smooth operators use the same tactics as in the previous booby trap. In this case, they formulate and promote their own mutant strains of matrimony. I classify these men and women as marriage missiles. Like laser guided missiles, they have a two-fold mission to find a target and explode. Once a marriage missile gets married, eventually they are going to send their marriage crashing into the jagged rocks. Either they or their bewildered spouse will end up pulling the divorce trigger. Read these alarming examples.

Divorcees filing uncontested divorces who want to avoid paying exorbitant attorney's fees have websites such as **www.Completecase.com** and **www.Legalzoom.com** that cater to their increasing demands. They log on to these self-help websites and input their information: name, address, social security number, and financial data. They also input information about their soon to be ex, click the submit button and their completed divorce papers are mailed to them ready to file.

Each of those websites presently (*as of April 2003*) assists about 6,600 spouses a year to file for divorce. Those are only two of the many websites used to file uncontested divorces.

The number of people seeking divorces who logged on to the divorce section of the California court system's self help website **www.courtinfo.ca.gov**, soared to about 15,000 in April of 2003. That is just one month, in one state. By the time you add up the number of people who file for divorce using these websites, along with the people who retain attorneys, plus those who purchase self-help divorce kits, the figures are beyond staggering. The numbers do not lie; these people know how to get married! They are also experts on how to shred a marriage into pieces. There are three levels of marriage missiles:

(Level Three)

• ***Those who do not know the sacredness of the marriage covenant*** - Take the case of Kendall and Lorena. These two had been dating sporadically for about six months. Kendall showed up at Lorena's apartment one night, unannounced, banging on her door like a madman.

He woke her up and passionately pleaded with her to marry him, (*or else he would kill himself*). With tears running down his eyes, this millionaire businessman got on his knees and convinced Lorena that his life was not worth living unless she married him.

Lorena had never felt so wanted and so needed by a man in her life! Touched by his passion filled plea, the two took a road trip to Las Vegas, Nevada, found one of those 24-hour drive through marriage mills, and made the **One Hundred Yard Dash To The Wedding Altar**.

When they returned home from their honeymoon, they looked at each other and wondered, "What's next?" From that moment on, Kendall and Lorena behaved like many lost spouses. They became marital combatants. They yelled, screamed and shouted at one another until their fights escalated to physical violence. Eight months and four days from the day they said, "I do," their marital roll of the dice was over. Kendall and Lorena were legally divorced.

What these individuals know about the sacredness of the marriage covenant can be summed up in one word, "nothing!" They know how to spell marriage and that is where their knowledge base about the marriage covenant ends. I am going to show you what every potential mate must know, understand, and respect concerning the marriage covenant *before* they get married. First, let's examine the other two levels of marriage missiles.

(Level Two)

• ***Those who do not understand the sacredness of the marriage covenant*** - This group has received some information about marriage and they sincerely believe they have matrimony figured out.

So what makes them so dangerous? They do not understand what they know. This next point is so critical that I'm going to take my time to break it down into bite size pieces. Follow me closely. There is a big difference between knowing and understanding. For example, most men, including those who don't even read the Bible and don't go to church, will tell you that a wife must obey her husband.

Their position on marriage is that their wife is bound to obey them or else! A good percentage of the widespread marital abuse and domestic violence that permeates our society stems from the men who have adopted this, "you'd better do what I say, woman," philosophy.

Read this actual police report of a man who whipped his wife because he said, *"she was snoring too loud when she fell asleep and it bothered me."* I changed the names for the family's safety and protection. (Please note: **R/O** stands for Reporting Officer, **Perp.**, stands for Perpetrator, **dep.**, stands for Deputy and **(DBL)** stands for double).

On Saturday 5/31/03 at approx. 0026 hrs, unit 317, manned by dep., (name withheld) was dispatched to (Street Address withheld) relative to a signal 103 (D) (Disturbing The Peace By Domestic Violence) and a signal 34 (Aggravated Battery). Upon arrival R/O met with two family members, teenage son and teenage daughter. Both youths were standing outside the residence at the curb edge. Both youths told R/O their father, (name withheld) was in the bathroom area inside their residence with their mother, (name withheld). Both youths told R/O their father was beating their mother with a belt.

R/O immediately entered the residence. R/O observed both subjects in the bathroom area. R/O observed the female victim laying in the bathtub and the male subject standing over her. R/O then ordered the Perp. out of the bathroom. Due to numerous firearms, the safety of everyone involved, the Perp was detained and removed from residence. The R/O then met and spoke with the victim who then stated she came home from work and was very tired. The Perp. started a verbal altercation with the victim which turned physical. The victim told R/O the Perp. started striking her in the kitchen area with an unknown object. The Perp. then dragged her down the hall to the bathroom. The victim stated the Perp. punched her multiple times to the head, face, and body area before being thrown into the bathtub. After the Perp. had the victim in a down position inside the tub, he began striking her multiple times with a leather belt to the legs, arms, and head areas.

Note: The R/O observed several marks on the victim's legs. Also (1) brown leather belt was taken into evidence. The R/O then spoke with both eye witnesses who acknowledged the incident. Both witnesses observed the Perp. strike the victim multiple times with his fists and belt. The R/O later questioned the Perp. as to the incident. The Perp. stated his wife was snoring too loud when she fell asleep and it bothered him. At this point the R/O advised the Perp. he was being placed under arrest for the above said charges. The Perp. was placed into handcuffs (DBL) and advised of his constitutional rights after Miranda.

Sorrowfully, there are millions of men worldwide from all cultures, religions, educational, social and financial backgrounds, who believe they have a right to whip their wives into subjection. When they feel their wife is not obeying their house rules, not following their commands or not fulfilling their sexual demands, they believe they are justified in using intimidation, coercion, threats, whippings, beatings, and other physical violence to force her into obedience.

I followed one case in which the husband built a sound proof room in the house. He would drag his wife into the room and mercilessly beat her, thinking the altered room would shield their children and neighbors from hearing his wife's tormented cries.

Then there are cases like Marilyn Joyce (*real name*). She was married to a wife beating pastor. She wrote a book about her harrowing experience, entitled: **If He Doesn't Deliver**. Her *ex*-husband would preach messages on the Holy Spirit and then come home and punch, kick and attack her. On one occasion, to the horror of their two children, her husband pummeled her into unconsciousness. The assault was so vicious, a doctor said it was a miracle Marilyn lived. She was five months pregnant at the time and lost their precious child. May I remind you, her violent prone *ex*-husband was the pastor of a large church!

Where do these men get these eerie beliefs? They adopt them from being influenced by philosophers like Milton. Read his subversive slant on marriage: **To thy husband's will Thine shall submit. —Milton.** Do you see the implications? "You are my wife and you will obey me! I am the man of this house and you will submit to me now!"

They develop this mindset by sitting under the tutelage of ignorant ministers who only carelessly glance at the Bible periodically. Using the Scriptures below as their foundation, these impudent ministers and erroneous preachers belch out fiery sermons and spew out fanatical doctrines about a wife's absolute obedience to her husband's iron fist rule and dogmatic dictatorship.

> Ephesians 5:22-23 [Emphasis added]
> [22] WIVES, SUBMIT YOURSELVES UNTO YOUR OWN HUSBANDS, as unto the Lord.
> [23] For the HUSBAND is the HEAD OF THE WIFE... [Many ministers replace the word "head" with the word "boss," "master," or "commander"]

> I Peter 3:6 [Emphasis added]
> EVEN AS SARA OBEYED ABRAHAM, calling him lord...

In chapter three, I showed you numerous paths smooth operators travel to get this training. What I did not fully explain was the mass number of relationship assassins who are indoctrinated by corrupt or sincere but ignorant ministers. What do you think happens to a man's psyche after a preacher tells him, "Brother, you are the king of your castle and you have to make your wife obey you!" That is how these half-baked, half-cocked ministers talk, preach and teach.

To compound the matter, some religions gleefully perpetuate wife beating and domestic violence. Examine this verse taken from the Muslim's Bible commonly known as the Holy Quran or Holy Koran:

Koran 4:34 [Emphasis added]
Men have authority over women because God has made the one [*male*] superior to the other [*female*], and because they spend their wealth to maintain them. Good women are obedient. They guard their unseen parts [*by wearing veils*] because God has guarded them. As for those [*wives*] from whom you fear disobedience, admonish them, forsake them in beds apart, AND BEAT THEM. Then if they obey you, take no further action against them. Surely God is high, supreme. [If she doesn't obey him, what actions is he to take? Stab, kick, whip or strangle her?]

You just read wife beating 101. How did this prophet end his violent diatribe? By forging God's signature, falsely making God the initiator of spousal abuse. Another way these domestic violence coaches fuel other *mis*-guided men is by using these trumped up marriage vows.

I Suzy Q, do take thee John Doe, to be my legally wedded husband, to have and to hold from this day forward, for better or for worse, for richer or for poorer, in sickness and in health, to love, cherish **AND TO OBEY**, till death do us part, **ACCORDING TO GOD'S HOLY ORDINANCE**, and thereto I give thee my troth.

Did you pay attention to how the vow ends? "...according to God's holy ordinance..." Pay close attention - there is no *ordinance* from God that commands a wife to obey her husband. That is why that vow is trumped up. The command of God is for a wife to submit to her husband but God didn't stop there. He gave commands of submission to both the husband and to the wife, (*we'll examine those commands later*). Remember, this part of this booby trap is not understanding the sacredness of the marriage covenant, and here is what these men come to ~~understand~~ *mis*-understand about the female gender and marriage:

A woman is a man's piece of property. She must completely give up her will, opinions, tastes, observations, thoughts, dreams and desires. She must be under his absolute dominion. A man is bound to completely control his wife at all times, including policing her feelings and emotions. This is the will of G-O-D!

These men vigorously believe God has commanded them to own, dominate, and control their girlfriend, fiancée or wife. Ladies, listen to me carefully. If you ignore this booby trap and make the fatal mistake of dating, courting, or walking down the aisle with one of these *mis*-guided marriage missiles or relationship assassins, here are just a few samples of some of the day-to-day atrocities you will experience:

- The complete mutilation of your self-esteem
- Frequent visits to the emergency room
- Shame, bewilderment, and astonishment
- Broken bones, black eyes, welts, scars, etc.,
- Arrival at a hospital - (DOA) Dead On Arrival
- Living in a shelter for abused women

- Unprovoked attacks
- Frantic emergency calls to 911
- Extreme stress and depression
- Abandonment and destitution
- Rejection, hurt, and pain
- Intense fear and distrust of men

After inflicting you with such cruel maltreatment, these *mis*-guided males will masterfully attempt to persuade you, the emergency medical technicians, the arresting officer, a judge, your parents and theirs, your pastor, a therapist, an anger management counselor and anyone else who will listen, that it is your fault!

According to them, you are the reason they will with no regret or remorse, bushwack you in the middle of the night. Their control is so methodical and their training is so in-depth, they become foremost experts at apologizing but not repenting!

Please note: these men are smooth operators and during the dating, courting, or engagement process, they will do or say just about anything to hide their fiendish, hellborn beliefs concerning women. You think you can change these tyrannical heathens with your beauty, love, care, sense of humor, kindness, femininity or walk with Christ? For your sake... I plead with you to think again!

It does not matter if you look like Halle Berry, Pamela Anderson and a Victoria Secret's lingerie model all rolled into one. You can prepare meals so scrumptious that Chef Emeril Lagasse requests your recipes. You can smell like Oil of Olay twenty-four hours a day, and sing him to sleep with the voices of Anita Baker, Celine Dion and Mariah Carey.

You can be funnier than a Whoopi Goldberg-Gildna Radner female comedy tag-team and make him giggle so hard that he falls out of his seat in uncontrollable laughter. You can take care of the house far better than Martha Stewart ever dreamed and care for the children so well that even the folks at Parent Magazine would envy you.

You can personally bring more money to the marriage than Oprah Winfrey and Athina Roussel-Onassis combined. Your personality could be sweeter than nectar and your disposition more flexible than play dough. You can be more spiritual than Juanita Bynum, Joyce Meyers, and Paula White grouped together.

You can fast and pray for him five hours a day, wash his back daily, clip his toe nails weekly, belly dance for him nightly, and fulfill all of his sexual fantasies. After you have done all of the above, he's still going to slap you in your face, grab you by your neck, make you cry, curse you out, stress you out, break your heart, try to have sex with your friend, and try to kill you if you object to his heathen ways!

With these men, no matter how great you are, you will never be great enough! Engrave this point into your mind and heart:

You will never get a good mate by making bad choices

That is why you must not under any circumstances: date, become engaged, or marry someone unless they also (a) **Know,** (b) **Understand,** and (c) **Respect** the sacredness of the marriage covenant. There are other areas of *mis-*understanding to which men and women vehemently subscribe, but I focused on that particular area, because domestic violence is so prevalent in our society and so destructive. I'll deal with the other areas later in this chapter.

(Level One)

• *Those who do not respect the sacredness of the marriage covenant* - To respect means: **1)**. to regard with honor. **2)**. to esteem, and **3)**. to avoid the violation of. This is the highest level of marriage missiles because the damage these men and women cause, in most cases, is first degree premeditated matrimonial mutilation. They completely understand the consequences of their actions and they fully realize how their sinful lifestyles will harm their spouse, children, and loved ones.

They know well in advance their irresponsible behaviors will tear their family or someone else's family apart. Apparently they don't care. They seem to numb their consciences and go for the gusto. The end result of their actions is either: (a) **your marriage is ruined,** (b) **their marriage is ruined,** (c) **they take someone's husband,** (d) **they take someone's wife,** or (e) **they ruin a child's right to have both their father and mother present in their life.**

To help you clearly understand the dangers of love, sex, relationships and marriage, I have given you numerous real life examples throughout this book. I have a few more examples from which we can learn. Take a deep breath, brace yourself, then examine the attitudes, mindsets and acts of these individuals.

• In February of 1999 in a Louisiana courtroom, Dr. Richard J. Schmidt (*real name*) was convicted of injecting his adulterous lover with a mixture of contaminated blood he cleverly extracted from two of his patients. One patient had full blown AIDS. The other was infected with Hepatitis C. Court testimony revealed that Dr. Schmidt and his lover were both married with children, but were secretly seeing each other. As their illicit affair progressed, they both agreed to divorce their spouses and marry one another. She divorced her husband, but the philandering doctor reneged on his promise. His mistress eventually gave him an ultimatum to leave his wife and marry her or else.

Instead of leaving his wife, Dr. Schmidt decided to inject his lover with the deadly blood concoction, apparently to end their ten year sexual tryst - *permanently*. In the end, the other woman endured a volatile decade long affair that left her infected with the HIV virus and with Hepatitis C. Dr. Schmidt ended up receiving a fifty year sentence of hard labor in an overcrowded Louisiana state prison.

• In the summer of 2003, in southern California, a well known pastor announced to his congregation at Crossroads Community Church that he was stepping down due to a moral transgression. While church members were trying to recover from Church Shock Syndrome, the pastor's brother filled in the blanks. Apparently, the pastor's transgression was a long term adulterous affair with his brother's wife.

• The *ex*-mistress to husband, father, political figure, businessman and preacher, the Reverend Jesse Jackson, granted an interview to the media after she gave birth to their illegitimate child. Pay close attention to her words.

> "...calls their daughter her "miracle baby" and expresses no regrets over her relationship with the civil rights leader.
> She says they were in love with one another but accepted that their circumstances precluded a conventional relationship.
> "He didn't make any promises," she says. "I didn't think we'd have a future together. I just thought it was something we were doing for the moment."
> Says it did not bother her that Jackson was married. "From what I understood about Rev. Jackson's marriage, was that it was basically a political marriage," she says.
> "I was very comfortable with our relationship, and I knew that while we were together, his heart was nowhere else."
> "I know it's caused a lot of pain," she says. "I know it's caused a lot of problems for people, but she's here, and she's happy and she's healthy. I think it was a good decision."

• In the summer of 2000, Michael Thompson, (*real name*) husband, father and pastor of the flourishing Tabernacle Church in Melborne, Florida, was essentially defrocked after he admitted to having affairs with three different married women who came to him for counseling.

• When Charlie Sheen (*real name*), Hollywood actor, filed for divorce after a five-month marriage, he declared, "I couldn't breathe, I had to come up for air." He said in a media interview: "You buy a car, it breaks down, what are you gonna do?"

I could give you numerous other examples. If you knew the true beliefs some potential mates held concerning love, sex, relationships, and marriage, I guarantee you, the next thing you said to them would be, "good-bye!"

There should be no argument in your quest to find and experience *True Love.* You must identify and avoid individuals who *dis*respect the sacredness of the marriage covenant. I have said this before but it bears repetition, so I'll say it again.

I do not care if your potential mate is a deacon, prophetess, Sunday school teacher, reverend, bishop, pastor or has some other impressive religious title. If they do not know, understand and respect the sacredness of the marriage covenant - leave them alone! I wish it was not so, but this is the cold brutal fact. Some people who sit in the pews and who stand in the pulpit are there to pimp the Lord's name and to prostitute the church for their personal pleasures.

They say they are Christians. They say they are saved, delivered, cleansed by the Blood of Christ, and filled with the Holy Spirit. Publicly they may not drink, smoke, curse or swear. Publicly they may be against all forms of sin including adultery, fornication, and pornography.

Publicly they may stand for family values, but privately they will violate the sacredness of the marriage covenant, (*yours or theirs*) with the poise of a serial check forger. You need to understand, marriage missiles know no boundaries. The sanctum of the church or the sacredness of the pulpit means absolutely nothing to them. Your potential mate may have graduated from an Ivy league university, or earned a doctorate. BUT! As impressive as those accomplishments are, you still must establish the fact that they (a) **know,** (b) **understand,** and (c) **respect** the sacredness of the marriage covenant.

If they do not, refrain from dating, courting or getting engaged to them. For your sake, do not under any circumstances marry them. Here is what you must know, understand and respect concerning the sacredness of the marriage covenant. Please note: these three areas must be firmly established before he says, "Will you marry me?," before she says, "Yes!," and before they walk down the aisle and say, "I do."

Presently our society is filled with various groups, organizations and individuals who dispense concepts and philosophies they passionately claim are the true models for marriage.

Among the broad list of experts who claim to be authorities on this subject are prominent social scientists, high-paid divorce attorneys, relationship experts, homosexuals and lesbians, politicians, polyamorists, certified marriage counselors, licensed therapists, polygamists, bitter divorcees, fuming radical feminists and scripturally illiterate ministers. These various entities define marriage as:

- A social contract
- An open marriage
- A common law marriage
- A formal commitment
- A 50/50 partnership
- A civil agreement

If you are contemplating marriage, you and your potential mate must sit down and thoroughly discuss and come to terms on this next vital issue long before the two of you have a wedding ceremony:

Which marriage model are both of you going to follow?

Are you going to have a **formal commitment marriage**? A **50/50 partnership marriage**? An **open marriage**? What type of marriage are you going to have? As you will learn, just because someone says, "*marriage*" does not mean they are saying and believing the same thing you are saying and believing. When they say, " Will you *merry* me?" You must check the spelling and definition. They don't mean to marry you, they mean to *merry* you! Like the people who create their own brands of love, some men and women have manufactured their own brands of marriage. Their marital beliefs and philosophies will leave you gasping for air. The next critical point you must understand is this: each marriage model has its own distinct *foundation* and *reference source*. It is vitally important that you grasp this next point, so read it carefully.

The *foundation* of a professional football team is its playbook and the *reference source* of that playbook is the coach. If a team or a player is having an issue with their opponent's defense or offense, they call a time out and go to their *reference source*, the coach. The coach goes to his *foundation,* the *playbook*. It is the same with each marriage model.

When a couple is having a challenge or if they have hit a marital road block, they go to their *reference source*, their *coach*, and their coach refers them to his or her *foundation*, their *playbook*, on how to handle the problem or issue. Do not make the mistake the average person makes prior to getting married, by not knowing what marriage model they or their spouse will follow. If you wait until after the wedding bells to figure this out, take note of this. You waited way too late!

Why? Each marriage model has its own distinct *foundation* and *reference source*. If a couple is not following the same marriage model, one problem should be clearly obvious. They have two different *coaches* and consequently, two different *playbooks*. No matter how you perceive it, that is a major disaster waiting to happen.

Before deciding which marriage model you are going to follow, I'll describe each marriage model and show you their *foundation, reference source* and *playbook*. This will allow you to perform a critical side-by-side analysis. Only then will you be able to make a prudent decision and answer this all important, life-altering question:

Which marriage model am I going to follow?

- 12 -

"Yes, I Will 'Merry' You!"

In an **open marriage** one or both spouses consider it acceptable to have sexual relationships with someone other than their spouse. The foundation of open marriages are books such as:

Open Marriage: A New Life Style for Couples
by Nena O'Neill, George O'Neill

The New Intimacy: Open-Ended Marriage and Alternative Lifestyles
by Ronald M. Mazur

Recreational Sex: An Insider's Guide to the Swinging Lifestyle
by Patti Thomas

The coaches for open marriages are highly educated experts and others who believe in having what they classify as sport or recreational sex. According to their *playbooks*, a spouse can have sex with someone other than their husband or wife as long as they do not form any emotional ties with that sex partner, hence the phrase, "sport sex."

These experts [*coaches*] claim that monogamous marriages are outdated and that humans are like animals. They assert that we cannot control our sexual urges, so why try. (*Ironically, rapists, pimps, prostitutes, johns, pedophiles, pornographers and adulterers all follow the same theory about sexual urges*). Open marriage advocates teach that the way to reduce divorce and infidelity, and increase communication and commitment is to swap spouses and engage in recreational sex.

So why do they get married in the first place? Why don't these men and women just find a group of sex partners, rent a room, and go for it? Why do they write books, launch websites, recruit others to get married and then swap spouses? Answer: they are part of a defiant faction of individuals who are intent on eroding the family and making a mockery of the sanctity of marriage. The *foundation* of the **50/50 partnership** is the mantra, "50/50." The *coaches* for these partnerships are the self-appointed marriage experts who teach that a marriage is in disarray if a spouse is not delivering their fifty percent of the union.

Some experts teach spouses to keep a log of the chores they perform and money they contribute and compare their log to their spouses log. Per their marital philosophy, if things do not balance out exactly, the marriage is in trouble! These experts claim that a wife has no marital equality unless she is contributing fifty percent or more of the household income. If she is not, she is considered less than a wife.

Even if she is pregnant or has just given birth, she is still expected to bring home her percentage of the income and perform her percentage of the chores. You would be surprised at the number of couples who get divorced because one spouse was adamant about everything being split right down the middle. If he isn't cut out for cooking and she isn't cut out for yard work, watch out because there will be no compromise!

Once a person has bought into this marriage model, all of the talking or pleading in the world for them to change is usually going to be moot. Why? Because they learned about marriage from the experts, and surely the highly educated experts could not be wrong, could they?

The *foundation* of the **common law marriage model** is cohabitation. What is cohabitation? It is commonly referred to as "**living together, shacking-up, test driving, taste testing, domestic partnering** and **living in sin.**" It describes a relationship between a man and a woman who are sexually involved with each other and share a household but are not legally married.

Note: At times they try to ease their guilt ridden conscience or fraudulently obtain benefits legally married people enjoy. They do this by introducing themselves as husband and wife, fully knowing they are not legally married. Blatant lying simply goes with the territory. Their *reference sources* [*coaches*] are a diverse group of organizations who teach their alternatives to the covenant marriage on websites such as:

- www.cohabitationnation.com
- www.polyamorysociety.org
- www.lovemore.com
- www.libchrist.com
- www.palimony.com
- www.unmarried.org

Their *reference sources*[*coaches*] also include a list of universities that teach cohabitation as an alternative or a replacement to marriage. In 1997, the New York based **Institute for American Values** released a report entitled, *"Closed Hearts, Closed Minds."* This detailed report included a list of twenty social science textbooks used in over 8000 college courses.

These textbooks (*filled with rhetoric, blatant lies, false statistics and mysticism*), were written to convince students, (*especially women*), that marriage is an evil plot invented by the male species designed to oppress the female gender. Using frivolous scientific data and godless lectures, these scholars have influenced many students to join their mission to convert our society into a marriageless cohabitation nation.

Their sphere of influence is unmistakable. Read these woefully compelling book titles:

Shacking Up: The Smart Girls Guide To Living In Sin Without Getting Burned
by Stacy Whitman, Wynne Whitman

The Ethical Slut: A Guide to Infinite Sexual Possibilities
by Dossie Easton, Catherine A. Liszt

Unmarried to Each Other: The Essential Guide to Living Together as an Unmarried Couple
by Dorian Solot, Marshall Miller

The final list of *reference sources* [*coaches*] who fancy living together and proudly boast that marriage is not necessary, is antiquated, was never sacred, or must be abolished are people who:

- come from broken homes
- have been through a divorce
- are already living together
- are children of divorcees
- are not financially stable (*men*)
- are fearful of getting a divorce
- are in financial desperation (*women*)
- hold bitter anti-marriage sentiments
- are young or immature
- are radical flaming feminists
- have drug and alcohol addictions
- have no family values or principles
- have limited or no education
- have no God-based morals or integrity

Read the various reasons why these people say they live together:

- it's the final *pre*-marital test
- it's the best way to get to know someone
- it's guaranteed sex...
- cohabitation is a natural evolution of love
- to learn his or her bad habits/nuances
- frankly, we consider ourselves married
- it makes sense, since we're engaged
- to make sure he's house trained
- to see if he or she is marriage material
- it lets you work out the kinks
- only church people need to get married
- to see if you love the person
- all the couples I know are doing it!
- to confirm our sexual compatibility
- we're together most of the time anyway
- it's more accepted in this generation
- you try on a coat before you buy it, a spouse should be no different
- it's the best way to take the relationship to the next level
- it is the only way to learn about someone before you decide to marry them
- if you're planning on getting married, why delay the fun?
- to make sure you know every little thing about a person before taking the plunge
- with divorce so rampant, cohabiting first is simply a prudent decision
- people who believe in marriage are secretly insecure with themselves
- to save money on rent, food, gas, etc... you can literally cut your bills in half!
- no more clubs or bars and you don't have to worry about STD's
- it gives you a chance to see a person in their natural habitat
- it gives you the confidence you need to take the next step and tie the knot
- a marriage license and vows don't prove or confirm anything
- marriage is not natural, it is created by religion and forced upon us by a prude society

Did you see their main reasoning for cohabiting? *"To test compatibility."* At first glance, it sounds great, but here is a side of living together cohabiting proponents do not want you to know about: (*all real names*)

- **Gladys Ricart** was at home posing for pictures just moments before her wedding ceremony was to take place. She wrote on her wedding invitations,"This day, I will marry the one who loves me without end, the one who brightens my life and gives love a new meaning…" All seemed perfect until her ex-live-in lover, Agustin Garcia entered the house, pulled out a gun and opened fire, hitting Gladys with three bullets, soaking her pure white wedding gown with blood, killing her. RIDGEFIELD, NJ, September 1999
- **Ryan O'Hare** - police arrived on the scene to find Ryan's live-in girlfriend bloodied. They say he beat her in the face with a hammer. Then, as stunned witnesses watched in horror, he chased her down, forcing her to jump from a three story building to avoid more of his brutal attack. FALL RIVER, MA, August 2003
- **Quinshala Gray** had been living with her boyfriend, Waymon Jenkins, about two months when police say he killed her after they argued over a water bill. BELLE GLADE, FL, August 2003
- **Michael Dodson** - friends say Michael was not pleased when he saw his live-in girlfriend flirting with another man. He went home and tossed some of her belongings on the front lawn and set them on fire. When she approached Michael, witnesses watched him pick her up, toss her into the fire, put his foot on her back and then yelled at her to die. ST. CHARLES TOWNSHIP, IL, November 2002
- **Jessica Mencia** had been with Felix Rondon, her live-in lover for 8 years. She had two daughters by him. She informed him that she was ending their relationship. She said, hours later, Felix brutally attacked her while she slept. Thankfully, someone dialed 911. When police arrived, they said they found Felix on top of Jessica, biting off chunks of her face. QUEENS, NY, February 2002
- **Sabrina Goodman** was murdered by her live-in lover after she threatened to leave him. Police say Shelly Lee Crayton's wife had left him and he was determined not to let another woman exit his life. He shot Sabrina three times, then dialed 911. They had lived together for six months. GRANITE QUARRY, NC, June 1999
- **Christelle Peterson** had planned on taking her two kids roller-skating but police say her live-in lover, John Scott changed her plans. After the two had an argument, John shot Christelle three times, then dialed 911. Sources said they believe John had become jealous because the biological father of Christelle's children had been spending time with the kids. QUEENS, NY, August 2003
- **Carolyn Green** was murdered by the 12-year-old son of her live-in boyfriend. The child told investigators that he resented his dad's girlfriend telling him what to do, so he shot her twice then dialed 911. NEW MIDDLETON, TN, June 2003
- **DeAngelo Shelton** moved in with Tracy Walker, then turned her life into a living nightmare. She had become afraid of him. After he assaulted her, Tracy would call the police but would not testify against him at the trial. Two months after the last attack, DeAngelo ended his cat and mouse game with his live-in lover by killing her, then committing suicide. CINCINNATTI, OH, July 2003
- **Lyric Benson**, a 21-year-old Yale graduate who was featured in an American Express ad, was returning to her apartment when her *ex*, Robert Ambrosino, ambushed her and shot her in the face. Acquaintances said Benson broke off her relationship with Robert just weeks prior to her murder after a religious reawakening prompted her to rethink living together. BROOKLYN, NY, April 2003

You just read a few incidents out of thousands. Each of those individuals discovered what most live-in lovers find out when they reside with someone. If they determine they are not compatible or that their live-in lover has issues, they learn the hard way that breaking up and moving out is not as easy as their cohabitation [*coaches*] portrayed it would be. Repeatedly, I hear from people who are living with someone but feel trapped in the relationship. They know they should leave, but the pressure to stay is too intense. Here are the reasons they say they stay when they know they should breakup and move out:

- the reduced income would hurt them financially
- their lover is a manipulator or controller
- she intentionally got pregnant to trap him
- he keeps telling her he's going to marry her
- they can't give up the sex
- they have a child together
- she's fearful of her boyfriend
- they're afraid of starting over

To say, *"If things don't work out, I'll just pack my bags and move..."* is utter insanity! Your partner might not let you walk away. As you have read, some live-in lovers will attempt to kill you if you try to leave them.

I need to pause and remind you, this book was written with a two-fold purpose: (1) to help you *avoid* choosing the wrong mate, and (2) to help you avoid becoming the wrong mate. Therefore, you need to know that live-in lovers have two glaring character flaws that make them extremely volatile and severely dangerous potential mates.

• *Flaw #1: Live-in lovers do not understand the potent threefold power of flesh ties, spiritual ties or soul ties* - This goes back to what you learned on pages 48 & 49, about being spiritually immature. Live-in lovers reject or simply do not understood these critical spiritual laws. Let's start with the flesh. Here is what the Word of God says about flesh ties...

> I Corinthians 6:16 AMP [Emphasis added]
> Or do you not know *and* realize that when a man joins himself to a prostitute, HE BECOMES ONE BODY WITH HER? The two, it is written, SHALL BECOME ONE FLESH.

Once a man and woman have sex together, they become one flesh. They do not have to be husband and wife. She could be a prostitute. They could have had a one night stand or they could consider themselves to be meaningless casual sex partners. All it takes for a man and woman to become *One Flesh* is to have sex with each other.

If a person has had two sex partners, they have become one flesh with each partner. The same is true if they had three, four, or more sex partners. You may adamantly disagree with what you just read. But just like the unseen law of gravitation, this truth is a spiritual law. It cannot be repudiated nor changed.

A flesh tie can become magnified if: (a) **one sex partner gives the other a sexually transmitted disease, especially if it's incurable,** (b) **she becomes pregnant, especially if they do not want the child,** (c) **their relationship involves abuse or domestic violence,** or (d) **one partner wants to sever the flesh tie but the other refuses.** Now read what the Word of God says about spiritual ties...

> I Corinthians 15:33 AMP [Emphasis added]
> Do not be so deceived *and* mislead! Evil companionships (communion, associations) corrupt *and* deprave good manners *and* morals *and* character.

Remember what you learned in chapter 3 about **influence by association**? This Scripture is the basis of that spiritual law. Spiritual ties are formed by the people with whom you associate. If your best friend is a liar, you will take on a spirit of lying. If your close friend is a fornicator, you will take on a spirit of fornication. If a person you have a close association with is rebellious and has rejected God, you will take on a spirit of rebellion and you will reject God also.

You say, "Oh noooo, Gillis, not me!" Yes, you! Read the Scripture again! Do not deceive or mislead yourself. Evil (*companionships, communions or associations*) will destroy your good manners, corrode your godly morals, and stain your sterling character. The moment you convince yourself that you cannot be influenced by evil associations, you have misled yourself. In August of 2003 in Baghdad, Iraq, two American soldiers married Iraqi women they met during the war against Saddam Hussein.

One of the soldiers said, "He was a Christian." Part of the process of marrying this woman is that he had to convert to Islam. Before witnesses, he had to confess, *"There is no God, but God, and Mohammed is the messenger of God."* His companionship with that woman caused him to renounce Jesus Christ as his Lord and make the god of Islam his god. The spiritual law of **influence by association** is irrefutable.

Finally we have soul ties. What is a soul tie? A soul tie is exactly what it sounds like. It is a tie (*or a bond*) between two or more people formed in the soul realm. Our soul is the seat of our will, intellect, emotions, feelings and memory.

When you ignite feelings for someone and the two of you develop a relationship, you establish a soul tie with that person. Your feelings will affect your will, your intellect, your emotions and become etched into your memory. There is no way around it. Pay attention to what happens when you form ties with someone in all three of these areas:

> Ecclesiastes 4:12
> "... a threefold cord is not quickly broken.

Here is Gillis Triplett's Relationship translation of that same verse:

Ecclesiastes 4:12
"... when a man and a woman establish a spirit tie, a soul tie and
a flesh tie, this threefold bond is going to be hard to break.

Although this powerful connection was only designed for husband
and wife, live-in lovers take all of these elements and form their own
threefold bond, (*albeit a counterfeit one*). Since they are having sexual
relations, that makes them have a flesh tie. Their companionship
propels them to have a spiritual tie, which causes them to come under
the law of **influence by association**. Their soul tie causes them to commingle
their souls... fusing together their wills, their intellect, their emotions,
and their feelings. As they talk and play with one another, engage in
sex, have disagreements, make up and do other things that spouses
do, those memories become etched into their soul.

To tell someone they can simply walk away after they have formed
such a potent threefold bond borders on blasphemy. It would not be so
hard to breakup if a person had only formed a soul tie, or if they just
had a soul tie and a spiritual tie. But when they add a flesh tie to the
equation, plus live together... and possibly have intertwined their
finances, exiting the relationship is not going to be a simple ho-hum
case of packing suitcases and walking out.

Quite frankly, in most cases, breaking up and moving out will be
just as stressful and tense as getting a divorce! I am going to answer
some questions that have puzzled various therapists, prosecutors,
ministers, police officers, and counselors for a long time.

Why do women stay with abusive men? Why do abused women go
back to men who have threatened to kill them or who have choked,
slapped, kicked, or nearly strangled them to death? Why do people
stay in volatile or stormy relationships? Why do sane people stress
themselves out by wallowing in painful dead-end unstable
relationships? It is because of this potent bond.

It is exactly as the Word of God declares. Once a man forms a
threefold bond with a woman, whether married or not, it becomes
extremely difficult to walk away from that emotional, sexual, physical
and spiritual attachment. However, once all three ties in a threecord
bond are severed, it does not matter how smooth, controlling or
manipulative a person is. That relationship is over!

• *Flaw #2: Live-in lovers have no morals or family values* - This is a truth
every live-in lover will vehemently try to deny. On page 191, you read
some of their absurd reasons for living together, (*to test their sexual*

compatibility, to cut their bills in half, they claim marriage is not natural, they want guaranteed sex, etc.). These individuals have yanked any semblance of morals or family values from the shelf of their hearts. To have morals means to know the difference between what is right versus what is wrong and to hold firmly to what is right.

When you talk to live-in lovers about fornication, adultery, promiscuity, or sexual immorality, they will either laugh in your face, laugh at you, or make chide remarks about you behind your back. Even those who sit in church and claim to follow the Lord will find your stance on morals to be highly constrictive and painfully irritating.

To have family values means to esteem the sacredness of the marriage covenant and all that it embodies, (*husband, wife, children, grand children, great grand children, family legacies and family traditions*). People who have morals and strong family values will not dishonor the sacredness of the marriage covenant by cohabiting. The real reasons most people choose to cohabit is because: (a) he wants steady sex available without any commitment or responsibility, (b) it's a great way to supplement their income, or (c) this is her backdoor method of snagging a husband.

At best, it is a fool's paradise. What happens when these live-in lovers are forced to deal with a severely critical issue such as pregnancy? It is a known fact, that even with the availability of condoms and other forms of birth control, the unplanned pregnancy rate amongst live-in lovers is high. So how do they deal with this issue? Their *coaches* gleefully advise them to get an abortion. Problem solved, right? Wrong!

What if he adamantly insists that she get an abortion but she cannot bring herself to commit such a brutal act? If she refuses, the mass number of bitter single mothers, murdered pregnant women, child support cases involving *ex*-live-in lovers, incarcerated *ex*-boyfriends, live-in lover murder-suicides and angry newlyweds prove that her live-in boyfriend is going to either...

(a) **attempt to coerce or force her to get an abortion,** (b) **attempt to force or cause her to have a miscarriage,** (c) **stay with her but kick himself for getting her pregnant and despise their child,** (d) **regrettably and grudgingly marry her,** (e) **dump her and move out,** (f) **start abusing her,** or (g) **murder her to prevent her from collecting child support.** Only a tiny portion of the men who shack-up with a female welcome their child with the same joy as loving husbands and caring fathers. Here is another common dilemma cohabiting females face everyday. Let's say they agree to discuss marriage after monogamously cohabiting for a year. After a year, she is ready for a committed relationship, but he decides he wants to test drive her for another twelve months. Does she (a) **move out?** Or, (b) **let him test drive her further?** If she moves out, does she let another man test drive her?

How many live-in lovers do the cohabitation *coaches* say a woman should allow to sample her **Eros Love**, test drive her wifely skills and toy with her emotions before she says no more sampling and no more test drives? Two, four, or more? Cohabitation *coaches* refrain from addressing this critical issue. They will not talk about the down side of shacking-up. To compound the matter, it is widely known that women who cohabit suffer from a high rate of depression. They spend an awful lot of time worrying about their live-in boyfriend just suddenly leaving.

Women with children have it the worst. Once they move in with a man, they soon realize the fleeting nature of their relationship. They receive no commitment from their lover and no one with any morals or strong family values will support their (*room mates having sex*) hookup.

When they hit a snag in the relationship and seek help, if they pray to God for guidance, the only thing He's going to show them is their sin, (see John 4:15-19, I Corinthians 6:18 and Proverbs 1:10). If they go to a true minister of God, he's going to show them the exact same thing God showed them. If they go to one of their cohabitation *coaches*, they will usually hear the standard speech for live-in lovers in trouble.

• **For the men it is:** *"Hit the booty as long as you can and then leave! She's not your wife. You're not married to her. You don't owe her a thing... not even a ring! When she moved in with you, she should have known the deal!"*

• **For the women it is:** *"Hang in there girl as long as you can, he said he loves you, maybe he's just afraid. He may be a commitment phobic. Try counseling, see if that works. He just might come around, but if you feel you can't stay, you have no choice but to love yourself first and leave him!"*

As popular as it is, if you allow someone to talk you into this marriage model, your chances of marital success are slim. The best way to describe living together first, then getting married is this: it is divorce preparation 101. Here are some more critical issues about cohabiting. Cohabition is one of the reasons the divorce rate is so high. There are only two groups with a higher divorce rate than live-in lovers who get married. **1). Pregnant teenagers who get married.** Their divorce rate is about eighty percent, and **2). Divorcees who remarry.** Their divorce rate hovers around sixty percent. Why is the cohabitation divorce rate so high? It goes back to their second character flaw. Remember - they have no morals and no strong family values.

They have no motivation to uphold the sacredness of the marriage covenant. They bring their cancerous cohabitation attitudes into their marriages. To them, divorce is synonymous with moving out. That is why they are more inclined to divorce than to solve problems. Since their conscience is not troubled about having *pre*-marital sex, most of them have no qualms about committing adultery either. After their wedding ceremony, they both know from firsthand experience that their newly christened spouse believes in having sex outside of marriage. Faced with that alarming knowledge, the trust level between them starts off tarnished. The possibility that their spouse may cheat on them is almost always on the back of their minds.

They also have a tendency to get married but hold firm to their live-in lover's mindset which is, *"what's yours is yours and what's mine is mine!"* Most live-in lovers have poor conflict resolution skills.

That flaw makes them more prone to domestic violence while living together and carries over into their marriage. Nothing about this model for marriage is appealing to people who are serious about choosing the right mate and having a lasting marriage endued with vibrant love.

The spouses who elect the **formal commitment** marriage model have made the philosophies and beliefs of man their sole *foundation*. To fully understand the malignancy of this model for marriage, let's define the words "formal" and "commitment." One definition of the word formal means: **to have an outward appearance but lack no substance**. The word commitment is defined as **1). the trait of sincere and steadfast fixity of purpose. 2). the act of binding yourself (intellectually or emotionally) to a course of action.** People who choose this marriage model make lofty promises and noble commitments to their spouses but their words are only mere formalities.

There is absolutely no substance to their matrimonial commitment. When marital issues surface, and they will, these people run to experts who can only be described as mentally unzipped.

Their *reference sources* [*coaches*] are men and women who are licensed, board certified, highly trained or heavily degreed. These *coaches* hold impressive titles such as clinical sexologist, resident relationship expert, romance coach and certified marriage psychologist.

Their *coaches* not only have degrees but they also have numerous initials behind their names such as: Dr. Suzy Quaint, Ph.D., M.S.W., Dr. John Doe, L.M.F.T., B.C.D., N.L.P., Dr. Jane Pain, M.Ed, L.C.S.W., C.I.C.S.W., and Dr. Joe Schmoe, C.A.D.C., C.C.H. You would think their education, training, and expertise would inspire them to give sane advice, but that is not the case.

This rebuke is not directed towards legitimate professionals who respect the sacredness of the marriage covenant and counsel spouses from that vantage point. They are not the problem. My concern lies with these critically acclaimed passionate pop psychologists and other experts. They influence millions of people with their fluffy love, sex, relationship, and marital advice. Read how they advise their patients, clients, readers and listeners.

A certified sexologist asserts that having sexual fantasies will spice up your marriage. These are her words: *Fantasies are a safe way to explore your sexual desires and I encourage both men and women to have them. They allow you to imagine having sex with various people without experiencing any of the real-life consequences. Just be aware that your fantasies can become all consuming and so lifelike, that you find it hard to hold back from trying to fulfill them in real life..."*

Another relationship expert gives her take on pornography. Read her eerily deceptive words: *"There is nothing particularly sinister about the majority of pornography. Some women think pornography is degrading to the female gender but that is not the case. Many 21st century women are finding that pornography can fulfill their sexual desires as well as their financial needs. A woman shouldn't feel threatened by her husband's attraction to view sexually explicit pictures of other women. It doesn't mean he's going to cheat on you nor does it mean that he finds you unattractive... it's just a guy's way of expressing his sexuality..."*

One marriage therapist, like many of her modern day colleagues, brazenly encourages infidelity. Read how she cleverly promotes adultery and mocks the virtue of being faithful: *"Infidelity can actually stabilize a marriage... to the joy of their spouse, the extracurricular sexual activity will teach a partner how to become a better and more sensitive lover..."*

Amazingly, the average person classifies these so called "experts," as knowledgeable, credible, and correct. And why wouldn't they? These experts have syndicated radio talk shows and television programs. They become syndicated columnists. They write bestselling books. They put on mega conferences that draw millions. They make guest appearances on the big networks... they become media darlings.

No wonder people who choose the **formal commitment** marriage model believe their mentors wholeheartedly. Their advice causes their clients, listeners, and readers to join the swelling ranks of heartbroken divorcees. Yet many of these people still hold firm to the pop-psychology philosophies of their renegade experts.

This next relationship expert specializes in counseling single women. She is licensed, has a Ph.D. degree, and is a board certified sex therapist. She has a list of accomplishments that would make even top notch professionals in her field glimmer with envy.

This is her advice to young women who have acknowledged they are suffering from depression, guilt and shame for having had numerous sex partners: *"Guilt, shame, depression and sex are usually paired together when a woman has developed beliefs about her sexuality that are restrictive in nature. We (females) are in the midst of a sexual awakening. Enjoy your new found sexual freedom and don't be bound by societal or by outdated religious beliefs about sex. Today's men want women who are sexually skilled. Women with sexual experience are less likely to cheat because they have sampled a variety of men and know what they want. They also demonstrate to their men that they enjoy sex and most importantly they bring their sexual experiences to their marriage and are not forced to rely solely upon their husband to lead them to sexual gratification..."*

Another relationship expert suggests having an extramarital affair as a means of getting your spouse's attention. Read her words, *"One way to communicate to your spouse that your physical, sexual, emotional, or financial needs aren't being met is by having an affair. This act will get your spouse's attention and communicate to them that you mean business, and that things must change..."*

The objective of these experts should be obvious: to seduce as many people as they can into becoming relationship assassins and marriage missiles. But why would a seemingly sane, intelligent person follow the shoddy advice of these rogue counselors? It goes back to what you learned on page 49, about being feeble minded. They believe these demented whacko pop psychologists because they are easily influenced.

If you make the fatal mistake of choosing a potential mate who believes in this model for marriage, you might not kiss your marital happiness good-bye on your wedding day. It may take three to seven years but eventually, these people will make you cry tears of ~~joy~~, pain.

To fully understand these individuals, you have to understand the characteristics of a leech, also known as common blood suckers.

There are three type of leeches. **1) Predators 2). Parasites, and 3). Predator-parasites.** Predators attack worms, snails, etc., and digest their flesh. Parasites attach themselves to a host, (*i.e., an animal, a human, turtles, frogs, etc.*) and slowly suck the blood out of them. Predator-parasites do both. People who choose this model for marriage are like the parasite type of leech.

They attach themselves to their host, (which is their spouse), then they proceed to slowly suck the life out of them by draining them spiritually, emotionally, physically, financially and socially. Have you ever heard any of these incriminating expressions, *"...their spouse dragged them through the mud, raked coals over their face, put them through a living hell, might as well have spat in their face or, they're married but live separate lives?"*

If you marry one of these parasites, people will be making those statements about you. Engrave this truth into your mind and do not ever forget it: *"A parasite has no capacity to love its host."* The objective of the parasite is to find and attach itself to a host (*spouse*) and then suck the blood out of them. That is their only objective! You can do everything in your power to make a marriage to one of these parasites work.

If you believe in prayer, the parasite will have you constantly praying for their deliverance but they will not change. At some point in the marriage, one party is going to opt for therapy or counseling, (*anger management, sexual addiction, drug or alcohol addiction, batterer's counseling, etc.*) but the parasite will not change. The intention is not to discourage anyone. However, no matter how much you believe in these kind of spouses, they will not change. Remember that to them, marriage is only a commitment born of formality.

When they say, "I do!," there is absolutely no substance to their words. When they go to counseling or therapy it is also a formality. They will not change. Yet, one group that parasitic spouses will frantically avoid are individuals with spiritual discernment. They do not mind being around Church pew warmers or other religious slackers, but they cannot tolerate being in the presence of people who are born-again, Spirit-filled, obedient to the Word of God, sensitive to the voice of the Holy Spirit, and who speak the truth of the Word of God in love.

Why not? True Christians will expose their rebellion, divulge their spirit of compromise, confront their spirit of adultery, rebuke their spirit of abuse, and make a clarion call for them to repent. Their therapists, psychologists, and counselors require no repentance.

These experts, for the most part, do not believe in sin or self-accountability. They treat sexual immorality, volatile tempers, pathological liars, abusers, contentious women and wife beaters with medication therapy, behavior therapy, art therapy, post-modern therapy and other psychotherapy. In the end, after all of their therapeutic measures have been exhausted, they and their clients will come to understand this irrefutable truth:

It is better to have not married than to have been in a bad marriage with a leech.

How do we define a **civil agreement** marriage? It is a union between two people who have chosen to exclude God and the church from their marital procession. These individuals use a justice of the peace, a judge, self-proclaimed ministers, or anyone with a license to perform weddings. However, they refuse to use a true minister of God. Their ceremonies are held in courtrooms, drive-thru marriage mills, 24 hour marriage joints, foreign countries that sponsor quickie marriages, strip clubs, night clubs and sporting events, anyplace but in the presence of God.

The key element in a **civil agreement** marriage is this. Marriage is seen as an agreement between two people. God has no input or say in their weddings or subsequent marriages. The people who opt for this model for marriage usually fall into these categories:

- lone rangers, **(see Chapter 4)**
- wife beaters, gold-diggers, paternity fraud predators etc., **(see Chapter 9)**
- homosexuals, lesbians, transgendered, transsexuals, etc., **(see Romans 1:24-28)**
- haters of God, fornicators, those who cohabit, **(see Romans 1:29-30)**
- wayward, carnally-minded and rebellious Christians, **(see Romans 8:1-13)**
- people who follow man-made religions and philosophies, **(see Colossians 2:8)**
- sexually active females who use quickie marriages as a tool to cover up their unplanned pregnancies, **(see Chapter 6)**

Their *foundation* can range from absolutely nothing, to astrology and horoscopes, palm readings and psychics, to yoga and Zen Buddhism. If you marry one of these individuals, you will know what it is like to have a marriage built on sand. Their *reference sources* [*coaches*] can be best described as a crew of sacrilegious marital juggernauts.

The **social contract** marriage model downgrades marriage to the same level as a cellular telephone contract, recording contract or any other contract. The *foundation* of these marriages is a piece of paper such as a prenuptial agreement, postnuptial agreement, or some other contract. These spouses subscribe to the theory that divorce attorneys, family law attorneys, and judges invented marriage.

Their marriages are set up like military preemptive strikes. Before they go to the altar, one or both spouses gets an attorney to separate and protect their individual money, personal belongings and treasures from their soon to be bride or groom. With their legal beagles at their sides, they *pre*-determine property settlements in the event either spouse decides to pull the divorce trigger. When conflict or disagreement arises in a **social contract** marriage, one or both spouses promptly consults with their *coach,* a.k.a. their attorney, to determine if it is time to engage their spouse in the war of all wars, the brutal divorce war.

Once the divorce papers are filed, the divorce attorney advises his or her client to go into the spousal combat mode. ***Warning*** Brace yourself as I reveal some of the training these spouses receive once they decide to go from *One Flesh* to torn flesh. I apologize in advance for the vile language, but you need to know three critical points.

1). The fiendish evil attitude of these spouses once they file for divorce. They make a word like "backstabber," look like child's play.

2). I had to reveal the titles of these books to help you to understand what is at stake. These spouses are indoctrinated to slam you to the ground and then trample on you without mercy.

3). You might become appalled when you read at least one of the book titles. Just know that I felt the same way when I discovered them. They appalled me! I wanted to keep quiet or just allude to them, but if I shielded them from you or acted as though they did not exist, some people might not grasp the seriousness of this issue.

Divorce War! 50 Strategies Every Woman Needs To Know To Win
by Bradley A., Esq. Pistotnik

Screw the [XXXXX]: Divorce Tactics for Men * See note below
by Dick Hart, Victor Santoro

*The authors of this book used extremely offensive language that I could not repeat.

Tao of Divorce: A Woman's Tactical Guide To Winning
by Sun Yee, Lee Fong

The Lion's Share: A Combat Manual for the Divorcing Male
by J. Alan. Ornstein

The Woman's Book of Divorce: 101 Ways to Make Him Suffer Forever and Ever
by Christine Gallagher

Like pit bulls deliberately bred to have ferocious temperaments, these spouses are trained by their attorneys and others to take a menacing attitude toward their soon to be *ex*. The focus of their newly developed fierce demeanor is to get the lion's share of the finances by attacking their spouse with the viciousness of a blood thirsty Rottweiler. To the chagrin of God, even people who claim to be Christians have adopted this brutal, *"I will destroy my spouse divorce combat mentality."*

I have witnessed the devastation first hand as I sat through divorce case after divorce case. I have stood in the halls of the divorce court and listened as divorce attorneys advised their clients, "don't worry, we'll keep the pressure on them, they'll break sooner or later." I have watched husbands and wives transfixed like deer staring at headlights, baffled at the treacherous acts of their soon to be *ex*. They had no idea their spouse had been prepped by their attorney to go for their jugular vein. Here is a short list of some of the **Guerilla Warfare Tactics** these spouses have been influenced to use and commit:

- File false domestic violence charges
- Illicit perjured testimony from experts
- Use kids as bribery or extortion tools
- Make false financial & asset declarations
- Get restraining orders obtained by fraud
- Make false accusations of child abuse
- File trumped up Ex Parte Motions
- Implement the **Scorched Earth Policy**

What is the **Scorched Earth Policy**? During World War II after Hitler invaded Germany, Stalin went on the radio and announced his **Scorched Earth Policy** for Ukraine. He ordered the people to completely destroy any and all valuable property, including nonferrous metals, grain and any fuel they could not use or move. Anything the enemy could get their hands on was sabotaged or set on fire. This included food, vehicles, cattle, railway cars, forests and buildings, they torched them all.

Some divorce attorneys advise their clients to implement the **Scorched Earth Policy** by instructing them to sell, give away, or destroy their possessions. That includes houses, cars, furniture - everything. They are told to put all the bills in their spouse's name and if possible, get paid under the table. They are advised to close or cancel all accounts, utilities, credit cards, and services in their name and to open offshore accounts and use other schemes to smuggle cash and hide assets. The objective is to dump all the bills on their spouse and leave them with no assets. If questioned about the sudden disappearance of cash or valuables, they are advised to claim they gave the money to a church or lost it gambling.

Once a spouse puts their marriage into the domain of divorce attorneys, judges, divorce court and family court, they have unknowingly thrust themselves into a forty billion dollar a year fully automated human grinding machine. This machine is specifically designed to crush hearts, shred emotions, and dash dreams.

Do not be surprised that the divorce attorney's mantra is: **"DIVORCE IS WAR!"** That mantra is their code of ethics. Most men who follow the **social contract** marriage model claim that marriage is just an insurance policy for women and these men will cancel that policy at the drop of a dime. Most women who follow after the **social contract** marriage model take this position, *"If he doesn't work out, I'll exercise my termination clause."*

If your potential mate follows after the **social contract** marriage model, you must face the facts; this is what you get. If you are expecting justice or fairness from a divorce or family court, forget it! These are the same people who banished the Ten Commandments from being displayed and who refused to recite the Pledge of Allegiance because it contains the phrase, *"...one Nation under God..."* The forty billion dollar a year divorce court machine is primarily comprised of these three groups.

• *Corrupt judges* - In April of 2003, Judge Gerald Garson (*real name*), a well known Supreme Court Judge was arrested for fixing divorce cases in Brooklyn, New York. Most of the people employed in his courtroom were also arrested for their participation in the alleged scheme. Prosecutors say some of the payoffs included cash, a trip to Bali, bottles of Scotch and dinners at fine restaurants. Judge Garson is currently awaiting trial. I have seen trials in which the judge was the father of one of the divorce attorneys trying cases before him.

There is no way an opposing attorney could get a fair shake for his or her client in such a courtroom. Isn't that an ethics violation? Shouldn't that judge have made full disclosure and informed all parties, (*i.e., the opposing attorney and both litigants*), that one of the attorneys was also his beloved biological child? Behind the laced curtain of the divorce court gestapo, the answer to those questions is a resounding, "NO!"

Such infractions are the norm. Countless divorcees have no idea they are being violated by an unethical judicial militia motivated by money, politics, and power. Even people within the system are starting to acknowledge the corruption.

In February of 2003, Judge Edith Jones (*real name*) of the U.S. Court of Appeals for the Fifth Circuit, addressed the Federalist Society of Harvard Law School. She said and I quote, *"...the American legal system has been corrupted beyond recognition..."* That scathing review came from someone in the system! Robert Seidenberg exposed the true nature of the divorce court system when he wrote:

The Father's Emergency Guide to Divorce-Custody Battle:
A Tour Through the Predatory World of Judges, Lawyers,
Psychologists & Social Workers, in the Subculture of Divorce
by Robert Seidenberg, William Dawes, Lawrence Peckmezian (Illustrator)

• *Female judges who are confirmed radical feminists* - These women despise men. When a man shows up in a courtroom presided by one of these male emasculators, his wife could be a confessed drug addicted stripper on parole, facing serious child neglect charges, but he still has no chance of getting a fair or equitable divorce settlement.

• *Unethical attorneys* - The divorce court system is filled with these bloodthirsty barracudas. In addition to the ruthless tactics they teach their clients, they also employ a set of dirty tricks against their clients. These tactics include churning cases, overbilling, intentionally not filing forms or motions, manipulating spouses into long drawn out divorce court battles and trials and other unethical schemes.

Understand this fully. Attorneys are trained to rip spouses apart, not keep them together. Divorce attorneys do not get up in the morning praying for the marital success of this nation. They pass out business cards, run ads on television and in the Yellow Pages and plaster divorce billboards all over town to attract their next pool of clients. These attorneys live, breath, and eat to see the day when a couple is having marital tension.

Their solution is to file for divorce and grill the dazed spouse until they scream! When an attorney works for a firm that specializes in divorces, they get pay raises, promotions, company cellular phones, expense accounts and company cars based on how many couples they can inspire, influence, trick or lure to travel down the cold, dark, painful and lonely halls of divorce. If anyone tells you differently, they are not being truthful! If a divorce attorney develops a knack for reconciling estranged spouses, they will quickly receive a stern rebuke from their law partners. If they do not change their healing ways, a sizzling pink slip will be the next case load they'll have to manage.

A large portion of people who use divorce attorneys as their *coach*, did not need to divorce. With the proper mentoring, they could have worked things out and turned their marriage into a vibrant love.

But once he or she consulted with an attorney [*coach*], to figure out what to do, their union was doomed. Here is a portion of a cheat sheet questionnaire used by some divorce attorneys to help their clients determine when it's time to file for divorce:

- Are you bored and simply ready to move on?
- Has your love for your husband or wife faded, waned, or cooled off?
- Do you need your freedom to find a new man or woman?
- Do you feel his commitment to his work takes priority over your needs?
- Has your marriage changed since having children?
- Is your wife too busy with chores, children and job, that she leaves your needs unmet?
- She showers before going to bed, (That's a sign that she's cheating)
- You're attracted to other females, (Your wife just doesn't turn you on any more)
- The normal amount of food is not in the house, (A sign that she has other interests)

If a person follows after this marriage model, this mentality comes with the package. Be advised: if a person attempts to get you to sign a prenuptial, post nuptial or other marital contract, they are trying to steer you into a **social contract** marriage. Even if they do not push for you to sign a contract, that does not mean they do not adhere to the **social contract** marriage model.

If they define marriage as being some sort of contractual agreement, they are followers of the **social contract** marriage model and their *reference sources* [*coaches*] will be attorneys, judges, and court appointed mediators. At the drop of a dime, with no provocation, these spouses will drag you into the vicious blood sucking divorce court grinding machine. Concentrate on this powerful statement:

How a person views marriage determines how they will value marriage.

People who view marriage as a contractual agreement, will value marriage as they value an insurance policy or cellular telephone contract. They are subject to cancel or terminate their marital contract at will. Why is it so easy for them to divorce?

It goes back to the world's commonly accepted view of contracts. Read it carefully: *"All contracts were made to be broken."* That includes the **social contract** marriage. Here is another powerful statement to digest.

When a person's view of marriage is distorted,
their value of marriage will be distorted also.

To distort means: **1). to take out of the original or natural state, 2). to make a perverted translation of the original, 3). to cause to work in a disorderly fashion, and 4). to give a false or misleading perception of.**

I have now shown you six different models for marriage:

- A social contract
- A 50/50 partnership
- A common law marriage
- An open marriage
- A civil agreement
- A formal commitment

Each of these models was invented by taking the original model for marriage and adding a different twist, or omitting a major element, thereby distorting the original.

Each was designed to pervert the original design for marriage, causing matrimony to work in a disorderly fashion. Ultimately, each of these six models for marriage gives a misleading and false perception of true marriage. That was the bad news. Now the good news. We need to learn how marriage was created and designed to function:

> Mark 10:6-8 AMP [Emphasis added]
> 6 But FROM THE BEGINNING OF CREATION God made them male and female.
> 7 For THIS REASON a man shall leave [behind] his father and his mother and be joined to his wife and cleave closely to her permanently,
> 8 And THE TWO SHALL BECOME ONE FLESH, so that they are no longer two, but ONE FLESH.

Notice the Scripture says, "...from the beginning of creation GOD..." This was not the Pope, the United States Supreme Court, or the Canadian Parliament. This was the doing of Almighty God, by Himself, with no one else. Remind yourself of this critical point everyday. God did not ask your opinion or mine concerning marriage.

God did not consult with the Prime Minister, the polygamists, the homosexuals, the lesbians, the Muslims, the Chief Justice, a consortium of bishops, the feminists, the Scientologists, a divorce attorney, a family law expert, or a relationship coach. He did not seek the profound insight of a clinical psychologist, a social scientist, the Mormons, the Catholics, a PhD, an Adjunct Professor or anyone else.

Until you accept and acknowledge that critical point in your mind and heart, how you view and value marriage will always be distorted. In verses 6, 7 and 8, God established the institution of marriage as a union between one man and one woman in which they are permanently joined together and become *One Flesh*.

This *One Flesh* union is called a **Covenant Marriage**. The *foundation* of the **Covenant Marriage** is the Written Word of God and the only *reference source* [*coach*] for the **Covenant Marriage** is God Himself through prayer. The **Covenant Marriage** consists of five essential elements.

• *Element #1* - The **Covenant Marriage** is sacred. It was declared sacred by the Lord, (See Hebrews 13:4). To be sacred means: **1). To be made holy, 2). Due to it's divine sanction, the Covenant Marriage is not to be defiled, profaned, violated, corrupted, transgressed, betrayed or dishonored, 3). To command honor and respect, 4). To be reserved solely for the exclusive use of a husband and wife.**

• *Element #2* - The **Covenant Marriage** is the fusing of a man and woman into *One Flesh*. When you see the word "marriage" or "married" in the Bible, (See I Timothy 5:14 and 1 Corinthians 7:28), it is the Greek word, "gameo." Our English translation of the word "gameo" is the word, "gem," as in precious gem. Remember in the seventh booby trap, when I showed you the four facets of *True Love,* and how *True Love* is like a precious diamond?

Scientists cannot really explain it, but once carbon is exposed to the heated pressure of the earth's convection oven, it combines with other elements and minerals. They are fused together into a tight crystalline format we call a diamond.

The **Covenant Marriage** mysteriously fuses a husband and wife together in the same manner, (See Ephesians 5:31-32). Instead of carbon, heat, gases, water, serpentine and calcite, the elements and minerals used to fuse a husband and wife together are *Agape love*, *Phileo love*, *Storge love, Eros love* and prayer.

• *Element #3* - The **Covenant Marriage** is just that - a covenant. Notice the Word of the Lord in Malachi 2:14 AMP [Emphasis added], "...she is your companion and THE WIFE OF YOUR COVENANT..." She is not the wife of your contract. Nor is she the wife of your civil agreement. After the discovery of this Scripture, we must answer two questions:

1). What is a covenant? **2).** How are covenants made? We will answer the second question first. To see how a covenant is made we have to go back to: Malachi 2:14 AMP [Emphasis added], "...she is your companion and the wife of your covenant [MADE BY YOUR MARRIAGE VOWS]. It is your marriage vows that make a covenant.

Pay attention as we determine the seriousness of your marriage vows. To do that we have to revisit Malachi 2:14, AMP [Emphasis added], "...Because THE LORD WAS WITNESS [to the covenant made at your marriage] between you and the wife of your youth..."

When you exchange marriage vows, the Lord becomes a witness to those vows. This is another critical point most newlyweds fail to comprehend. As an expert witness, the Lord listens to your marriage vows. He repeats your vows back to you, (*through the person officiating the wedding ceremony*) and then He records your vows in heaven as a testament, (*proof of evidence that you made them*). Now read how He commands you to handle your marriage vows.

Ecclesiastes 5:4-6 AMP [Emphasis added]
4 WHEN YOU VOW A VOW *or* make a pledge TO GOD, do not put off paying it: FOR GOD HAS NO PLEASURE IN FOOLS (those who witlessly mock Him). PAY WHAT YOU VOW.
5 IT IS BETTER THAT YOU SHOULD NOT VOW than that you should vow and not pay.
6 Do not allow your mouth to cause your body to sin, AND DO NOT SAY before the messenger [THE PRIEST] [A pastor or other minister of God] that IT WAS AN ERROR *or* MISTAKE..."

The Lord takes your marriage vows and uses them to convert you from being a mere man and woman into being lawfully wedded husband & wife... Malachi 2:15, AMP [Emphasis added], "And did not GOD MAKE [YOU AND YOUR WIFE] one flesh?..." Once He, (*through your vows*) converts you into *One Flesh*, the Lord takes your union quite seriously.

Mark 10:8-9 AMP [Emphasis added]
8 And THE TWO SHALL BECOME ONE FLESH, so that they are no longer two, but ONE FLESH.
9 What THEREFORE GOD HAS UNITED (joined together), LET NO MAN SEPARATE *or* DIVIDE.

Once God has joined a man and woman together, they become *One Flesh* and He admonishes both spouses to not let any man or woman separate, divide, or tear them apart. That includes a divorce court judge, an attorney, in-laws, a child, an *ex* flame, sickness, parents, a job, a business, a friend, a neighbor, a coworker... nothing and no one! Read why God stands behind the **Covenant Marriage** with such adamant vigor.

Malachi 2:16 AMP [Emphasis added]
For the Lord, the God of Israel, says: I HATE DIVORCE AND MARITAL SEPARATION..."

The Lord not only hates divorce, but He hates marital separation with equal hatred. Why? It goes back to the first element of the **Covenant Marriage**. When the Lord created marriage, He made it to be sacred. And! When a husband and wife separate or divorce, they are tearing apart a sacred creation that belongs to Almighty G-O-D!

That is why the Lord gave us this sizzling hot two part command in Ecclesiastes 5:2 NIV, Do not be quick with your mouth, do not be hasty in your heart to utter anything before God..." Rejecting this command has been the Achilles heel for more marriages than we will ever know. Although you will find some, there are not many individuals who were quick to say: *"I love you," "Will you marry me," "Yes,"* and *"I do,"* who have love stories worth telling anyone about. Performing all of the *Booby Trap Acid Tests* protects you from being quick with your mouth and hasty in your heart concerning falling in love. Let's define a covenant.

A covenant means: **1). To become allies, 2). To band together, 3). To form a confederacy, and 4). To dispose.** The one detail about the **Covenant Marriage** that eludes most people, (*including most ministers*) is that prior to joining a man and woman together in Holy matrimony, God requires that both the man and the woman be disposed. This is a must!

This process can take place through a pastor or other minister, through a *pre*-marital or marriage counselor or through someone who understands the process. To dispose means: (a). **To set in the correct and proper order, and** (b). **To define the duties, responsibilities and codes of conduct.** Read how the Lord sets a marriage in order:

> Malachi 2:16 AMP [Emphasis added]
> For the Lord, the God of Israel, says: I HATE DIVORCE *and* MARITAL SEPARATION and him who covers his garment [his wife] with violence. Therefore KEEP A WATCH UPON your spirit [that it may be CONTROLLED BY MY SPIRIT], that you deal not treacherously *and* faithlessly [with your marriage mate].

Before you proceed any further, *re*-read that verse to make sure you understand who is speaking. The Lord starts putting the marriage in its proper order by commanding the man to put a watch upon his spirit. That word "watch" means to guard, to protect, and to preserve. Remember on pages 51 through 53, when I gave you the five areas to guard? This is where I got guarding your spirit from. He goes on to command the man to let his spirit be controlled by the Holy Spirit. The Lord echoes this critical command all throughout the Scriptures. You can read it in: Romans 6:13, James 4:7.

When a man obeys the command to guard his spirit and yields himself to being led by the Holy Spirit, he will not cover his garment, (*his wife*) with violence. That word violence means: **1). To treat unrighteously 2). To divorce without cause, 3). To be cruel towards, 4). To oppress, 5). To abuse emotionally, mentally, financially or socially, 6). To physically assault, 7). To damage, bruise, or hurt, 8). To be unkind to, and 9). To deal with deceitfully.**

From God's standard, a man has committed violence against the wife of his covenant if he commits any of these acts. Now you can see why the Lord ordains that a man and woman be disposed with the Written Word of God before they get married.

When a couple exchanges marriage vows without clearly understanding their duties, responsibilities, and codes of conduct, they have acted with haste in their heart and they have been quick with their mouths. That brings us to the next essential element.

• *Element #4* - The foundation of the **Covenant Marriage** is the **Written Word of God**. It is the code of conduct revealed in the Written Word of God that sets the marital temperature to release that warm, deep, heart-to-heart connection that eludes so many spouses. Here are a few key examples of those codes of conduct...

For the Husbands:
- Husband love your wife as Christ loved the church, **(Ephesians 5:25)**
- Husband do not cover your wife with abuse or domestic violence, **(Malachi 2:16)**
- Husband dwell with your wife according to knowledge, **(I Peter 3:7)**
- Husband honor your wife, **(I Peter 3:7)**
- Husband be not bitter against your wife, **(Colossians 3:19)**
- Husband, as you get older, rejoice with the wife of your youth, **(Proverbs 5:18)**

For the Wives:
- Wife, when you speak, let the law of kindness rule your tongue, **(Proverbs 31:26)**
- Wife, love your husband, **(Titus 2:4)**
- Wife, submit to your husband, that is follow his leadership **(Colossians 3:18)**
- Wife, when you open your mouth speak with wisdom, **(Proverbs 31:26)**
- Wife, honor your husband, **(Esther 1:20)**

For Both The Husband & Wife:
- Submit yourselves to God... to His Word and to His code of conduct, **(James 4:7)**
- Submit yourselves to and be flexible to each other, **(Ephesians 5:21)**
- Be gentle and kind to one another, **(I Thessalonians, 2:7, James 3:17, Titus 3:2)**
- Walk in agreement and be on one accord with each other, **(Amos 3:3, Acts 2:1)**
- Spend time together in prayer, **(I Peter 3:7, Matthew 18:19-20, Luke 18:1)**

• *Element # 5* - The last essential element of the **Covenant Marriage** is one of the most exhilarating. Your source [*coach*] is not some wacko pseudo-psychologist whose advice will ruin your life or come back to haunt you ten years down the road. The Lord God Almighty is your *source* and He is called, the Wonderful Counsellor, (See Isaiah 9:6) for a reason. He created matrimony and His counsel will not mislead you, nor fail you. He will show you how to turn your marriage into a masterpiece. He is, wonderful in counsel, and excellent in working." (See Isaiah 28:29). With His counsel, a husband and wife can withstand the tests, trials, and temptations of life without ever bending or breaking.

What *Booby Trap Acid Tests* must you perform to protect yourself from self-destructive marriage missiles and relationship assassins who do not: (a) **know,** (b) **understand,** or (c) **respect the sacredness of the marriage covenant?** Here they are; you must study them carefully:

1). Which of the seven marriage models are you and your potential mate going to follow? This decision will determine the temperature and atmosphere of your marriage and love life, so choose wisely.

2). Does your potential mate, know, understand and respect the sacredness of the marriage covenant? You find out by asking them what they know, believe and understand about marriage, then listen to their answers.

3). Have you and your potential mate had in-depth pre-marital training? If the answer is "no," you are already in trouble. In our society, before a person can drive a bus or fly an airplane, they must be licensed. To get a license, they must first receive the proper training. A major reason we have so many brokenhearted divorcees is because unlike the truck driver or pilot, they received a marriage license with zero training. At minimum, this pre-marital training must include:

(a) **understanding the covenant marriage**, (b) **understanding true love** (c) **understanding his needs - her needs**, (d) **the duties of the husband**, (e) **the duties of the wife**, (f) **spousal communication 101**, (g) **conflict resolution 101**, (h) **marital sex 101**, (i) **marital finances 101**, (j) **dealing with life's issues, setbacks, stresses and pressures**, (k) **understanding soul ties, flesh ties and spirit ties**, (l) **clearing emotional baggage**, (m) **the dangers of being unequally yoked**, (n) **adultery's ripple affect, and** (o) **fatherhood and motherhood 101.**

A good *pre*-marital training course is going to take at least eight to twelve weeks. If your potential mate has not had or refuses to take *pre*-marital training, bid them farewell. A person who has not had or refuses to submit to *pre*-marital training but insists on getting married does not want to have a vibrant lasting marriage. This can be compared to a person who dreams of being a premier trial lawyer but refuses to go to law school and then take the bar exam.

4). As a couple, have you had in-depth pre-marital counseling? Pre-marital training gives a person the foundation and tools they need to be a great marriage partner. *Pre*-marital counseling is designed to: (a) **disprove or confirm compatibility**, (b) **assist a couple in evaluating these areas:**

- Criminal History Check and Evaluation
- Communication Skills Evaluation
- Family Background Evaluation
- Financial and Credit Evaluation
- Spirit, Soul and Flesh Ties Evaluation
- Spiritual, Moral and Emotional Evaluation
- Life's Purpose and Plan Evaluation
- Psychological and Mental Evaluation
- STD Evaluation
- Extended/Blended Families Evaluation

Marriage is an extremely serious undertaking. It is not to be trifled with or entered into impulsively or casually. *Pre*-marital counseling protects you from becoming *One Flesh* with a marriage missile. Read this next powerful truth as if your life, peace of mind, and sanity depended on it because it does.

It is much better to have a broken engagement than to have a broken marriage and go from *One Flesh* to torn flesh.

- 13 -

He Kept Trying To Warn You!

By now you understand that when it comes to finding *True Love*, it is a lover's jungle out there. This jungle can become so dark, you may believe it is impossible to see your way out. At times you won't know what to think. He says he loves you, yet you have this lingering feeling in your heart. Is he *The One*? You ponder the relationship. He seems like he's a good man. You check your emotions and ask yourself, "Are these normal feelings to have when you are in love?"

You wonder, "Does she have a dark side? Could there be more to her than meets the eye?" Those are all valid questions. If you do not ask them and get the answers to them, you are setting yourself up for a major heartbreak. Aside from the obvious, (*abuse, domestic violence, sexual immorality, being manipulated or controlled*), how do you know when you should walk away? Do you have a plan for detecting the host of men and women who are adept at deception, seasoned at lying, and ingenious at defrauding? Do you have a system for immediately detecting stealthy wife beaters or females shopping for disposable dads?

What if they show no signs? Do you have a procedure for unmasking these individuals? You already know that some smooth operators are going to look normal and say and do all of the right things. What is your plan to expose their sinister intentions? Here is another riveting truth you must honor with the highest state of respect:

There are some people, who, when they say "hello," you must say "goodbye!"

If you allow things to proceed any further, you, your family and your friends will regret your decision for the rest of your lives. Remind yourself of this vital point as often as possible: you do not go on a date with these individuals. You do not give them your telephone number or e-mail address, nor do you ask for theirs. When they say, "hello," you say, "good bye," end of story! The question arises, "How will I know when one of these relationship assassins or marriage missiles crosses my path or comes knocking at the door of my heart?"

I have shown you numerous accounts of men and women who died at the hands of the person who claimed to love them. Had those victims been able to look into and see the true intent of that person's heart, they never would have proceeded into a relationship or marriage with them. There are certain men and women who are domestic violence ticking time bombs. They use phrases such as, "Honey, please, you need counseling," "I can't take this anymore," "it's over, this is not going to work," and, "you hurt me for the last time," as detonators.

Mention or say those words to this bunch and you have just heated up or shaken nitroglycerin. People who knew Chantay Bishop, (*real name*) described the budding 19-year-old New Yorker as an angel. She was kind to everyone she met. Chantay never got a chance to fully blossom because in choosing her first boyfriend she chose the wrong mate. At some point she realized she had to end things and she did. However, once you get involved with a relationship assassin, you should know by now, your life is earmarked for a grim explosive tragedy.

It may happen immediately or it may take years, but it is going to happen. If you try to break up, leave, or divorce them, they are going to hurt or kill you, your child, children or family members. On March 29th, 2002, Chantay's first love, Dwayne Reed, (*real name*), went to her condominium but was met at the door by her new beau. Dwayne assured the man that he only wanted to end things with Chantay.

He said he just wanted to say a proper goodbye. Once inside, police say Dwayne became enraged because Chantay was with another man. He brandished a Tec 9 semiautomatic handgun and fired at her new boyfriend, who fled the apartment in fear of his life.

Dwayne then turned his attention to Chantay. As she cowered in the bathroom, completely helpless, Dwayne shot the supposed love of his life four times. I was not there, but I can hear Chantay screaming... pleading for her life... wondering, "God, what did I do to deserve this? How could this happen to me?" There is no need to ask...

She got booby trapped by a smooth operator! With Chantay's death, Dwayne showed us the point most smooth operators are out to prove. They are the ones in control. Westchester County Judge Lester Adler said this to Dwayne Reed during his sentencing, *"(You decided) if you could not have Chantay Bishop as your girlfriend, she could not live," "You terminated the life of a young woman because you could not have her."*

Chantay did not have a system in place to guard her from men like Dwayne. Is there an available warning or radar system to protect you from such individuals? I submit to you, the answer to that question is, "Yes!" Let's examine some fundamental facts. You cannot see into a potential mate's heart nor can you read their mind. But God can!

Psalm 139:1-4 NIV [Emphasis added]
¹ O Lord, YOU HAVE SEARCHED ME and you know me.
² You know when I sit and when I arise; YOU PERCEIVE MY THOUGHTS from afar.
³ You discern my going out and my lying down; YOU ARE FAMILIAR WITH ALL MY WAYS.
⁴ BEFORE A WORD IS ON MY TONGUE you know it completely, O Lord.

Zero in on verse 3. The Lord God Almighty is familiar with all of our ways, yours and your potential mate's. He knows the women of virtue and the men of honor. He also knows the wife beaters, the controllers, the pornography addicts, and the cheaters. He has identified and tagged the ruthless gold-diggers and the master manipulators.

What about the bold-faced liars, the deceivers and the con artists? Read verse 4, again. God has pegged them also. In verse 1, He reveals that He searches each of us. What type of search does He use?

Hebrews 4:12-13 AMP [Emphasis added]
¹² For the Word that God speaks is alive and full of power [making it active, operative, energizing, and effective]...
...EXPOSING *and* SIFTING *and* ANALYZING *and* JUDGING the very thoughts and purposes of the heart.
¹³ And NOT A CREATURE EXISTS THAT IS CONCEALED FROM HIS SIGHT, but ALL THINGS are OPEN *and* EXPOSED, NAKED *and* defenseless to the eyes of Him with Whom we have to do.

He uses a full-fledged strip search. We are all exposed and naked before Him. He judges our thoughts and the very purposes of our hearts. Verse 13 says, not one individual escapes God's thorough examination. Let's learn how God uses the vital information He has gathered about a potential mate, to warn and protect us from relationship assassins and marriage missiles. It starts with this critical question.

II Corinthians 10:7 [Emphasis added]
Do you look on things after the OUTWARD APPEARANCE?...

If you answered, "yes," that is your first mistake! You must make the following mental and spiritual adjustment.

John 7:24 [Emphasis added]
JUDGE NOT ACCORDING TO THE APPEARANCE, but judge righteous judgment.

Translated: you must see a potential mate exactly as God sees them. Here is an account of some men who, on election day, were prepared to choose a leader based solely on outer appearances. Pay attention to how the Lord rejected all of their shoe-in candidates:

> I Samuel 16:7-10 NIV [Emphasis added]
> ⁶ When they arrived, Samuel SAW ELIAB and thought, "Surely the Lord's anointed stands here before the Lord."
> ⁷ But the Lord said to Samuel, "Do not consider his appearance or his height, FOR I HAVE REJECTED HIM. The Lord does not look at the things man looks at. Man looks at the OUTWARD APPEARANCE, but the Lord looks at the heart."
> ⁸ Then Jesse called Abinadab and had him pass in front of Samuel. BUT SAMUEL SAID, "THE LORD HAS NOT CHOSEN THIS ONE EITHER."
> ⁹ Jesse then had Shammah pass by, BUT SAMUEL SAID, "NOR HAS THE LORD CHOSEN THIS ONE."
> ¹⁰ Jesse had SEVEN of his sons pass before Samuel, BUT SAMUEL SAID TO HIM, "THE LORD HAS NOT CHOSEN THESE."

God searched the hearts of these seven men and rejected them all. Why? The reasons do not matter because as long as you are star gazing at a person's outer appearance, you will not believe or respond to what the Lord tells you about them. For example, in November of 2003, Bishop Anthony Glenn Owens, (*real name*) was arrested in Shreveport, Louisiana, on bigamy charges stemming from a fraud investigation. Detectives in Gwinnett County, Georgia, said the minister fraudulently wed nine different women. From a jailhouse interview in February of 2004, Owens said what he did was based on his religious beliefs.

He said his intentions were not to hurt and marry women. He said the reason there were so many marriages was because he was searching for a mother figure which he could never find. He said his mom died when he was twelve years old and he was trying to replace her.

Some of his wives paint a different picture. They said Owens wooed them with religious talk. They said he posed as a minister, married them, then stole their money. One of his wives said she once thought Bishop Anthony Owens was everything. Read what she later said about him, *"He's a smooth talker;" "When I married him I had five cars and a house;" "When he got through with me, I was dead broke."* Clearly these women were hurt and their pain goes way beyond their financial losses. Some of them have holes in their hearts, most people would never understand.

Write this next statement down and endeavor never to forget it. Once the Lord performs a strip search of a person, He judges and exposes the purposes and intents of their heart. If he or she: (a) **won't be compatible with you,** (b) **won't be equally yoked with you,** (c) **is going to play games with your heart,** (d) **is going to use, misuse, hurt or try to harm you, or**

(e) has secret sins, addictions, soul, flesh or spiritual ties or emotional issues that makes them an unstable or dangerous potential mate, the Lord will always warn you. This brings us to our next *Booby Trap Acid Test*.

Do you know God's voice?

If you do not know God's voice, unless you have figured out an iron clad, fool proof way to know the condition of a person's heart and discern their true intentions, you are at a severe disadvantage. You have no one to expose, sift, analyze and judge the true intent of your potential mate's heart. There are seven methods God uses to speak us.

• *He Speaks Directly To Our Hearts* - I remember being introduced to a certain young lady. After conversing with her for about an hour, I was thoroughly impressed. She told me that she loved God and how she wanted nothing more than to be at the center of God's will.

She seemed to be the answer to my prayers and I could not resist asking her for her telephone number to continue our invigorating conversation. She gave me her contact information, then we parted ways. As soon as I walked away from her, the Lord spoke to me and said, "She has a dark cloud over her life." Admittedly, when He said that to me, I thought, "No way, not her, she's born-again and she seems so yadda, yadda, yadda, blah, blah, blah..."

Do you see where I am going with this? I was looking at her outer appearance and how she sounded, but God knew her heart. At that time, there were many things I did not understand about love, sex, relationships, marriage or women. However, there was one thing I did know. I knew the Lord's voice!

Remember He said, "She has a dark cloud over her life." The Lord was warning me, "Son, if you proceed in a relationship with this female, she is going to cause you much heartache." You need to know this - the Lord will not yell at you or brow beat you to get you to listen. When He speaks to your heart, you will have to make the decision to reject or obey His voice, (See Hebrews 3:7-12). If you make the wrong decision, you will most likely experience some painful consequences.

• *He Speaks To Us Through His Written Word* - Another way the Lord speaks to us is through the Written Word. The Scriptures show men the type of females to avoid. For instance, in Proverbs 6:20-33, men are warned to avoid strange women. Most men are unable to describe a strange woman until they find themselves victims of paternity fraud, false domestic violence or false rape charges. The Written Word describes evil men and then warns women not to open up their hearts, submit their emotions, or expose their bodies to these men.

The average female is usually speechless when asked to describe these type of men. **Break The Cycle** is a nonprofit organization with offices in Los Angeles, San Francisco and New York. They provide free and confidential legal advice, advocacy and representation to victims of emotional and physical abuse. Their clients are females between the ages of sixteen and twenty-two.

Many are pregnant or have young children. These young girls are forced to file restraining orders, check into shelters for abused women, make frantic calls to 911 and find ways to escape their tormenting boyfriends. Do you understand what two things have occurred?

1). These females are entering into relationships and yet they are clueless about *True Love*. They know nothing about relationship assassins, marriage missiles or the 9 deadly booby traps.

2). Their boyfriends have been indoctrinated and trained to commit abuse and domestic violence at very early ages. These boys have been indoctrinated to enjoy abusing women. Some of them eagerly boast about their ability to seduce, manipulate and control females.

The scary thing is, as you learned in the 3rd chapter, these teenage boys are taking their abusive tactics and their domestic violence arsenal into their adult relationships. Learn this point. God uses His Written Word to speak to your heart, to educate, edify, and empower you concerning the true dynamics of love, sex, relationships, and marriage.

If you do not read or study the Word of God, you will lack critical insights to help you understand how to choose the right mate. You can resort to using scientific, psychological, and educational means in attempts to gain these needed insights, but none of those methods gives you the capabilities of exposing a person's heart.

• *He Speaks To Us Through Prayer* - It takes prayer to become sensitive to God's voice. Without prayer you will consistently miss when He is leading you to the love of your life or warning you about a relationship assassin or marriage missile. With prayer, you will not miss those desperately needed warnings or critical promptings.

• *He Speaks To Us Through People Who Truly Love Us And Sincerely Care About Us* - We looked at this vital method in chapter 8.

• *He Speaks To Us Through Pre-Marital Counseling* - We looked at this critical method in chapter 12.

• *He Speaks To Us Through His True Messengers* - The Lord uses His messengers to assist you in making the proper decisions concerning love, sex, relationships and marriage. We may use tools such as this book, conferences, the preaching or teaching of the Word of God. Either way, you need to be spiritually alert so that you do not miss His voice when we speak.

• He Speaks To Us Through Dreams or Visions There are times when God will warn you or speak to you about a person or situation through a dream, (See Matthew 2:12 and Matthew 2:22), or in a vision, (See Acts 9:10-15 and Acts 18:9). How He decides to speak to you is His decision. But once he speaks, what will your response be if He says, "He or she is not *The One?*" Will you date that person anyway?

Will you proceed into a relationship or marriage after God has warned you that you are headed into a lover's hailstorm or a marital tsunami? Will you cop an attitude against God? Those critical questions bring us to our final *Booby Trap Acid Test,* which is:

Will you turn a deaf ear when God speaks to you?

Will you do as some of the victims you read about within these pages? I have interviewed multitudes of victims and family members of victims, (*victims of domestic violence, abuse, paternity fraud, marital fraud, STD's, etc.*). The truth is - some of them mocked God... even after He kept trying to warn them. They scoffed at His Written Word or laughed at His messenger. The Lord spoke to their hearts and said, "I have not chosen this one," and their rebuttals were along these lines, "It's my life, it's my body, and I'll do what I want!"

I have personally counseled numerous women who were so ashamed after being date raped, that they could not bring themselves to call the police and report the crime. God, in some way, warned these young ladies not to go out with these creeps. The Lord knew these men were unrepentant sexual predators and He alerted these women through a dream or a vision. Yet they either did not recognize they were being warned of God or they brazenly shrugged off His warnings.

Some erroneously believed God would protect them regardless of who they dated. That simply is not the case. When the Lord warns you, His objective is to prevent you from going on a dangerous date, protect you from entering into a hazardous relationship and to stop you from exchanging vows with a marriage missile!

If you turn a deaf ear when He speaks, you will find yourself groping through an enormously dangerous lover's jungle. This jungle will be filled with booby traps, liars, contagious diseases, pitfalls, abusers, fakes, cheaters, predators and gold-diggers who are salivating at the scent of your flesh. In this menacingly dark wilderness, your only hope is to have a bright light to dispel the darkness.

That ray of hope, the one that illuminates your path like beams of sunlight piercing through a cluster of dark clouds, is the voice of God. His voice is your lie detector, illuminator and heart chaperone.

His voice is the defender of your emotions and the guardian of your physical well being, but only if you listen when He speaks. This next point should be glaringly apparent by now. There are good men and women in our society: men and women who will make great mates, men and women who will never use, misuse or abuse the person they love. They will always do what is just and what is right, but these men and women do not come a dime a dozen.

In reality, they are rare gems. Remember - you have three groups of dangerous men and women. **1)**. Those who have been indoctrinated by immoral men and women. **2)**. Those whose minds and consciences have been corrupted by the media, music and Hollywood, and **3)**. The victims of circumstances. Between them, when it comes to finding the love of your life, you are looking for a needle in a hay stack! The good news is, when you make God your metal detector, sifting through the massive pile of hay becomes a painless process.

Where do you go from here? Take these three steps... First and foremost, you must put your **Dream Team** together. In chapter 8, I showed the importance of having people in your life who truly love you and sincerely care about you. This special group of individuals is called your **Dream Team** because their hearts are set on seeing God's glorious plan for your love life fulfilled. They are vital to God's glorious plan for your love life because they always have your best interest at heart. Think of your **Dream Team** as your life guards.

While you are in the deep waters searching for the love of your life, your **Dream Team** is on duty, waiting to warn you about the sharks, sea urchins, moray eels and rip tides. With your **Dream Team** of advisers in place, you won't waste valuable time with individuals who look, sound and act like *The One*, but turn out to be harmful impostors.

For the women, putting together a **Dream Team** is usually a cinch. Women are more prone to talk about these issues. However, with many men, because of a lack of proper training, that is not the case. The average man has a bad tendency of not discussing his love life with others until after he has been booby trapped into a lover's nightmare, (See Proverbs 5:1-13). Therefore, I must issue this crucial warning to all men. Do not go seeking the love of your life until you have your **Dream Team** in place. This next Scripture clearly illustrates why:

> Proverbs 7:26 [Emphasis added]
> For she hath cast down many wounded: yea, many strong *men* have been slain by her.

These cunning females have wiped out a mass number of men and not just any men, but men of stature.

Solomon aptly classified these female mantraps as seductive but evil women who seduce men by using their beauty and feminine wiles as bait, (See Proverbs 6:24-26). They then slay these men using weapons such as: paternity fraud, false rape and false domestic violence charges, spousal defraud, false child abuse charges and child custody extortion.

The good news is that you can avoid these lethal females by having a **Dream Team** to help you navigate through this menacing dark lover's jungle. Whether you are male or female, rich, middle class or poor, educated or uneducated, eighteen years of age or sixty-seven, get a **Dream Team**! If you need help in putting your **Dream Team** together, go back and *re*-read chapter 8. List your **Dream Team** here:

1. _____

2. _____

3. _____

4. _____

The second step is, you must become proactive concerning your love life. To be proactive means to prepare in advance to prevent a foreseeable calamity. That means your **Dream Team** must have detailed knowledge of each of the nine deadly booby traps and be clear on how to help you use the *Booby Trap Acid Tests* as a protective shield.

Another gigantic step you can take to be proactive is to put together a discussion group using **Why People Choose The Wrong Mate - Avoiding The 9 Deadly Booby Traps** as your starting point. Time and time again, I have talked and prayed with family members of victims of domestic violence. In many cases, God kept trying to warn the victim through family members, friends or coworkers. But they rejected His advice because they did not understand or perceive the grave danger they were in.

Discussing these issues ensures that everyone within your circle of influence understands that relationship assassins and marriage missiles exist and why they must be avoided at all costs. I urge you not to take this matter lightly. Think about those you care about and love... the statistics prove that they desperately need this vital information!

Finally, thoroughly examine your heart. Perform a self examination to ensure you are not harboring any ungodly behaviors or destructive personality traits. If you don't know how to perform this self examination, go back and *re*-read chapter 9. You don't want to be guilty of sabotaging God's glorious plan for your love life.

Resource Guide

Are you a victim of domestic violence? Experiencing abuse? Dating and marital violence has become rampant in our society. Know the tell-tale signs:

National Domestic Violence Hotline
- **1-800-799-SAFE**
- **www.ndvh.org**
- **www.break-the-cycle.org**
- **In emergencies dial 911!**

Are you a stalking victim? Do you have an *ex* that won't let go?
- **www.stalkingvictims.com**
- **www.ncvc.org**

Have questions or concerns about being sexually active?
- **www.getthetruth.net**
- **www.lovematters.com**

Questions or concerns about a sexually transmitted disease(s)?
- **www.medinstitute.org**
- **www.ashastd.org**

Much false information has been published about safe sex. Here are the facts:
- **www.gillistriplett.com**
- **www.thefactsproject.org**

Are you dealing with an unplanned pregnancy? Don't know what to do, where to go, or who to talk to? Need someone to talk to? Before you do anything start here first:
- **www.birthright.org**
- **24 hour hotline 1-800-550-4900**

Are you considering having an abortion? Get the facts first:
- **www.abortionfacts.com**
- **www.pregnantpause.org**

Have you had an abortion already? Has your decision affected you psychologically, spiritually, mentally or physically? Are you suffering from (PAS) Post Abortion Syndrome? To find out, go here immediately!:
- **www.safehavenministries.com**
- **www.silentvoices.org**

Are you paying child support? In a custody dispute? Divorced? Are you 100% sure you are the biological father? You have reason to be concerned! One third of the men who take DNA tests *turn out* not to be the baby's daddy. It is called paternity fraud. Don't be a victim. Know the truth...
- **www.paternityfraud.com**
- **www.4truthidentity.com**

Have you been falsely accused of rape, domestic violence or child abuse by your estranged spouse, soon-to-be ex-spouse, live-in lover or by your ex? Go here ASAP!
- **www.abuse-excuse.com**
- **www.innocentdads.org**

Obtaining criminal records - in the criminal history evaluation, each individual must agree to share the results with their potential mate during the *pre*-marital counseling. This is another necessary part of the 'bare all' *pre*-marital process. Contact your local police department to find out how to retrieve this information. You must cover all three levels: (a) **city**, (b) **state, and** (c) **federal**. Include a check for outstanding warrants, domestic violence incidents, suspended license and probation and parole. Remember: *truth invites examination, sincerity of heart does not shun it, trustworthy people expect it, and true love demands it!*

About The Author

Gillis Triplett is passionate about helping others find and fulfill their God-ordained destiny. As a versed communicator, motivator, pastor and teacher, he addresses the critical issues of the heart through intense training sessions that educate, edify and empower his hearers and readers. As a devoted advocate of the family, Gillis masterfully gets to the heart of the issues that affect our families and society.

The central theme of his vision and mission is to protect and flourish the family. He is founder of Gillis Triplett Ministries, the flagship of a potent network of ministries that are re-shaping the way men and women think and act. He is also founder and CEO of Mastering Manhood. The focus of this high-powered men's ministry is transitioning men from meandering manhood into Mastering Manhood.

With his gift for reaching and impacting men at the very core of their being and his no-nonsense approach to training, Gillis is raising up the next generation of men who will serve as society's leaders: spiritually, economically, politically and socially. Most importantly, he is raising up men who are faithful fathers, honorable husbands, effective mentors and true role models.

Gillis is the author of many powerful life-changing articles and books, including the spiritual warfare essential: **How To Make The Devil Obey You!!!** For information about speaking engagements, to bring this dynamic communicator to your church or organization, or to send your comments, praise reports or questions, you can write:

Gillis Triplett Ministries
P.O. Box 310900
Atlanta, Georgias 31131

For immediate 24 hour access, log on to our website:

www.Gillistriplett.com

My final word is in the form of a poetic prayer... one that prophetically declares that you find *True Love* in God's perfect timing.

May your love life be a vibrant love,
Ignited and fueled from up above.
One that stands firmly against the tests of time,
And brings to your heart: warmth, joy and peace of mind.

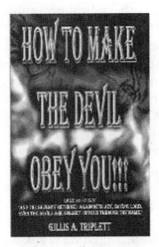

About The Author

Gillis Triplett is passionate about helping others find and fulfill their God-ordained destiny. As a versed communicator, motivator, pastor and teacher, he addresses the critical issues of the heart through intense training sessions that educate, edify and empower his hearers and readers. As a devoted advocate of the family, Gillis masterfully gets to the heart of the issues that affect our families and society.

The central theme of his vision and mission is to protect and flourish the family. He is founder of Gillis Triplett Ministries, the flagship of a potent network of ministries that are re-shaping the way men and women think and act. He is also founder and CEO of Mastering Manhood. The focus of this high-powered men's ministry is transitioning men from meandering manhood into Mastering Manhood.

With his gift for reaching and impacting men at the very core of their being and his no-nonsense approach to training, Gillis is raising up the next generation of men who will serve as society's leaders: spiritually, economically, politically and socially. Most importantly, he is raising up men who are faithful fathers, honorable husbands, effective mentors and true role models.

Gillis is the author of many powerful life-changing articles and books, including the spiritual warfare essential: **How To Make The Devil Obey You!!!** For information about speaking engagements, to bring this dynamic communicator to your church or organization, or to send your comments, praise reports or questions, you can write:

Gillis Triplett Ministries
P.O. Box 310900
Atlanta, Georgias 31131

For immediate 24 hour access, log on to our website:

www.Gillistriplett.com

My final word is in the form of a poetic prayer... one that prophetically declares that you find *True Love* in God's perfect timing.

May your love life be a vibrant love,
Ignited and fueled from up above.
One that stands firmly against the tests of time,
And brings to your heart: warmth, joy and peace of mind.